ST. AUGUSTINE
ON THE PSALMS

ENARRATIONES IN PSALMOS

ANCIENT CHRISTIAN

WRITERS

THE WORKS OF THE FATHERS IN TRANSLATION

EDITED BY

JOHANNES QUASTEN
Catholic University of America
Washington, D.C.

WALTER J. BURGHARDT, S.J.
Woodstock College
Woodstock, Md.

No. 29

ST. AUGUSTINE
ON THE PSALMS

TRANSLATED AND ANNOTATED
BY

DAME SCHOLASTICA HEBGIN
AND
DAME FELICITAS CORRIGAN

*Benedictines of Stanbrook
England*

VOLUME I

PSALMS 1–29

PAULIST PRESS
New York / Mahwah

De Licentia Superioris S.J.
  Nihil Obstat:
        J. Quasten

Imprimatur
        Patricius A. O'Boyle, D.D.
        Archiep. Washingtonen.
        die 16 Decembris 1959

COPYRIGHT 1960
BY
REV. JOHANNES QUASTEN
AND
REV. WALTER J. BURGHARDT, S.J.

Library of Congress
Catalog Card Number: 60-10722

ISBN: 0-8091-0104-1

PUBLISHED BY PAULIST PRESS
997 Macarthur Blvd.
Mahwah, NJ 07430

PRINTED AND BOUND IN THE UNITED STATES OF AMERICA

CONTENTS

ST. AUGUSTINE
ON THE PSALMS

INTRODUCTION

St. Augustine's authorship of the *Enarrationes in psalmos*, by far his longest and undoubtedly one of his most important works, has never been open to question. Not only has Possidius, Bishop of Calama, his contemporary biographer and friend, included these commentaries on the Psalter in his *Indiculus librorum*, the detailed catalogue of Augustine's works, but the Saint himself has rendered any dispute as to their authenticity impossible. In his short Preface to Psalm 118, he states:

All the other Psalms contained in that book which according to the Church's usage is known as the Psalter, I have explained partly in sermons to the people, partly in writing, as far as I was able with the help of our Lord. I have deferred the explanation of Psalm 118, however, not so much because of its length, which is known to all, as because of its depth, which is recognized by few. My brethren were much concerned that an exposition of this one Psalm, which after all is a necessary part of the complete Psalter, was missing from my work. They therefore urged me with great insistence to complete my task. . . . I have at length decided to set it out in sermons, such as the Greeks call homilies, which may be preached to the people. For I think it better that our congregations should not be denied an understanding even of this Psalm, seeing that, as with the other Psalms, they ordinarily derive great pleasure from singing it.

These words of Augustine make it clear that while not composed in the form given in the manuscripts and printed editions, the whole work has come down to us very much

3

as its author finally arranged it. The now universally accepted title *Enarrationes*, however, derives solely from Erasmus, who has used it to indicate a running explanation of a Psalm, verse by verse. The manuscripts, even the most ancient, are inconsistent in their various appellations; they employ seemingly at random the terms *expositio, sermo, tractatus, commentum,* or *explanatio.*

In the Preface to Psalm 118 already quoted, St. Augustine has shown that he did not always approach his subject matter in the same way. Broadly speaking, the *Enarrationes in psalmos* fall into four classes, in which the written commentaries often differ considerably from those delivered orally:

1: brief exegetical notes (Pss. 11–32);
2: more detailed commentaries (Pss. 1–10 etc.);
3: dictated expositions in sermon form—possibly read aloud in church by his priests;
4: sermons proper.

The Maurists have prefixed the words *Sermo ad plebem* or *Sermo ad populum* to each of the discourses preached to a congregation. This note has been retained in the texts of Migne's Latin Patrology and the *Corpus christianorum* from which the present translation has been made. References to sermons so delivered will be found in the notes appended to each volume. Certain Psalms demanded more than one commentary: there are two on many of them; three on Psalms 32, 33, and 36; four on Psalms 30 and 103; and no fewer than thirty-two on Psalm 118. Possidius states:

1: Psalms 1–32. Of these were publicly treated: Psalms 18, 21, [25], 26, 29, 30, 31, 32.
2: Others were dictated: Psalms 67, 71, 77, 78, 82, 87,

89, 104, 105, 107, 108, 110, 111, 112, 113, 114, 115 (joined with 116), 117, 135, 150.

3: All the rest, excepting Psalm 118, were discussed in public, to the number of ninety-seven.

4: All the discourses on the Psalms delivered in public, therefore, amount to 123, for Psalm 121 is expounded twice.

Just as the methods of treatment vary, so the dates at which the commentaries were composed differ widely. While the *Enarrationes* on Psalms 1–32 belong to the year 392, that on Psalm 118, which is the last, is assigned to 418. Nor were all the sermons delivered in the same place. Some were preached at Hippo or at Carthage, seven at Thagaste, and one at Utica.

In this series of sermons the harmony of the themes grows ever richer and fuller; threads which at first apparently have no connection are woven together, and in this respect the last thirty Psalms gain much from the constructive work of the earlier ones. Almost all the discourses bear the stamp of free improvisation (138.1); they often allude either to Psalms which have just been sung by the people during divine service (Pss. 18.2; 21.2; 30.2; 37 etc.), or to epistles which have been read a moment before (65.4). They have the freedom, the forcefulness, and the penetrating simplicity of the spoken word, added to the inexorable realism which characterizes all Augustine's sermons to the people. One gathers the impression from many of these lively homilies that they are the addresses of a pastor of souls to a flock whom he loves and knows intimately. Their homely metaphor and flashes of wit, their wordplay, assonance, and rhymes must have sent many a listener home chuckling with appreciation. The chimerical good old days, the scolding wife, the mother scrubbing her baby boy, the swindling servant, the surgeon, the place-hunter, the stumbling donkey—all are as true to life today as when Augustine used them to illustrate his truly amazing insight into human nature and its problems. But above and beyond all the oratorical brilliance and psychological penetration, he opens up wide horizons at every turn, initiating his simple hearers into the most sublime truths of Christianity.

Hans Urs von Balthasar, whose valuable Introductions to his *Augustinus* and *Über die Psalmen* have been extensively used here, has likened Augustine's commentaries to a landscape too full of detail to be taken in at a glance. He aptly compares them to those mile-long Chinese scenic representations painted on strips which are never completely unrolled. The flow of the preacher's words moves in leisurely, sometimes sluggish fashion, winding in and out of all the bends and caprices of the text. The frequently incomprehensible readings of the Old Latin Psalter are precisely those which reveal the commentator's skill and surpassing beauty of thought. Patiently he follows the text verse by verse, interpreting, referring backwards and forwards, often wandering from the main theme in digressions which are not seldom the finest passages in the commentary. He never forces an external unity of form on his material. Both form and medium spring solely and naturally from the subject matter. The work itself is ever repeating the same themes, often in almost identical words. It sometimes gives an impression of looseness of construction, disorder, and abrupt transition. Yet what at first appears to the reader outwardly disconnected, presently with ever-increasing clarity is seen to fit together into a wonderful organic unity, that of the Church as seen through Augustine's eyes.

For it was the Church which increasingly occupied Augustine's mind from the time of his conversion until his death. He had journeyed from a philosophizing youth to theological maturity, from a speculative life devoted to private, personal problems, to the life of a priest and bishop devoted entirely to the Church. Augustine's works show a development and gradual change of emphasis, from the relations of God and the soul in his *Soliloquies*, written at Cassiciacum in the year of his baptism, to the general problem of truth as shown in the Christian Platonism of *De quantitate animae* and his earlier philosophical works, composed either at Rome or in Africa after the death of his mother, and finally to the conflict between the truth of the Gospel and the heresies which attack that truth, forced upon his mind after his elevation to the priesthood.

Augustine received sacerdotal ordination in 391, and four years later was consecrated Coadjutor Bishop to Valerius, Bishop of Hippo. From 396 until his death in 430 he ruled the See as sole Bishop. His influence over the Church in Africa was immense from the beginning. Possidius, who wrote Augustine's life after living in closest intimacy with him for forty years, remarks that with his advent "the Catholic Church in Africa began to lift up its head." During his episcopate the Saint was called upon to deal with three heresies, all of which were confronting the Church with problems of the greatest moment. It can have fallen to few to fight so many battles and see them won so triumphantly. He routed the Manicheans of his day, broke the Donatist schism, and spent the last eighteen years of his life combating the insidious heresy of Pelagius. All three campaigns have left their mark upon the *Enarrationes in psalmos*, but in particular the war against the Donatists.

Of the three, this last was the more urgent on the practical side, since it had rent the African Church for precisely one hundred years. It had originated when a schismatic body in the Church refused to accept Caecilian, Bishop of Carthage, consecrated 311, on the ground that his consecrator, Felix of Aptunga, had been a *traditor*. This was the name given to Christians who had surrendered the Scriptures when their possession was forbidden during the persecution of Diocletian. The Numidian bishops, supporting the objectors, consecrated Majorinus as a rival to Caecilian, and he was soon afterwards succeeded by Donatus, from whom the schism takes its name. The keynote of the schism was the Donatist claim to exclusive sanctity (*Enarr.* 1.5 on Ps. 10; *Enarr.* 2.2 on Ps. 21), a claim flagrantly contradicted by the incredible enormities perpetrated by the roving bands of armed ruffians called Circumcellions, employed by the Donatist bishops. The Donatists further held that sacraments conferred by *traditores* were invalid and that all who communicated with them were likewise infected. They therefore insisted upon rebaptizing converts, maintaining that since the Church is one and holy, the Donatists alone formed the Church. At the instance of the Emperor Honorius, a public debate was held at Carthage in 411 between the opposing Donatist and Catholic bishops. As a result, the imperial commissioner pronounced finally against the schismatics. The conflict forced Augustine to formulate his ideas and so to carry the doctrines of the sacraments, sacramental grace, and the Church as the Mystical Body of Christ, to a stage beyond that reached by any of his predecessors. His influence on all subsequent Western theology has thereby been immense.

What Augustine defended in the Church was not an exterior institution but the very locus and centre of the dogma of God and Christ. Dogma for him is formal ecclesiastical dogma or nothing at all. The kernel of his dogmatic teaching is the teaching on the whole Christ, Head and members. For him the theology of the Mystical Body is nothing but the theology of the Incarnation. Neither he nor the Fathers in general recognize a human being in isolation. The Incarnation of God in the human nature of Christ is a union—not of course a hypostatic union—of God with the whole *corpus humanum*. Redemption is a work done by the Head alone, but communicated to the whole Body: not a bare, external, and juridical application to a passive community, but one which enables the members to share in the activity of the Head; not a mere forgiveness of sins, but a deeper and richer communication to the members, of the mission, life, activities, and sufferings of the Head. It is the communion of Christ, the Bridegroom, with His bride, the Church, in the mystery of redemptive fruitfulness.

St. Augustine's theory, like Catholic theology, has three points of light: God, Christ, the Church. These three, however, are not juxtaposed; they are inseparably one. God is revealed and accessible to us only through Christ, Christ only through the Church. This idea of God-Christ-Church is not to be conceived as a kind of chain, as if the Church were superfluous once she had led a soul to Christ, and Christ superfluous once He had led a soul to God. The Church is the horizon of Christ—not a narrow horizon, for the Church is universal—and Christ is for us the horizon of God. Augustine devotes all his energies to warding off any attempt to found a religion apart from the Catholic faith, any tendency to depart from the unity of the Church. For him the last will and testament of the ascending Christ is the unity of the *Catholica*.

Any attempt to leave it, even from the best and purest motives, is indisputably wrong.

Although it was a thought already familiar to the Fathers that the whole of the Old Testament foreshadows Christ in types and symbols, and that the Psalter especially throws light upon our Saviour's inward prayer, it was left to St. Augustine to develop this line of thought, and so to reveal with amazing richness the soul of the One Man as He prays, suffers, or rejoices. The Psalms, which in their diversity of feeling embrace all the possibilities of human life, actually become the Book of Hours of the Mystical Christ, whom we hear praying to God now as Head, now as Body—or at times we even overhear a mysterious dialogue between the two. Once we have grasped this idea, we have found the whole theme of the *Enarrationes in psalmos,* a book bewildering in the wealth of its content. The material of a whole world—for what human experience is beyond the ken of this Man?—is controlled and ordered by the consciousness of the whole Christ as He thinks, prays, works, and suffers. In this way we are able to learn and enter into the mind of the Church, as we listen to what is as it were her inward voice, reflecting upon her own life, the story of which Augustine has set forth in his *City of God.* It is a life which began with Adam and will continue until the Last Judgment—outwardly a struggle with another mystical body, that of the Evil One, indeed so closely interlocked with it as to be at times scarcely distinguishable from it. Augustine, who like St. Paul had much to endure from false brethren and grave scandals within the Church itself, does not evade the problem of what may be called Christ in the form of a slave. Catholic existence stands or falls with endurance of the cross of the mystical Christ. The very signs of this existence are laments, anxiety, and frustration, but deeper still, endurance and an all-conquering patience. So it is that Augustine never tires of hammering into his audience at every turn the necessity of bearing with the chaff among the grain, the cockle amid the wheat, the bad fish along with the good. All heresy is for Augustine impatience—easy to understand when one considers the greatness of the provocation, but unpardonable when one grasps what the Church stands for. The very suffering of the Church resulting from her own form of a slave is her share of the passion of Christ (Col. 1.24). The Church is Catholic unity because she is the bond of charity and peace and love of the brotherhood, the reflection of the love of God in Christ through the Holy Ghost, and every "purification" of the Church which attacks this unity would injure the Church herself.

Throughout these sermons on the Psalms, St. Augustine does not hesitate to initiate his audience into the deepest secrets of the allegorical interpretation of Scripture. This interpretation is based on the application of theology to history. If the mystical Christ has really been living since the beginning of the human race, then the Old Testament, and the Psalms in particular, can be nothing else but the first phase of His revelation, still veiled under carnal types which point forward to the future. And so the Christian will seek Christ everywhere in it (*Enarr.* on Ps. 98.1), discover Him with ever new joy (*Enarr.* on Ps. 96.2), and that by a method of interpretation sanctioned, or rather enjoined, by the Apostle in 1 Cor. 10.1–11. Thus Augustine invariably interprets the title *In finem*, "Unto the end," prefixed to so many Psalms, in the Pauline sense of Rom. 10.4, *Finis legis est Christus:* "We must refer everything to Christ," he says in his Discourse on Ps. 96.2, "if we are to follow a method of reasonable interpretation; we must never depart from the cornerstone, if we would avoid the road of ruin."

This spiritual interpretation as employed by the Fathers may at times betray a certain ingenuous delight in unveiling mysteries. It cannot be denied also that St. Augustine occasionally makes texts which modern exegesis has discarded, either the starting point or the whole foundation of his exposition, yet his *Enarrationes* are in general far less dependent on the text of the Psalm under discussion than might be expected. The bad Latin text of the Psalms which confronted Augustine undoubtedly lent itself to somewhat arbitrary interpretations. The titles of the Psalms especially, which for the most part result from a complete misunderstanding of the Hebrew, gave rise to elucidations which may nowadays appear fantastic. Nevertheless St. Augustine's spiritual method serves as an indispensable counterpart to the modern historical and literal exegesis.

In his Encyclical *Divino afflante Spiritu*, Pope Pius XII, while praising present-day methods, clearly shows that modern scriptural studies have by no means consigned the exegetical works of the Fathers to oblivion: "Although sometimes less well equipped with profane erudition and linguistic knowledge than the interpreters of our own time, yet, by reason of the office in the Church with which God entrusted them, they excel in a delicate perception of heavenly things and in a wonderful keenness of understanding, which enable them to penetrate far into the depths of the word of God and bring to light all that can contribute to explaining the teaching of Christ and to promoting sanctity of life" (*Divino afflante* § 34). Not that preoccupation with textual criticism was entirely absent from the mind of Augustine. On the contrary, he begged St. Jerome to revise the Septuagint, and when the latter preferred to make a translation from the Hebrew, Augustine proceeded to the task himself and revised the entire text of certain books, including the Psalter. In his translation of the Psalms, he had three clearly-defined aims:

1: to correct the Latin meaning by the Greek, as closely as possible;

2: to make the meaning clear and unambiguous;

3: to improve their Latin style.

The Saint was unsparing in his efforts to collate manuscripts and secure reliable texts. In the Encyclical already quoted, the Sovereign Pontiff pays special homage to Augustine's labors in the field of literal exegesis: "The study of ancient languages and recourse to the original texts had already been strongly recommended by the Fathers of the Church," the Pope writes, "and especially by St. Augustine. . . . But the condition of letters at that time was such that only a few possessed any knowledge of Hebrew, and even that knowledge was imperfect" (*Divino afflante* § 19).

It is true that in his *De doctrina christiana*, begun in 397, revised and published in 426, Augustine had laid down precise and necessary rules for textual criticism. Ignorance must be remedied, he says, by a knowledge of languages, especially Greek and Hebrew (2.11). Moreover in the same Book 2 he draws a sharp distinction between the literal and figurative sense of Scripture, declaring that ignorance and ambiguity arise from failing to distinguish between the two. Nevertheless, as an exegetist there was an irremediable gap in Augustine's knowledge: his almost total ignorance of Hebrew, an ignorance he admits in the *Confessions* 11.3: "If he [Moses] spoke in Hebrew, his voice would beat upon my ear to no purpose, nothing of what it said would reach my mind." His knowledge of Greek was not to be compared with St. Jerome's, yet he was sufficiently cognizant of the Septuagint to produce a Latin Psalter which, so Dom D. de Bruyne asserts, merits to bear Augustine's own name. In his *Enarrationes in psalmos* there is an evident disproportion between the number of citations from Greek in the earlier compositions and in the later ones. In the course of his thirty-two homilies on Psalm 118 he has recourse to the Greek original forty-four times, whereas he uses only nineteen Greek quotations throughout all the rest. The *Enarrationes* on Psalm 118 were composed after the others in response, as we have seen, to the appeal of the faithful, who wanted a complete exposition of the Psalter from his pen. As Possidius informs us, they were not preached or hastily improvised, as were many of the others. We may picture the Saint, therefore, in old age, perhaps with the Vandals at his door, seated at his desk before numerous Latin codices which he has time to collate and compare with the Septuagint—hence the abundance of Greek quotations. Perhaps also this serves to show that as he advanced in years St. Augustine became more and more preoccupied with the literal sense of Scripture.

The textual tradition of Augustine's Psalter has been minutely discussed and analyzed by Dom A. Wilmart and Dom D. de Bruyne. It seems probable that he used the Italic Psalter and the Old Milanese which he had taken to Africa from Italy. This last is best known to us through St. Ambrose and through three extant codices of which the finest is that of Verona. These witnesses, in a form more or less pure, show the text which Augustine tried carefully to emend, so that as far as its Latin dress was concerned it should be more elegant, and especially that it should follow the Greek meaning more closely. But after the year 415 he increasingly admitted the readings of the Gallican Psalter. Nevertheless, whatever his shortcomings as a Greek or Hebrew scholar, Augustine remains, in Alexander Souter's phrase, "assuredly the greatest man that ever wrote Latin."

* * *

ACKNOWLEDGMENTS

The present translators would like to express their appreciation and thanks to the Reverend Francis D. Dorman, Chaplain to the Augustinian Canonesses Regular of the Lateran, Haywards Heath, Sussex, England, whom ill-health compelled to abandon his task of translating Volume 1 of the *Enarrationes in psalmos* after he had devoted much time and labor to it. With the utmost generosity and unfailing kindness, he freely placed his manuscript and notes at their disposal, thus considerably facilitating and expediting the work.

They are also very grateful to the Editors of *Corpus christianorum* for kind permission to reproduce (with slight revisions) their chronological list of St. Augustine's *Enarrationes in psalmos* at the head of the series.

* * *

BIBLIOGRAPHY

TEXT USED FOR TRANSLATION

Sancti Aurelii Augustini Enarrationes in psalmos (Corpus christianorum, series latina 38–40; Turnhout 1956), edited by Dom Eligius Dekkers, O.S.B., and J. Fraipont. This text

follows almost exactly that of Migne, ML 36–37, and the
Maurist edition, both of which have also been consulted.

TRANSLATIONS

Exposition on the Book of Psalms by St. Augustine (A
  Library of the Fathers; Oxford 1848).
Oeuvres complètes de saint Augustin, traduites sous la
  direction de M. Raulx (Bar-le-Duc 1869).
Les plus belles homélies de saint Augustin sur les psaumes,
  choisies et commentées par le Chanoine G. Humeau
  (Paris 1942).
Über die Psalmen. Auswahl and Übertragung von H.
  von Balthasar (Leipzig 1935).

WORKS OF REFERENCE

Balthasar, H. von, *Augustinus: Das Antlitz der Kirche*
  (Einsiedeln 1955).
Capelle, P., *Le texte du psautier latin en Afrique* (Rome
  1913).
Miscellanea Agostiniana 2 (Rome 1931); in particular:
  De Bruyne, Dom D., "*Enarrationes in psalmos* prêchés à
  Carthage."
  De Bruyne, Dom D., "Saint Augustin reviseur de la
  Bible."
  Lapeyre, G. G., "Saint Augustin et Carthage."
  Wilmart, Dom A., "La tradition des grands ouvrages de
  saint Augustin."
Pope, H., O.P., *Saint Augustine of Hippo* (Westminster,
  Md. 1949).

*   *   *

Chronological List of the Enarrationes

DATE	ENARR.	PLACE	PSALM	
392	Written down		1-32	
393-394	Preached	Hippo	94	
393-394	Preached	Hippo	97	
395, March	Preached	Hippo	37	
395, Apr., Paschal Time	Preached	Hippo	101	Sermon 1
395, Apr., Paschal Time	Preached	Hippo	101	Sermon 2
395, Apr., Paschal Time	Preached	Hippo	148	
395, Apr., Paschal Time	Preached	Hippo	145	
395, Apr., Paschal Time	Preached	Hippo	56	
395, Apr., Paschal Time	Preached	Hippo	63	
395, Apr., Paschal Time	Preached	Hippo	54	
395, Apr., Paschal Time	Preached	Hippo	100	
395-405	Preached	Hippo	33	Sermon 1
395-405	Preached	Hippo	33	Sermon 2
396, 399, April	Preached	Hippo	96	
403, August	Preached	Hippo	57	
403, Aug. 25, Tuesday	Preached	Hippo	42	
403, Aug. 26, Wednesday	Preached	Carthage	32	Enarr. 2, Serm. 1 (morning)
403	Preached	Carthage	32	Enarr. 2, Serm. 2 (afternoon)
403, Sept. 2, Wednesday	Preached	Hippo	44	
403, Oct. 19, Monday	Preached	Hippo	80	
403, Oct. 25, Sunday	Preached	Carthage	36	Sermon 1
403, Nov. 1, Sunday	Preached	Carthage	36	Sermon 2
403, Nov. 8, Sunday	Preached	Carthage	36	Sermon 3
After 410	Preached	Hippo	84	
After 410	Preached	Hippo	41	
After 410	Preached	Hippo	25	Enarr. 2
411-413	Preached	Carthage	98	
411-413	Preached	Carthage	39	
411-413	Preached	Carthage	40	
411-413	Preached	Carthage	50	
411-413	Preached	Carthage	149	
411, 412, July	Preached	Carthage	30	Enarr. 2, Serm. 1
411, 412, July	Preached	Carthage	30	Enarr. 2, Serm. 2
411, 412, July	Preached	Carthage	30	Enarr. 2, Serm. 3
411, Sept. 14, Tuesday	Preached	Carthage	72	
412-413	Preached	Carthage	55	
End of 411 or beginning of 412	Preached	Hippo	106	

End of 411 or beginning of 412	Preached	Hippo	18	Enarr. 2
End of 411 or beginning of 412	Preached	Hippo	26	Enarr. 2
End of 411 or beginning of 412	Preached	Hippo	69	
End of 411 or beginning of 412	Preached	Hippo	74	
End of 411 or beginning of 412	Preached	Hippo	75	
End of 411 or beginning of 412	Preached	Hippo	134	
End of 411 or beginning of 412	Preached	Hippo	88	Sermon 1
End of 411 or beginning of 412	Preached	Hippo	88	Sermon 2
412, Lent	Preached	Hippo	92	
412, Lent	Preached	Hippo	46	
412, Lent	Preached	Hippo	43	
412, Lent	Preached	Hippo	45	
412, Lent	Preached	Hippo	47	
412, Lent	Preached	Hippo	35	
412, Lent	Preached	Hippo	48	Sermon 1
412, Lent	Preached	Hippo	48	Sermon 2
412, Lent, Saturday	Preached	Hippo	91	
412, Lent, Sunday	Preached	Hippo	65	
412, Lent	Preached	Hippo	60	
412, Lent	Preached	Hippo	73	
412, Lent	Preached	Hippo	79	
412, Lent	Preached	Hippo	49	
412, Lent	Preached	Hippo	62	
412, Lent	Preached	Hippo	109	
412, Sept. 13, Friday (Vigil of St. Cyprian)	Preached	Carthage	85	
412, Sept. 14, Saturday (Feast of St. Cyprian)	Preached	Carthage	86	
412, Sept.-Dec., Saturday	Preached	Carthage	146	
412, Sept.-Dec., Tuesday	Preached	Carthage	147	
412, Sept.-Dec., Thursday	Preached	Carthage	103	Sermon 1
412, Sept.-Dec., Friday	Preached	Carthage	103	Sermon 2
412, Sept.-Dec., Saturday	Preached	Carthage	103	Sermon 3
412, Sept.-Dec., Sunday	Preached	Carthage	103	Sermon 4
412, Sept.-Dec., Monday	Preached	Carthage	102	
412, Sept.-Dec., Tuesday	Preached	Carthage	66	
412, Sept.-Dec., Wednesday	Preached	Carthage	38	
412, Sept.-Dec.	Preached	Carthage	61	
412, Sept.-Dec.	Preached	Carthage	76	
412, Sept.-Dec.	Preached	Carthage	90	Sermon 1
412, Sept.-Dec.	Preached	Carthage	90	Sermon 2
412, Sept.-Dec.	Preached	Carthage	99	
412, Dec. 5 (Feast of St. Crispina)	Preached	Carthage	120	
6/7	Preached	Carthage	121	

7/8	Preached	Carthage	122
9/10	Preached	Carthage	123
412, Dec. 11/12	Preached	Carthage	124
12/13	Preached	Carthage	125
14/15	Preached	Carthage	126
412, Dec. 17 (Feast of St. Felix)	Preached	Carthage	127
18	Preached	Carthage	128
19	Preached	Carthage	129
20	Preached	Carthage	130
21	Preached	Carthage	131
22	Preached	Carthage	95
23	Preached	Carthage	132–133
26/28	Preached	Carthage	64
27/29	Preached	Carthage	138
28/30	Preached	Carthage	143
31	Preached	Carthage	136
413, Jan.	Preached	Carthage	51
413, Jan.	Preached	Carthage	53
413, Thursday	Preached	Carthage	31 Enarr. 2
413	Preached	Carthage	58
413	Preached	Carthage	59
412-414, Aug. 16/18	Preached	Utica	144
414, Paschal Time	Written down and preached	Hippo	110–117
414, Summer	Preached	Thagaste	34 Sermon 1
414, Summer	Preached	Thagaste	34 Sermon 2
414, Summer	Preached	Thagaste	68 Sermon 1
414, Summer	Preached	Thagaste	68 Sermon 2
414, Summer	Preached	Thagaste	52
414, Summer	Preached	Thagaste	93
414-415	Preached	Hippo	29 Enarr. 2
414-415	Preached	Hippo	70 Sermon 1
414-415	Preached	Hippo	70 Sermon 2
414-415	Preached	Hippo	83
414, Dec. 5 (Feast of St. Crispina)	Preached	Hippo	137
414-415 (Vigil of Martyr Saints)	Preached	Hippo	140
414-415 (Vigil of Martyr Saints)	Preached	Hippo	141
414-415, next day	Preached	Hippo	142
414-416	Written down		67, 71, 77, 78, 81, 82, 87, 89, 104, 105, 107, 108, 135, 150
418	Written down		118

1. [Verse 1] *Blessed is the man who hath not walked in the counsel of the ungodly.* The blessing applies to our Lord Jesus Christ, *homo dominicus,* the Man of the Lord.[1] *Blessed is the man who hath not walked in the counsel of the ungodly,* as did the man of earth[2] whose wife the serpent beguiled; her husband agreed to her proposal and ignored God's command.[3] *Nor stood in the way of sinners.* It is true that our Lord came by the way of sinners: He was born as sinners are; but He did not stand still, for He was never captivated by the world's allurements. *Nor sat in the chair of pestilence:* He spurned an earthly throne and the pride of it. This interpretation of the chair of pestilence is a legitimate one, because scarcely a man is immune from love of power or desire for human glory, and pestilence implies a disease so widespread as to infect all or nearly all. Yet perhaps the term *chair of pestilence* more truly symbolizes harmful doctrine, since its teaching eats in like a cancer.[4]

Then we must study the gradation: *walked, stood, sat.* Man walked in effect when he turned his back on God; he stood when he took pleasure in sin; he sat when, hardened in his own pride, he was incapable of retracing his steps unless He who had not walked in the counsel of the ungodly, nor stood in the way of sinners, nor sat in the chair of pestilence, came to deliver him.

2. [V. 2] *But his will is in the law of the Lord; and on His law he shall meditate day and night. The law,* says the Apostle, *is not made for the just man.*[5] It is one thing to be within the law, another to be under the law. He who is

21

within the law acts according to the law; he who is under the law is made to act according to the law. The one is a free man, the other a slave. So too, the law which is written and imposed on the slave is one thing, and the law seen by the mind of him who does not need the written text is another. *He shall meditate day and night:* this may denote either without a break; or *day* may signify in joy, *night* in trouble. For we read: *Abraham saw my day and was glad.*[6] And of trouble we read: *Moreover my reins have admonished me even till night.*[7]

3. [V. 3] *And he shall be like a tree which is planted near the running waters:* planted, it may mean, near Wisdom in Person, who has deigned to become man for our salvation so that man may himself be the tree planted near the running waters. Possibly it is in this sense also that another Psalm tells us that *The river of God is filled with water.*[8]

Or it may mean near the Holy Ghost. It is written of Him: *He shall baptize you in the Holy Ghost.*[9] Or again: *If any man is thirsty, let him come to me and drink;*[10] and: *If thou didst know the gift of God, and who He is that asketh water of thee, thou wouldst have asked of Him, and He would have given thee living water, whence whosoever drinketh shall never thirst, but it shall become in him a fountain of water, springing up into life everlasting.*[11]

Or again, *near the running waters* may signify near the people's sins. The Apocalypse, after all, interprets waters as peoples,[12] and we may reasonably construe running as falling, a word suggestive of sin. The tree in this case becomes our Lord. He it is who draws in the waters, the sinful peoples as they course along, into the roots of His own moral law. He will *bring forth fruit:* He will set up His churches, *in due season*—after He has been glorified by

His resurrection and ascension into heaven. For it was then that, having sent the Holy Spirit on the apostles, confirmed them in their faith in Himself, and despatched them among the nations, He reaped the fruit of the churches. *And his leaf shall not fall off*, for His word will never be ineffectual. *For all flesh is grass, and the glory of man as the flower of the field. . . . The grass is withered and the flower is fallen, but the word of the Lord endureth forever.*[13] *And all whatsoever he shall do shall prosper.* Whatever, that is to say, this tree shall bring forth: the general term obviously includes fruit and leaves, namely, deeds and words.

4. [V. 4] *Not so the wicked, not so: but like the dust, which the wind driveth from the face of the earth.* The earth here represents that steadfast abiding in God described in the words: *The Lord is the portion of my inheritance, for my inheritance is goodly to me;*[14] and also: *Expect the Lord and keep His way, and He will exalt thee to inherit the earth;*[15] and again: *Blessed are the meek, for they shall possess the earth.*[16] The point of the comparison here is this: that as the visible earth nourishes and supports the physical man, so does the invisible earth nourish and support the spiritual man. It is from the face of this invisible earth that the wind sweeps away the wicked—the wind of pride, in that it puffs up. The man on guard against this pride, being inebriated with the plenty of God's house and having drunk of the torrent of His pleasure, prays: *Let not the foot of pride come to me.*[17] Pride it was which swept away from this earth the one who declared: *I will place my seat in the north and I will be like the Most High.*[18] Pride likewise swept away from the face of this earth the man who gave his consent, partook of the forbidden tree in order to be like unto God, and then hid him-

self from God's face.[19] That this "earth" refers to the
spiritual man and that pride drives him away from it is perfectly plain from the text: *Why is earth and ashes proud?*
Because while he liveth he hath cast away his bowels.[20]
Considering why he has been driven away, it is not unfair
to say he has driven away his very self.

5. [V. 5] *Therefore the wicked shall not rise again in*
judgment. Why? Because they are swept away as dust
from the face of the earth. The speaker is right in declaring
that the ambition of the proud to sit in judgment will be
frustrated; this he explains more clearly in the next sentence: *Nor sinners in the council of the just.* The Psalmist
habitually repeats his first phrase with greater emphasis.
Here *sinners* denote the *wicked*, and *the council of the just*
reiterates *in judgment.* Possibly, however, the wicked are
one thing, sinners another. Every wicked man is a sinner,
but not every sinner is a wicked man. In that case the
phrase *the wicked shall not rise again in judgment* signifies that they will certainly rise but not with power to
judge, because they are already doomed to inescapable
punishment. *Sinners,* on the other hand, will not rise *in the*
council of the just, to act as judges, but rather to be
brought to judgment. Of such men it is written: *And the*
fire shall try every man's work, of what sort it is. If any
man's work abide, he shall receive a reward; if any man's
work burn, he shall suffer loss; but he himself shall be
saved, yet so as by fire.[21]

6. [V. 6] *For the Lord knoweth the way of the just.*
Precisely as we say: "Medicine knows the cure but not
the disease," and yet disease is diagnosed by the art of
medicine, so one can say the Lord knows the way of the
just but not that of sinners. The Lord, of course, is
ignorant of nothing, even though He tells sinners: *I never*

knew you.[22] But *the way of the wicked shall perish* is substituted, as if to say: the Lord does not know the way of the wicked. It is thus plainly stated that not to be known by the Lord spells death; to be known by Him spells life. With God, knowledge partakes of being; to be unknown is to cease to exist. *I am who am,* says the Lord; and, *He who is hath sent me.*[23]

DISCOURSE ON PSALM 2

1. [Verse 1] *Why have the Gentiles raged, and the people devised vain things?* [V. 2] *The kings of the earth stood up, and the princes met together, against the Lord and against His Christ.* The Psalmist asks *Why,* as much as to say: The futility of it! They have obviously not achieved their aim, which was Christ's destruction. The words are an allusion to our Lord's persecutors mentioned in the Acts of the Apostles.[1]

2. [V. 3] *Let us break their bonds asunder, and let us cast away their yoke from us.* Although this text admits of a different interpretation, it is better to apply it to those who are described as fabricating senseless plots. The verse *Let us break their bonds asunder, and let us cast away their yoke from us* then signifies: We must see that we keep free of the bonds and burdens of the Christian faith.

3. [V. 4] *He that dwelleth in heaven shall laugh at them, and the Lord shall deride them.* The same thought has been repeated: the Psalmist has substituted *Lord* for *He that dwelleth in heaven,* and *shall deride* for *shall laugh at them.* Neither of these expressions, however, must be taken literally, as though God wrinkled His cheeks to laugh or His nose to deride. What this context signifies is that power which God gives to His saints of reading the future,

of contemplating Christ's name and that kingdom of His
which is to extend to the last man on earth and make all
nations His own. By their vision they realize the futility of
wicked men's schemes. Now this power which unveils to
them the future, constitutes God's laughter and derision.
He that dwelleth in heaven shall laugh at them. If by
heaven we understand holy souls, then it is by their agency
that God, who knows what is to come, will deride and
laugh to scorn.

4. [V. 5] *Then shall He speak to them in His anger
and trouble them in His rage.* To define quite clearly the
effect of God's words, the Psalmist has said, *He shall
trouble them:* the phrase *in His rage* is identical with *in
His anger.* But we must not think of the Lord God's anger
as implying any disturbance of mind. Rather is it the power
whereby He asserts His rights in all justice, since every
creature is subject to His service. We should particularly
observe and remember the text in Solomon: *But thou,
Lord of power, judgest with tranquillity, and with great
favor disposest of us.*[2] God's anger, then, is the emotion
produced in a soul which knows God's law and sees this
law transgressed by the sinner. This indignation in the
souls of righteous men metes out many a penalty. Or else
God's anger in this context may very well allude to that
spiritual darkness which overtakes those who break the
law of God.

5. [V. 6] *But I am appointed king by Him over Sion,
His holy mountain, preaching the commandment of the
Lord.*[3] This is obviously spoken in the very person of our
Lord Jesus Christ. Now if Sion denotes contemplation, as
some interpret it, then we can apply it to nothing more perfectly than the Church, in which the members are urged to
rise each day to the contemplation of God's glory, accord-

ing to the Apostle's words: *But we all, beholding the glory of the Lord with open face.*[4] This, therefore, is the sense of the passage: "I am appointed king by Him over His holy Church," called here a mountain by reason of its eminence and solidity. *But I am appointed king by Him:* "I indeed, whose bonds they proposed to break asunder and whose yoke they thought to cast away." *Preaching His commandment.* Is there any one who can fail to understand this, seeing it carried into practice every day?

6. [V. 7] *The Lord hath said to me: Thou art my son, today have I begotten thee.*[5] It is possible to see in the word *today* a prophecy of the day on which Jesus Christ was born in His human nature. Yet as the word *today* denotes the actual present, and as in eternity nothing is past as if it had ceased to be, nor future as if it had not yet come to pass, but all is simply present, since whatever is eternal is ever in being, the words *Today have I begotten thee* are to be understood of the divine generation. In this phrase, orthodox Catholic belief proclaims the eternal generation of the Power and Wisdom of God who is the only-begotten Son.

7. [V. 8] *Ask of me and I will give thee the Gentiles for thy inheritance.*[6] This pertains no longer to eternity. It is addressed to Him who took upon Himself human nature, who offered Himself in a sacrifice which replaces all other sacrifices, and *who also maketh intercession for us.*[7] It is to Christ, therefore, against the background of the whole temporal economy which God has ordained for the human race, that the words *Ask of me* are addressed. Ask, namely, that all nations may be united under the Christian name, so that they may thereby be redeemed from death and belong wholly to God. *I will give thee the Gentiles for thy inheritance:* They shall be thine unto their own

salvation, and shall bring forth to thee spiritual fruit. *And the utmost parts of the earth for thy possession*. The same idea is repeated. *The utmost parts of the earth* replaces *Gentiles*, to show more clearly that all nations are meant, while the Psalmist uses the phrase *thy possession* instead of *thy inheritance*.

8. [V. 9] *Thou shalt rule them with a rod of iron*, in inflexible justice. *And shalt break them in pieces like a potter's vessel*.[8] Thou wilt shatter their earthly desires, the sordid doings of their animal self, everything which has become encrusted and ingrained in the clay-born sinner. [V. 10] *And now, O ye kings, understand. Now*, that is to say, when you are walking in newness of life; *now*, when you have shattered the outer crust of clay, those human vessels of folly which belong to your past; yes, *now understand*, O ye who are now kings, since you are able, on the one hand, to govern whatever is base and sensual in yourselves, and, on the other, to fight not as beating the air, but chastising your bodies and bringing them into subjection.[9] *Receive instruction, you that judge the earth*. This again is a repetition. *Receive instruction* replaces *understand;* and *you that judge the earth* replaces *ye kings*. The Psalmist implies that these judges of the earth are spiritual, for whatever we judge must be inferior to ourselves, and whatever is inferior to the spiritual man is rightly termed earth, since it has been marred by the earthly fall.

9. [V. 11] *Serve ye the Lord with fear*.[10] A warning that the title *kings who judge the earth* must not awaken pride. *And rejoice unto Him with trembling*. The word *rejoice* is happily chosen; otherwise the phrase *serve ye the Lord with fear* might seem to suggest distress. But as before, to avoid jubilation running to excess and rashness, the

Psalmist adds *with trembling:* an admonition to be circum-
spect and on our guard in the spiritual life.

These verses admit of another interpretation. *And now,
O ye kings, understand:* Now that I am henceforth enthroned as king, be not sad, ye kings of the earth, as though
robbed of your prerogative. Understand rather, and learn
the lesson that it is to your advantage to live under the protection of Him who trains and instructs you. This also is to
your advantage: not to set up an irresponsible rule of your
own, but to serve with fear the Lord of all, to rejoice in the
certitude of unalloyed happiness, and to act with prudence
and caution for fear pride should render it forfeit.

10. [V. 12] *Embrace discipline, lest at any time the
Lord be angry, and you perish from the just way.* This is a
repetition of *Understand and receive instruction,* for to
understand and receive instruction is to embrace discipline.
However, the expression *apprehendite,* embrace, implies
that discipline is a kind of protection and defense against all
that might harm us did we not cling to it assiduously. *Lest
at any time the Lord be angry* suggests uncertainty, not in
the prophet's vision—he feels none—but in the minds of the
men he warns, since those who have not received the full
revelation are liable to regard God's anger as somewhat
uncertain. This, then, is what they should say to themselves: Let us embrace discipline, otherwise we may risk
the Lord's anger and go astray from the path of justice.
Now we have already explained how the phrase *the Lord
is angry* should be interpreted.[11] *And you perish from the
just way.* Terrible punishment, and one dreaded by those
who have experienced something of the sweetness of holiness. The man who forsakes the road of justice will wander
in utter misery along the paths of sin.

11. [V. 13] *When His wrath shall be kindled in a short*

time, blessed are all they that trust in Him. When the vengeance laid up for sinners and the ungodly bursts forth, not only will it spare those who trust in the Lord; it will even serve to erect and establish for them a royal throne on high. For the Psalmist has not said: *When His wrath shall be kindled in a short time,* secure *are all they that trust in Him,* as though to escape punishment is to be their only reward. No, he calls them *blessed,* a word which expresses the epitome and crown of all possessions. The phrase *in brevi,* within a short time, signifies, I think, that it will blaze of a sudden upon sinners who imagine it hidden in a far-distant future.

DISCOURSE ON PSALM 3

1. [Verse 1] *The Psalm of David when he fled from the face of his son Absalom.*[1] The words of this Psalm: *I have fallen asleep and have taken my rest, and I have risen up, because the Lord will uphold me,*[2] lead us to believe that we must apply them to the Person of Christ. For they are more in keeping with our Lord's passion and resurrection than with the account which history gives of David's flight before the face of his own rebel son. And since it is written of Christ's disciples: *As long as the bridegroom is with them, the children of the bridegroom do not fast,*[3] it need not surprise us that the disloyal son should be the figure of the disloyal disciple who betrayed his Master. From a literal standpoint one may say, it is true, that Christ fled before him when, on the departure of Judas, He withdrew with the rest to the mountain. In a spiritual sense, however, when the Son of God, Power and Wisdom of God as He is, forsook the mind of Judas, the devil straightway took possession of it. *The devil,* so it is written,

entered into his heart.[4] One may therefore safely say that Christ fled from his face; not that Christ gave place before the devil, but that on Christ's departure the devil assumed the mastery. This departure of our Lord, I think, is termed a flight in the Psalm on account of its swiftness; a swiftness also indicated in our Lord's injunction: *That which thou dost, do quickly.*[5] We even use the expression in ordinary speech: The word has fled, we say, when it refuses to come to mind; and of a great scholar: Nothing escapes him. In the same sense, truth escaped the mind of Judas when it ceased to enlighten him.

Now Absalom, according to some interpreters, signifies in Latin *patris pax*, "peace of his father." It may very well seem puzzling that the name, "peace of his father," can be appropriate, either in the history of Kingdoms[6] where Absalom is at war with his father, or in the history of the New Testament where Judas is the betrayer of our Lord. But a careful reader will perceive in the first instance that during the struggle there was peace in David's heart towards the son whose death he even bewailed with bitter grief: *Absalom my son!* he cried. *Would to God I might die for thee.*[7] And when the history of the New Testament shows us the great, the truly wonderful forbearance of our Lord, who bore with Judas so long just as though he were upright, and although He was aware of his designs yet admitted him to the feast in which He set before and entrusted to His disciples His own body and blood under a figure, who finally in the other's very act of betrayal accepted his kiss,[8] we can easily see that Christ showed nothing but peace towards the man who betrayed Him, although the traitor's heart was prey to intentions so criminal. Absalom, then, is termed "peace of his father" because his father cherished the peace which the son lacked.

2. [V. 2] *Why, O Lord, are they multiplied that afflict me?* So multiplied, indeed, that even among my disciples one man has been found to swell the ranks of my adversaries. [V. 3] *Many are they who rise up against me. Many say to my soul: There is no salvation for him in his God.* It is obvious that unless they had disbelieved in His resurrection, they would never have put Him to death. Their taunts witness to this fact: *If He be the Son of God, let Him now come down from the cross;* and: *He saved others; Himself He cannot save.*⁹ Nor similarly would Judas have betrayed Him unless he had been one of those who said contemptuously of Christ: *There is no salvation for him in his God.*

3. [V. 4] *But thou, O Lord, takest me up.* Christ speaks to God in His human nature, since God's taking of human nature is the Word made flesh. *My glory.* He even calls God His glory, this Man whom the Word of God has so taken upon Himself that God and He are One. A lesson for the proud, who close their ears when asked: *What hast thou that thou hast not received? And if thou hast received, why dost thou glory as if thou hadst not received it?*¹⁰ *And the lifter up of my head.* Here, I think, is denoted Christ's human mind,¹¹ not without reason termed the head of the soul; and this soul was so united, so inextricably part of the surpassing excellency of the Word Incarnate, as it were, that it was not surrendered even in the deep humiliation of the passion.

4. [V. 5] *I have cried to the Lord with my voice:* not with the physical voice which produces sound by vibrations of the air, but with the voice of the heart, which man cannot hear but which rings out to God like a cry. By this

voice it was that Susanna was heard,[12] and with this voice
our Lord Himself has instructed us to pray in a room with
closed doors, or rather, noiselessly in the secret place of the
heart.[13] Let no one be too ready to say that there is not
much prayer in such a voice because not a single audible
word escapes from our lips, since in silent prayer of the
heart as long as any distractions interfere with the fervor
of our petition we cannot claim: *I have cried to the Lord
with my voice.* We are only entitled to say this with truth
when the soul, withdrawn in solitude from everything
physical and from all earthly considerations, speaks in
prayer to the Lord where He alone hears. Such prayer is
termed a cry by reason of its burning intensity.[14]

And He hath heard me from His holy mount.[15] Another
prophet applies the term mountain to our Lord Himself,
when he writes that *the stone that was cut out of a mountain without hands became a great mountain.*[16] Yet the
words of the Psalm can hardly be spoken in the Person of
Christ, unless possibly He were to say: The Lord hath
heard me "from myself" as from His holy mountain, since
He hath dwelt in me as in His heights. But it is clearer and
simpler to take it that God has heard him from the height
of His justice. For He owed it to His justice to raise from
the dead the innocent one who was slain, who had been
requited with evil for good, and to mete out to His persecutors their chastisement. We do in fact read: *Thy justice
is as the mountains of God.*[17]

5. [V. 6] *I have fallen asleep and have taken my rest.*[18]
Ego dormivi.[19] It may not be out of place to note that the
stress falls on *ego,* "I," to signify that our Lord underwent
death of His own free will. *Therefore doth the Father love
me,* He tells us, *because I lay down my life, that I may take
it again. No man taketh it from me, but I lay it down of*

myself. And I have power to lay it down, and I have power to take it up again.[20] It was not against my own will, He says, that you took me and put me to death, but I myself, *I have fallen asleep and have taken my rest, and I have risen up, because the Lord will uphold me.* Scripture contains numberless instances of sleep symbolizing death. The Apostle, for example, speaks thus: *I will not have you ignorant, brethren, concerning them that are asleep.*[21] Nor need we ask why the Psalmist adds *I have taken my rest* after having already said *I have fallen asleep.* Repetitions of this kind are usual in Scripture, as I have pointed out many times in the second Psalm. Some copies run: *I have fallen asleep and have been cast into a deep slumber.* Others give variant readings according to the possibilities of the Greek text: ἐγὼ δὲ ἐκοιμήθην καὶ ὕπνωσα. It may be that falling asleep symbolizes a dying man, while slumber symbolizes a man already dead, just as one passes from drowsiness to sleep, and from awakening to complete awareness. We must not regard these repetitions in the sacred writings as empty ornaments of speech. *I have fallen asleep and have taken my rest* is therefore an excellent way of saying: I surrendered myself to the sufferings which issued in death. *And I have risen up, because the Lord will uphold me.* It is noteworthy that in a single sentence one verb is in the past tense, the other in the future. For *I have risen up* is past, and *will uphold* is future; as if, indeed, Christ could not rise up without being upheld. In prophecy, however, past and future tenses are freely combined with the same signification. Predictions of things to come are future according to time, but in the minds of those who prophesy they are already accomplished facts. One also meets verbs in the present tense. These will be discussed as they occur in their context.

6. [V. 7] *I will not fear thousands of the people surrounding me*. The Gospel tells us of the crowds who surrounded our Lord as He hung suffering on the cross.[22] *Arise, O Lord; save me, O God*. The verb *Arise* is not addressed to a God who is asleep or lying down, but it is customary in the Holy Scriptures to attribute to the Person of God His own work in us. This is not always so, of course, but only when it can be done with propriety; as, for instance, God is said to speak when a prophet, or an apostle or some other messenger of the truth has received from Him the gift of speech. Hence the question: *Do you seek a proof of Christ that speaketh in me?*[23] St. Paul does not say: I speak through His enlightenment or at His bidding. No, he attributes his message directly to Him from whom he had received it.

7. [V. 8] *For thou hast struck all them who are my adversaries without cause*. We must not punctuate the words in such a way as to form a single sentence thus: *Arise, O Lord; save me, O my God, for thou hast struck all them who are my adversaries without cause*. If our Lord was saved, it was not because God struck His enemies; on the contrary, He saved Christ first, and struck them afterwards. This verse belongs therefore to what follows, so that the sense runs: *For thou hast struck all them who are my adversaries without cause, thou hast broken the teeth of sinners:* in the act of breaking the teeth of sinners, in other words, thou hast smitten my adversaries. It is precisely this punishment of the adversaries which constitutes the breaking of their teeth, the utter destruction, the crushing to dust, as it were, of the words spoken by the wicked who tore the Son of God to pieces by their execrations. These teeth, then, will signify abusive words in the sense in which the Apostle has said: *But if you bite and devour*

one another, take heed you be not consumed one of another.[24]

The *teeth of sinners* can also signify their ringleaders, who exert their influence in order to cut off men from the fellowship of the upright, and incorporate them into the society of evildoers. To these teeth are opposed the teeth of the Church, who does her utmost to tear away from the errors of paganism and heretical doctrines all true believers, and to transfer them into herself, the Body of Christ. It was with these teeth that Peter was told to kill and eat the animals.[25] In other words, he had to destroy the essence of the Gentiles by transforming it into his own.

Finally, concerning these same teeth the Church is addressed thus: *Thy teeth as flocks of sheep that are shorn, which come up from the washing all laden with twins, and there is none barren among them.*[26] Image of those who impart true doctrine and live as they preach; they fulfil the injunction: *So let your light shine before men that they may glorify your Father who is in heaven.*[27] Persuaded by the authority of preachers such as these, men believe in the God who speaks and acts through their agency, and they break with the world to which they hitherto conformed, in order to transfer their allegiance to the Church. The preachers to whom this is due are deservedly called teeth resembling shorn sheep, because they have laid aside the burden of earthly cares, they have risen from the bath, from the sacrament of baptism which has purified them from all earthly stain, and they are all laden with twins. They carry into effect, indeed, the two precepts of which we are told: *On these two commandments dependeth the whole law and the prophets.*[28] They love God with their whole heart, and with their whole soul, and with their whole mind, and their neighbor as themselves. There is none barren among them, since such is the fruit they bring forth unto God. The sense, therefore, in which we should interpret *Thou hast broken the teeth of sinners* is this: Thou hast brought the ringleaders of evil men to destruction by smiting those who wantonly assailed me. The Gospel narrative tells us that it was the ringleaders who in fact persecuted our Lord; the common people paid Him honor.

8. [V. 9] *Salvation is of the Lord, and may thy blessing be upon thy people.*[29] In the same verse the Psalmist both teaches men what they should believe and prays for believers. The first half, *Salvation is of the Lord*, is addressed to men, but not the latter half. That God's blessing may be upon His people is uttered entirely on man's behalf. The Psalmist turns in prayer to God Himself on behalf of the people whom he has told: *Salvation is of the Lord.* What does he mean? Surely this. No man should take any credit to himself, because God alone can deliver us from the death of sin. *Unhappy man that I am*, says the Apostle, *who shall deliver me from the body of this death? The grace of God, by Jesus Christ our Lord.*[30] But do thou, O Lord, bless thy people who look unto thee for their salvation.

9. Or we may regard this Psalm from a different angle and apply it to the Person of Christ speaking in His totality. I speak of the whole Christ by reason of the Body of which He is the Head, according to the teaching of the Apostle: *Now you are the body and the members of Christ.*[31] Christ is therefore the Head of this Body. For that reason St. Paul elsewhere says: *But doing the truth in charity, we may in all things grow up in Him who is the Head, even Christ, from whom the whole body is compacted and fitly joined together.* It is therefore both the

Church and her Head who, beset by storms of persecution throughout the whole world, as we have already seen, cry out with the lips of the prophet: *Why, O Lord, are they multiplied that afflict me? Many are they who rise up against me* in a desire to exterminate the Christian name.

Many say to my soul: There is no salvation for him in his God. For otherwise they could never have hoped to destroy the Church which was spreading on every side, unless they had supposed that God had no care of her. *But thou, O Lord, takest me up,* in Christ of course. For in taking His humanity, the Word, who *was made flesh and dwelt among us,*[32] has also taken upon Himself the Church, and has *made us sit together with Him in the heavenly places.*[33] Where the Head precedes, the other members will follow, for *who shall separate us from the love of Christ?*[34] The Church, therefore, has good reason to say to God: *Thou takest me up, my glory.* Far from attributing any excellence to herself, she realizes that she owes it to His grace and mercy. *And the lifter up of my head,* of Him, in other words, who as first-born from the dead[35] ascended into heaven.

I have cried to the Lord with my voice, and He hath heard me from His holy mountain. This refers to the prayer of all the saints, the odor of sweetness which rises up in the presence of the Lord. The Church is now heard from the height of this holy mountain which is also her Head, or from the heights of God's justice which delivers His elect and punishes their persecutors. The people of God may also say: *I have fallen asleep and have taken my rest, and I have risen up, because the Lord will uphold me,* in order to unite them inseparably to their Head. It is to them the words are addressed: *Rise, thou that sleepest, and arise from the dead, and Christ shall lay hold on thee.*[36]

They have been drawn from among that class of sinners summarized in the sentence: *For they that sleep, sleep in the night.*[37] The people of God may add moreover: *I will not fear thousands of the people surrounding me,* the heathen nations who press in on every side to exterminate the Christian name wherever they can. Why fear, when the martyrs' blood like oil feeds the flame of the love of Christ? *Arise, O Lord; save me, O my God:* such is the prayer of the Body to its Head. The Body was saved when its Head rose to ascend on high, leading captivity captive and giving gifts to men.[38] The prophet here speaks of things foreordained by God. He sees to the world's end, where that ripe harvest spoken of in the Gospel[39] has brought our Lord down; and this harvest finds its salvation in His resurrection who deigned to die for us. *For thou hast struck all them who are my adversaries without cause; thou hast broken the teeth of sinners.* Now that the Church is triumphant, the enemies of the Christian name have been covered with confusion, and their abuse like their power reduced to nothing. Firmly believe, then, children of men, that *salvation is of the Lord;* and as for thee, O Lord, *may thy blessing be upon thy people.*

10. Furthermore, when defects and evil desires swarm upon us to subject us to the law of sin in spite of our efforts,[40] each of us can cry: *Why, O Lord, are they multiplied that afflict me? Many are they who rise up against me.* And since the accumulation of evils very often gives rise to a feeling of hopelessness of being cured, the soul finds itself exposed to the ridicule of the very vices themselves. Or else the devil and his angels with their evil suggestions try to drive us to despair. Then in all truth can we say: *Many say to my soul: There is no salvation for him in his God. But thou, O Lord, takest me up.* For this is our hope,

that God has deigned to take up mankind in Christ. *My glory*, according to the principle which forbids us to ascribe any merit to ourselves. *And the lifter up of my head*, either of Him who is Head of us all, or of the spirit in each of us, which is the head of soul and body, for *the head of the woman is the man, and the head of the man is Christ*.[41] The spirit is uplifted, however, only when we can say: *With the mind I serve the law of God*.[42] What remains in human nature will be brought into peaceful unity[43] when, in the resurrection of the body, death is finally swallowed up in victory.[44]

I have cried to the Lord with my voice: with that interior, most urgent voice. *And He hath heard me from His holy mount*, or through Him whom He has sent to our aid, and by whose mediation He grants our prayers. *I have fallen asleep and have taken my rest, and I have risen up, because the Lord will uphold me.* Which of the faithful cannot make this language his own when he considers that his sins are no more by reason of the free gift of regeneration? *I will not fear thousands of the people surrounding me.* In addition to the trials which the Church in general has undergone and will yet undergo, every man also has his own temptations. When they beset him, he should cry: *Arise, O Lord; save me, O my God:* in other words, Make me rise above them. *For thou hast struck all them who are my adversaries without cause.* This prophecy with good reason refers to Satan and his angels who rage not only against the whole Mystical Body of Christ, but against every one of its members. *Thou hast broken the teeth of sinners.* Each of us has his ill-wishers; each has also his mischief-makers, who strive to sever us from the Body of Christ. But *salvation is of the Lord.* Let us guard against pride by exclaiming: *My soul hath stuck close to thee.*[45]

And finally, *May thy blessing be upon thy people,* upon each and all of us.

Discourse on Psalm 4

1. [Verse 1] *Unto the end, a psalm song for David. The end of the law is Christ, unto justice to everyone that believeth.*[1] This *end,* however, signifies completion, not destruction. One may wonder whether every song is a psalm, or rather every psalm a song. Or are there certain songs that may not be called psalms, psalms that may not be called songs? However, we must turn to the Scriptures to see whether the title "song" does not imply a joyful theme, whereas psalms properly so called are accompanied on a psaltery, deeply symbolic in meaning, which history reveals that the prophet David used.[2] This is not the place to make an elaborate study of a point which demands extensive research and much discussion. For the moment we must look for the words either of the man of the Lord[3] after His resurrection, or of the members of the Church who believe and hope in Him.

2. [V. 2] *When I called upon Him, the God of my justice heard me.* My prayer, the Psalmist says, has been heard by God, the author of my justice. *When I was in distress, thou hast enlarged me:* thou hast led me from the tight grip of affliction into the wide spaces of joy, for distress and anguish are the lot of every human soul that practices wrongdoing.[4] But the man who declares: *We glory in tribulations, knowing that tribulation worketh patience,* and so on up to the words, *because the charity of God is poured forth in our hearts by the Holy Ghost who is given to us*[5]—that man is enduring no anguish of heart, however hard-pressed he may be by persecutors from without. The

verb is in the third person when the Psalmist exclaims *God heard me*, and then passes at once to the second when he adds: *thou hast enlarged me*. If the change of person has been made simply for the sake of variety and style, it seems strange that the speaker should first of all set out to proclaim before men that he has been heard, and then call upon the God who heard him. Probably having told us that he has been heard in the very act of opening wide his heart, he has preferred to speak with God, in order thereby to show us the meaning of a wide-open heart. It means to possess a heart filled with God with whom the soul maintains intimate converse. All this applies to the faithful who believe in Christ and have received illumination from Him, but I fail to see how we can possibly extend it to the Man of the Lord, whom the Wisdom of God united to Himself, seeing that God never for a moment abandoned Him. Nevertheless, just as in His petition He emphasized our weakness rather than His own, so also in this sudden widening of the heart our Lord can speak in the name of His faithful whom He identified with Himself in this way when He said: *I was hungry, and you gave me not to eat; I was thirsty, and you gave me not to drink,*[6] and so forth. Here likewise our Lord can say: *thou hast enlarged me*, speaking in the name of one of His little ones who, when in converse with God, possesses His love poured forth in his heart, by the Holy Ghost who has been given to us.[7] *Have mercy on me and hear my prayer.* Why does He repeat the petition after declaring that He has already been heard and His heart widened? Has He done so for our sakes, of whom it is said: *But if we hope for that which we see now, we wait for it with patience?*[8] Or is He asking God to perfect in the faithful soul the work He has begun?

3. [V. 3] *O ye sons of men, how long will ye be dull of*

heart? Your deviation from truth, the Psalmist tells them, lasted at least until the coming of the Son of God; but why are your hearts still hardened? When will you put an end to unrealities if in the very presence of Truth you yet refuse? *Why do you love vanity, and seek after lying?* Why be content with the lowest? Truth alone, which gives to everything else its reality, can give happiness. Vanity is of deceivers,[9] and all is vanity.[10] What profit hath a man in all his toiling, wherein he toileth under the sun? Why therefore are you held fast by love of perishable things? Why follow after the meanest as if it were the highest? It is a delusion, a lie. You would set your heart, in fact, on keeping as your own forever what must pass away like a shadow.

4. [V. 4] *Know ye also that the Lord hath made His holy one wonderful.* Which holy one? Surely Him whom he has raised from the dead and enthroned on His right hand in heaven? The Psalmist therefore chides mankind of set purpose, to induce them to turn at long last from love of this world to God. If the addition of the connecting phrase *know ye* seems strange, it is easy to observe in the Scriptures how this manner of speaking is characteristic of the prophets. You will often find this introduction: And the Lord said to him, And the word of the Lord came to him. This conjunction, which has no preceding thought to link with what follows, may perhaps be an adroit way of suggesting the connection between the utterance of the truth by the prophet's lips, and the vision seen in his heart.

Here, however, one might observe that the foregoing sentence *Why do you love vanity, and seek after lying?* is as much as to say: Do not hanker after empty trifles and go in search of lies. After this statement the rest follows in direct speech: *Know ye also that the Lord hath made His holy one wonderful.* But the *diapsalma* which separates the two verses forbids our joining them together. One may, with some critics, regard *diapsalma* as a Hebrew word meaning "So be it," or as a Greek word denoting a pause in the psalmody. Thus *psalma* would mean what is sung, *diapsalma* a silent pause in the psalmody; and just as we speak of singing in unison as *sympsalma*, so a cessation marked by a certain pause or break in the continuity is called *diapsalma*. Whatever the explanation, be it this, that, or the other, one thing at least is all but certain, that after the *diapsalma* the sequence is broken and cannot be linked up with what precedes.

5. *The Lord will hear me when I shall cry unto Him.* We are here exhorted, I think, to implore God's help with great earnestness of heart, with an interior, soundless cry. As it is our duty to give thanks for our enlightenment during life, so we should beg for rest after death. We may therefore put these words either into the mouth of the faithful preacher of the Gospel or into that of our Lord Himself as meaning: The Lord will hear you, when you cry unto Him.

6. [V. 5] *Be ye angry, and sin not.*[11] Now the thought might strike someone: Who is worthy of being heard, or how should a sinner cry unto the Lord otherwise than in vain? The Psalmist therefore replies: *Be ye angry, and sin not*, a reply which may be interpreted in two ways. It may signify: Even though you are angry, do not sin. In other words, although there should arise in the soul an impulse which, as a penalty of sin, is now beyond our control, at least let us repudiate it with the rational mind which has been inwardly regenerated to the likeness of God. Thus with our mind we shall serve the law of God, even if with the flesh we still serve the law of sin.[12]

Or again it may signify: Do penance. Turn your anger against yourselves for your past misdeeds, and sin no more for the future. *The things you say in your hearts*, supply, say them out; so that the complete meaning would be: What you say aloud, echo also in your hearts, and do not be the kind of people described in the words: *With their lips they glorify me, but their heart is far from me.*[13] *Be sorry for them upon your beds*. The Psalmist has already expressed the same idea in the phrase *in your hearts*. These indeed are the resting places where our Lord advises us to pray interiorly with closed doors.[14] The advice *Be sorry for them* may denote either the penitential sorrow which drives the contrite soul to inflict punishment on itself in order to escape God's sentence of condemnation to torment, or else it is an incentive, a kind of spur, to keep the soul on the alert to watch for the light of Christ. Instead of *compungimini*, Be sorry, others prefer the reading *Aperimini*, Be ye opened, by reason of the expression κατανύγητε[15] in the Greek Psalter, which relates to that widening of the heart required to receive the inpouring of charity through the Holy Spirit.

7. [V. 6] *Offer up the sacrifice of justice, and trust in the Lord*. The Psalmist says elsewhere: *A sacrifice to God is an afflicted spirit.*[16] Now a sacrifice of justice may well apply to an act of penance. What more just than that a man should castigate his own sins instead of those of others, and by self-punishment offer a holocaust to God?

Or again, does the sacrifice of justice refer to good works done after repentance? For the *diapsalma* placed at this point may quite well suggest the transition from the old life to the new. When the old self has been destroyed or weakened by penance, the man born anew by regeneration offers to God a sacrifice of justice; the soul now purified offers and immolates itself on the altar of faith, to be consumed by the divine fire, the Holy Spirit. So that *Offer up the sacrifice of justice, and trust in the Lord* may amount to this: Live an upright life, and await the gift of the Holy Ghost, so that you may be enlightened by the truth in which you have believed.

8. Even so, the words *Trust in the Lord* are not yet fully explained. What precisely do we hope for? Doubtless, good things. But each one sets his heart on obtaining from God what he values, and rarely does one come across a man who sets store by the unseen good things that pertain to the interior life, which alone are worth our regard. We must use the others from necessity, not find in them our joy. Consequently, after saying *Trust in the Lord,* the Psalmist aptly proceeds: *Many say: Who showeth us good things?* This is the conversation, this the question which forms the daily topic of all fools and knaves who want to enjoy in the life of this world a peace and tranquillity which the perversity of human nature prevents them from attaining. In their blindness they even dare to find fault with the ordering of Providence, and being caught in the net of their own deserts, they think the present times worse than the past. Or else to the promise made to us of a future life they often enough retort in doubt and despair: Who knows if it is true? Has any one ever returned from the dead to tell us about it? Lucidly therefore and in few words, but only to those with eyes for the unseen, the Psalmist explains the good things we should seek. To the question, *Who showeth us good things?* he makes reply: [V. 7] *The light of thy countenance, O Lord, is signed upon us.* This light which shines upon the mind, not upon the eyes, constitutes mankind's whole and essential good. It is *signed upon us,* so the Psalmist has said, like a

coin stamped with the king's image. For man was made to God's image and likeness, and defaced it by sin.[17] His true and lasting good therefore is to be stamped anew by regeneration. This seems to me the sense which wise interpreters have applied to our Lord's words upon looking at Caesar's tribute money: *Render to Caesar the things that are Caesar's, and to God the things that are God's.*[18] It is as if He had said: God, like Caesar, demands from you the impression of His own image. Just as you repay his coinage to Caesar, so return your soul to God, shining and stamped with the light of His countenance.

Thou hast given gladness in my heart. Not in external things, therefore, is joy to be sought, as it is sought by the hardhearted who hanker after empty trifles and run in search of lies. No, it is to be looked for within, where the light of God's countenance is stamped upon us, for Christ has His dwelling place in a man's heart,[19] as the Apostle has told us. It rests with such a man to contemplate the truth, since our Lord has told us: *I am the truth.*[20] It was He too who spoke by the mouth of the Apostle. *Do you seek a proof of Christ,* he asked, *that speaketh in me?*[21] Obviously Christ was speaking not audibly, but in his inmost heart, in that secret place where we are to pray.[22]

9. But those enamored of perishable things—and what a great number there undoubtedly are—incapable of recognizing in their own hearts blessings of real and lasting worth, think of nothing to ask but, *Who showeth us good things?* Such men fully deserve what the Psalmist adds: *What time in their corn, wine and oil they are multiplied.* The addition of the word *their* is not superfluous, for there is a corn which is God's inasmuch as He is the living bread which came down from heaven.[23] There is a wine, too, which is God's. *They shall be inebriated,* says the Psalmist,

with the plenty of thy house.[24] There is also an oil which
is God's. *Thou hast anointed my head*, we are told, *with
oil.*[25] The innumerable men however who ask, *Who
showeth us good things?* and who fail to see that the kingdom of heaven is within,[26] are multiplied in the time of
their corn, wine and oil. Now multiplication does not
necessarily signify abundance; it occasionally signifies
want, as when a soul eaten up with an insatiable and burning desire for worldly pleasures falls prey to a horde of
disquieting images which prevent it from contemplating
the essentially simple good. Of a soul in this state we are
told: *For the corruptible body is a load upon the soul, and
the earthly habitation presseth down the mind that museth
upon many things.*[27] By the constant coming and going of
worldly possessions—its harvesting of corn, wine and oil, so
to speak—a soul like this becomes filled with countless
imaginings, and too dissipated to be able to fulfil the command: *Think of the Lord in goodness, and seek Him in
simplicity of heart.*[28] This simplicity is absolutely incompatible with such multiplicity. And so, leaving aside the
many who are distracted by the lure of worldly goods—
those who ask, *Who showeth us good things*, that one cannot see with the eyes but must look for inwardly in simplicity of heart—the man of faith cries out in delight:
[V. 9] *In peace in the selfsame I will sleep and I will take
rest.* He has the right to hope that his heart will become a
complete stranger to perishable things, that he will forget
the miseries of the present life; this state the Psalmist in
prophecy aptly terms sleep and rest, figures of that perfect
peace which no trouble can disturb. Bliss such as this, however, cannot be attained here and now; no, we must look
for it hereafter, as the actual words of the Psalmist in the
future tense teach us. For they are neither: I have slept and

have taken rest; nor are they: *I sleep and take rest*; but: *I will sleep and I will take rest*. Then shall this corruptible put on incorruption, and this mortal put on immortality; then shall death be swallowed up in victory.[29] Hence the Apostle's words: *But if we hope for that which we see not, we wait for it with patience*.[30]

10. Finally, in keeping with this line of thought the Psalmist concludes: [V. 10] *For thou, O Lord, singularly hast made me dwell in hope*. At this point he does not say "wilt make" but *hast made*. The man who has conceived such a hope will certainly see its fruition one day. The adverb *singularly* is full of meaning also, for it throws into relief that throng of men who have been multiplied in the time of their corn, wine and oil, and who ask: *Who showeth us good things?* This multiplicity will pass away, but simple unity will abide forever in the saints, as the Acts of the Apostles tell us: *The multitude of believers had but one heart and one soul*.[31] Single-minded and sincere, withdrawn from the swarming crowd of things which spring up only to die away, we must be lovers of eternity and unity if we would hold fast to the one God and to our blessed Lord.[32]

Discourse on Psalm 5

1. This Psalm is entitled: [Verse 1] *For her that obtaineth the inheritance*. The reference is to the Church, to whom our Lord Jesus Christ gives the inheritance of life everlasting in order that she may possess God Himself and find her blessedness in cleaving to Him. *Blessed are the meek*, so we are told, *for they shall possess the land*.[1] What land? Surely that spoken of in the words: *Thou art my hope, my portion in the land of the living*.[2] And even more

clearly: *The Lord is the portion of my inheritance and of my cup.*[3] The Church in her turn is called God's inheritance in the text: *Ask of me, and I will give thee the Gentiles for thy inheritance.*[4] Thus God is termed our inheritance because He sustains and holds us in being, and we are called God's inheritance because He governs and rules over us. This Psalm therefore is the song of the Church called to an inheritance in order to become herself the inheritance of our Lord.

2. [V. 2] *Give ear, O Lord, to my words.* In answer to His call, the Church in turn calls upon the Lord to help her pass through the wickedness of this world and so reach Him in safety. *Understand my cry.* This expression clearly shows the nature of this cry. It rises to God from within, from the bottom of the heart without audible sound; whereas the bodily voice strikes the ear, the spiritual voice is understood. It may be noted here that God listens, not with an ear of flesh but by the presence of His majesty.

3. [V. 3] *Hearken thou to the voice of my prayer:* that voice to which the Psalmist begs God to pay heed. He has already indicated its character in the words: *Understand my cry. Hearken thou to the voice of my prayer, O my king and my God.* It is true that the Son is God, the Father is God, and Father and Son together are but one God; and if asked who the Holy Spirit is, we must give no reply other than that He too is God; and when one speaks of all Three, Father, Son, and Holy Ghost, we must recognize one God alone. Nevertheless in the Scriptures the title of king ordinarily designates the Son. In accordance therefore with that declaration: *Through me do men come to the Father,*[5] the Psalmist rightly says *my king* first, and afterwards *my God.* Nor does he employ the plural "you" but the singular *thou,* for the Catholic faith proclaims not two

or three gods but very Trinity, one God. That is not to say the same Trinity may be termed now Father, now Son, now Holy Ghost, as Sabellius held.[6] No, the Father is none but the Father, the Son none but the Son, the Holy Ghost none but the Holy Ghost, and this Trinity none but one God. It is to the Trinity, we may suppose, that the Apostle alludes in the words: *Of Him, and by Him, and in Him are all things.*[7] He has not, however, added "to Them be glory," but rather, *to Him be glory*.

4. [V. 4] *For to thee will I pray; O Lord, in the morning thou shalt hear my voice.* Why has the Psalmist just said *Give ear*, as if he hoped to be heard at that very moment, when he now says *In the morning thou shalt hear*, not "thou dost hear"; then, *to thee will I pray*, not "I do pray"; and finally, [V. 5] *In the morning I will stand before thee and will see*, not "I stand and see"? May it not be that his earlier prayer expresses his petition? Blinded amid the storms of this world, the Psalmist realizes that he cannot see what he would, but he does not cease to hope, for hope that is seen is not hope.[8] He understands the cause of his blindness: it is because the dark night which is the punishment of sin is not yet ended. Therefore he says *For to thee will I pray, O Lord*, as much as to say: Such is thy might, O thou whom I shall beseech, that *in the morning thou shalt hear my voice*. Thou art not a God to be seen by men whose eyes are still dim by reason of the night of sin, but when the night of my error is past, and the darkness I have brought upon myself by my sins is gone, then *thou shalt hear my voice*.

Now why has the Psalmist said above not "Thou wilt give ear," but *Give ear*? Is it because having cried *Give ear* without being heard, he has realized how much he must get rid of before he can obtain a hearing? Or has he been heard

in the first place without being aware of it, because so far
he cannot see the hearer of his prayer? In that case the expression *In the morning thou shalt hear* would signify: In
the morning I shall realize I have been heard; just as the
phrase *Arise, O Lord*[9] is used in the sense of "Make me
arise." It is true that the latter refers to Christ's resurrection, but there can only be one correct interpretation of
the passage: *The Lord your God trieth you, that it may
appear whether you love Him,*[10] that through Him, in
other words, you yourselves are to learn; He will make
clear to you how much progress you have made in His
love.

5. [V. 5] *In the morning I will stand before thee and
will see.*[11] What does *I will stand* signify, if not "I will not
lie down"? But lying down implies resting on the ground,
does it not, it implies looking for happiness in worldly
delights. *I will stand*, says the Psalmist, *and I will see.* We
must sacrifice the things of earth if we would see God,
who is visible only to the clean of heart. *Because thou art
not a God that willest iniquity.* [V. 6] *Neither shall the
wicked dwell near thee, nor shall the unjust abide before
thy eyes.* [V. 7] *Thou hatest all the workers of iniquity;
thou wilt destroy all that speak a lie. The bloody and deceitful man the Lord will abhor.* Wickedness, treachery,
lying, murder, deceit, and suchlike form the night which
must pass away before the morning can dawn in which
God will be revealed. The Psalmist therefore has told us
why he will stand in the morning and see. *Because*, he says,
thou art not a God that willest iniquity. If God, in fact, as-
sented to evil, He could be seen even by evildoers; there
would be no need to await the morning which closes the
night of iniquity.

6. *Neither shall the wicked dwell near thee:* the evil-

doer will have no enduring sight of thee; and as a consequence, *Nor shall the unjust abide before thy eyes.* For
their eyes, or rather their minds, so long accustomed to the
darkness of sin, recoil from the light of truth, and they are
unable to bear the radiance of true knowledge. Therefore
even those who catch occasional glimpses, I mean those
who have a right conception of truth, are nevertheless still
unrighteous. They do not remain in the truth, because they
are attached to what is contrary to it. They carry within
themselves their own night, which consists in the habit, or
even more in attachment to sin. When this night comes to
an end, when they break with sin in other words, and drop
the habit of sin and attachment to it, then the morning may
dawn, and they will understand the truth to the extent of
remaining steadfast therein.

7. *Thou hatest all the workers of iniquity.* God's hatred
has the same signification as the hatred of every sinner for
the truth. It would seem as if Truth in its turn detests
them, since it will not permit to dwell in its presence those
who cannot endure it. *Thou will destroy all that speak a lie,*
for a lie is contrary to truth. No one must imagine, however, that there exists some substance or nature opposed to
truth; you must realize, on the contrary, that a lie partakes
of nonbeing, not of being. To speak of what is, is to speak
the truth; to speak of what is not, is to tell a lie. Therefore,
says the Psalmist, *Thou wilt destroy all that speak a lie,*
since in turning their backs upon that which has existence,
they turn aside to that which has none.

Many lies are apparently told out of kindness, not
malice, the object being someone's safety or advantage;
such were the lies told by the midwives in Exodus who
gave a false report to Pharaoh in order to save the male
infants of Israel from death.[12] But even here what is praise-

worthy is not the action but the motive, since those who
merely tell lies such as theirs will deserve in time to be set
free from all dissimulation, for in the perfect not even these
are to be found. *Let your speech be Yea, Yea: No, No*, we
are told. *And that which is over and above these is of evil.*[13]
Not without reason does Scripture elsewhere declare: *The
mouth that belieth killeth the soul*,[14] in order to teach us
that no perfect and spiritual man is free to tell a lie to save
this transitory life either for himself or another, since its
loss does not kill the soul.

On the other hand, it is one thing to tell a lie, another to
conceal the truth; one thing to speak falsehood, another to
pass the truth over in silence. If, for instance, we would
avoid exposing a man to the risk of visible death, we must
be prepared to conceal the truth but not to tell an untruth.
We must neither expose him nor lie, otherwise we shall kill
our own soul for the sake of another man's body. If this is
at present beyond us, we must at least admit of lies only in
strict necessity. We may then deserve to get rid even of
white lies, if we do no worse, and receive strength from
the Holy Ghost to make light of any suffering for truth's
sake.

To sum up: There are two kinds of lies which are no
great crime but not exactly free from sin, the lie spoken
in jest, and the lie spoken to render some service. The lie
spoken in jest does very little harm, since it deceives nobody. The man to whom it is told knows it is only banter.
And the second lie is all the less offensive because it means
well. As a matter of fact, where no duplicity is intended,
no lie can be imputed. A man, to take an example, has been
entrusted with a sword and has promised to return it at the
owner's request. What if the latter should demand it in a fit
of madness? Obviously he must not be handed it there and

then, for fear he may kill himself or other people. It must wait until he is restored to his right mind. Here, then, there is no duplicity, because when the friend entrusted with the sword promised to return it at the owner's request, he never imagined it would be demanded in a fit of madness. Even our Lord therefore concealed the truth when His disciples were unprepared for it. *I have yet many things to say to you*, He told them, *but you cannot bear them now.*[15] The Apostle Paul has likewise declared: *I, brethren, could not speak to you as unto spiritual, but as unto carnal.*[16] Hence it follows that to suppress the truth is not necessarily wrong. But you will never find lying conceded to the perfect.

8. *The bloody and deceitful man the Lord will abhor.* Probably this is a repetition of the previous statement: *Thou hatest all the workers of iniquity; thou wilt destroy all that speak a lie.* The bloodthirsty man corresponds to the worker of iniquity, the deceitful man to the liar. For it is cheating to do one thing and pretend to do another. Moreover the Psalmist has aptly chosen his phrase: *The Lord will abhor* him, an expression which is often another name for being disinherited, whereas this Psalm is a song *for her that obtaineth the inheritance.* The Church thereupon gives voice to her joyful expectation: [V. 8] *But as for me in the multitude of thy mercy, I will come into thy house.* The *multitude of thy mercy* refers perhaps to the host of the perfect and the sanctified who will form that city of men the Church at present bears in her bosom and will bring to birth in due time. Who indeed would deny that this throng of the regenerated and perfect should be called the multitude of God's mercy, when it is so true to say: *What is man that thou art mindful of him? Or the son of man that thou visitest him?*[17]

I will come into thy house. The metaphor, I imagine, is that of a stone in a building. What else, I ask you, is the house of God but God's temple, of which we are told: *For the temple of God is holy, which you are?*[18] And the cornerstone of this building is He who is clothed with the Power and Wisdom of God, coeternal with the Father.[19]

9. *I will worship towards thy holy temple, in thy fear.* The word *towards* signifies, I think, on the way to the temple; the Psalmist does not say, I will worship in thy holy temple, but *I will worship towards thy holy temple.* The phrase thus implies not attainment, but progress towards perfection, whereas *I will come into thy house* denotes achievement. In order to reach it, however, *I will worship,* he says first of all, *towards thy holy temple.* Possibly too, because fear is a great safeguard to travelers on the road of salvation, the Psalmist therefore adds, *in thy fear.* Those who reach the goal will experience how *perfect charity casteth out fear.*[20] No longer do they fear One who is now their friend. *I will not now call you servants,* our Lord tells them, *but friends.*[21] They have been led to the fulfilment of that promise.

10. [V. 9] *Conduct me, O Lord, in thy justice, because of my enemies.* The Psalmist here openly admits that he is on the road, advancing towards perfection without as yet having attained it, since he eagerly desires to be led thither. Notice *in thy justice,* not in that which appears so to men. For men consider it is justice to return evil for evil, but such is not the justice of Him *who maketh His sun,* we are told, *to rise upon the good and the bad.*[22] When God, for instance, punishes sinners, instead of inflicting evil, He simply leaves them to their own. *Behold,* says the Psalmist, *he hath been in labor with injustice; he hath conceived sorrow and brought forth iniquity. He hath opened a pit*

and dug it; and he is fallen into the hole he made. His sorrow shall be turned on his own head, and his iniquity shall come down upon his crown.[23] When God punishes, then, He does so as a judge punishes lawbreakers; He inflicts no penalty of His own, He merely casts them forth into the evil of their choice to fill up the cup of their misery. On the other hand, when man repays evil for evil, he does so with evil intent, so proving he is himself evil in the first place, when bent upon punishing it.

11. *Direct my way in thy sight.* Obviously the Psalmist is commending to God his whole course, for it lies along a road traversed, not in physical space, but in the powers of the soul. *In thy sight*, he says, *direct my way*, far from the eye of man, for mankind's praise or blame is not to be trusted. No man can possibly judge another's conscience, the path by which he makes his way to God. The Psalmist therefore adds: [V. 10] *For there is no truth in their mouth;* and since on no account should we trust their verdict, we must take refuge within, in our conscience and the presence of God. *Their heart is vain.* How, I ask, can truth be in the mouths of men whose hearts are blinded by sin and its penalties? That is why the voice recalls them with the question: *Why do you love vanity and seek after lying?*[24]

12. [V. 11] *Their throat is an open sepulcher.* One may apply this verse to greed, which is often the motive behind men's deceitful flattery. The Psalmist has used the excellent phrase *open sepulcher*, for greed is insatiably openmouthed, unlike sepulchers which are sealed up after receiving the corpse.

The text also admits of another interpretation. By means of lies and smooth-tongued flattery men attract to themselves those whom they entice to sin, and then they devour them so to speak by making them conform to their own manner of life. And since by sinning the victims suffer death, their seducers are rightly termed open sepulchers. They themselves are in a manner of speaking lifeless, being devoid of the life of truth, and they swallow dead men whom their lying words and cunning hearts have first murdered and then drawn into themselves. *They dealt deceitfully with their tongues,* with their wicked tongues, for that is what the Psalmist seems to imply in specifying *their tongues,* for evildoers have evil tongues, which speak evil in speaking deceitfully. *How can you speak good things,* our Lord asks such men, *whereas you are evil?*[25]

13. *Judge them, O God. Let them fall from their devices.* This is a prophecy rather than a curse. The Psalmist does not wish vengeance to fall, but he foresees that it will. It will befall them, moreover, not because he apparently invoked it but because they have brought it on themselves. In the same way when he afterwards says, *Let all them be glad that hope in thee,* the Psalmist is uttering a prophecy: he perceives their future joy. And likewise he predicted: *Stir up thy might and come,*[26] because he foresaw the Lord would come.

On the other hand, the phrase *Let them fall from their devices* might have signified an expression of good will, of the Psalmist's petition that they should abandon their evil designs and drop their machinations for the future. The subsequent phrase however, *Cast them out,* forbids such an interpretation. No favorable construction could possibly be put on any man's expulsion by God. So we must look at it as prophecy, not malediction, a prediction of what must inevitably befall those who persist in the sins under discussion. *Let them fall,* therefore, *from their devices.* That is the sentence. Let them fall beneath the accusations of their

own thoughts, before the testimony of their own conscience, according to the Apostle's words: *And their
thoughts between themselves accusing or also defending
one another, in the revelation of the just judgment of
God.*[27]

14. *According to the multitude of their wickednesses
cast them out.* Cast them far away. *The multitude of their
wickednesses* implies that He is to multiply their distance
from Him. Thus are the evildoers to be expelled from that
inheritance, which consists in the sight and knowledge of
God, just as injured eyes recoil from brilliant light and find
torture in what to others gives joy. Such men as these will
never stand in the morning and see.[28] Their rejection is a
penalty proportionate to the greatness of the others' reward as expressed in the verse: *But it is good for me to
adhere to my God.*[29] The words *Enter thou into the joy of
thy Lord* are the reverse of this punishment; identical with
it are those others: *Cast him out into the exterior darkness.*[30]

15. *For they have embittered thee, O Lord.*[31] Our Lord
has said: *I am the living bread which came down from
heaven;*[32] again: *Labor for the meat which perisheth not;*[33]
and: *Taste and see that the Lord is sweet.*[34] Sinners, however, find the bread of truth bitter; hence their hatred for
the mouth from which it issues. They have therefore found
God bitter, because sin has rendered them so sickly that the
bread of truth, delicious to souls in health, tastes to them as
unbearably bitter as gall.

16. [V. 12] *And let all them be glad that hope in thee:*
all those obviously who find the Lord sweet to their lips.
They shall rejoice forever, and thou shalt dwell in them.
This everlasting joy will commence when the righteous become the dwelling place of God; He, their indweller, will

Himself be their joy. *And all they that love thy name shall glory in thee,* because they can enjoy the object of their love. The phrase *in thee* admirably shows that they are to possess that inheritance which gave the Psalm its title, and in their turn are to be God's inheritance signified by: *thou shalt dwell in them*—a joy they forfeit whom God casts out by reason of their countless crimes.

17. [V. 13] *For thou wilt bless the just.* Their blessing is this: to glory in God and to possess God dwelling within themselves,. Such is the sanctification bestowed upon the just. In order to become just, they have first to be called, and this is a question not of any merit of theirs, but of God's free gift, for all have sinned and do need the glory of God.[35] For whom He called, them also He justified, and whom He justified, them also He glorified.[36] As, moreover, the call does not follow from our own merits but from the mercy and loving-kindness of God, the Psalmist adds: *O Lord, thou hast crowned us as with a shield of thy good will.* God's good will precedes ours; He first calls sinners to repentance. Such then are the weapons which ward off the enemy referred to in the words: *Who shall accuse against the elect of God?*[37] and again: *If God be for us, who is against us? He that spared not even His own Son, but delivered Him up for us all.*[38] *For if, when we were enemies, Christ died for us; much more being reconciled shall we be saved from wrath through Him.*[39] This is the unconquerable shield which hurls back our enemy when, at the height of affliction and temptation, he would drive us to despair of our salvation.

18. To sum up the whole Psalm: The verses *Give ear, O Lord, to my words* as far as *my king and my God* are a petition to be heard.

Next, the Psalmist passes in review the things which prevent him from seeing God and realizing he has been heard, from the verse *For to thee will I pray; O Lord, in the morning thou shalt hear my voice* until *the bloody and the deceitful man the Lord will abhor.*

Thirdly, from the verse *But as for me in the multitude of thy mercy* as far as *I will worship towards thy holy temple in thy fear* he hopes to become one day the house of God, and even in this life to draw near Him in fear until he reaches that perfection which casts out fear.

Fourthly, as he journeys onwards surrounded by the very things which seem obstacles, he prays for that inward help imperceptible to human eye, for fear that evil tongues should deflect him from his course. So run the verses *Conduct me, O Lord, in thy justice because of my enemies* up to *They dealt deceitfully with their tongues.*

Fifthly, from *Judge them, O God* to the final verse, the Psalm predicts the punishment awaiting evildoers, when the just man is to be saved only with difficulty, and prophesies the recompense awarded to the righteous who responded to the call and endured all trials manfully until they finally attained their goal.

DISCOURSE ON PSALM 6

1. [Verse 1] *Unto the end, in hymns for the octave, a Psalm of David.* This expression *for the octave* seems obscure. (For the rest of the title is fairly clear.) Some have thought that the phrase refers to the Day of Judgment, to that final advent of our Lord, who is to come to judge the living and the dead. According to this belief, the event will take place after seven thousand years reckoning from Adam. These seven thousand years will pass like seven days, and the eighth day as it were will be that of His

coming. But our Lord has declared: *It is not for you to know the times which the Father hath put in His own power.*[1] And again: *But of that day and hour no one knoweth: no, neither angel, nor power, nor the Son, but the Father alone.*[2] Finally St. Paul has written that the day of the Lord will come like a thief in the night.[3] All this proves obviously enough that no man may lay claim to knowledge of that day by any calculation of years. Now if it must come infallibly at the end of seven thousand years, any and every man can inform himself of the date by merely working out a sum. Then how would it come about that not even the Son knows it? Actually, of course, this phrase implies that the Son does not intend to reveal it to men, not that He Himself is ignorant of it. It is in this sense we are told: *The Lord your God trieth you, that He may know,*[4] that is, "may make you realize"; similarly, *Arise, O Lord,*[5] denoting "Make us rise up." If therefore the Son is said not to know this day, not because He is ignorant of it but because by withholding it He leaves in ignorance those to whom the knowledge would be inexpedient, what sense can there be in that unspeakable presumption which reckons up dates and expects the Lord's coming automatically after seven thousand years?

2. Let us then be content not to know what the Lord would not have us know, and let us inquire what the words of the title *for the octave* mean. Without recourse to any rash calculations, we may safely interpret the octave as the Day of Judgment, for the end of the world will admit us to life everlasting, and then the souls of the just will no longer be subject to the vicissitudes of time. Since all time advances by the repetition of the same seven days, the octave may very well signify that eighth day which is beyond such rotation.

There is a further sound reason why this phrase should
denote the Day of Judgment, in that it will follow upon
two economies, the one in the realm of the body, the other
of the soul. From Adam to Moses the human race lived
according to nature, that is, according to the flesh, which is
also termed the outward man and the old self.[6] To this
generation was entrusted the Old Testament, whose enact-
ments, religious yet still carnal, foreshadowed the spiritual
things to come. Throughout this whole period in which
men lived according to nature, *death reigned,* so the
Apostle says, *even over them who have not sinned.* It
reigned moreover, as the same Apostle observes, *after the
similitude of the transgression of Adam.* Consequently
unto Moses[7] means up to the time when, through a determined but hidden purpose, the works of the Law, those
sacred rites of corporal observance, became binding even
on those who served the one God. Since our Lord's coming, however, we have passed from bodily circumcision to
circumcision of the heart. We have been called to live
according to the spirit, in other words according to the inward man, the new man,[8] so termed because of our regeneration and the refashioning of our spiritual life.

Now it is obvious that the number four refers to the
body, from the four elements of which it consists, and the
four qualities, dry, wet, hot and cold. Hence it is regulated
by the four seasons, spring, summer, autumn and winter.
All this is familiar to you. Elsewhere, in a very subtle but
rather abtruse argument, I have discussed the number four
in its relation to the body. I must avoid it in this discourse,
which I wish to adapt to the less learned. The number
three, however, refers to the soul, as we learn from the
precept to love God in a threefold manner,[9] with our
whole heart, our whole soul and our whole mind; these

should be treated one by one in a discussion of the Gospel, not the Psalter. For my present purpose I have said enough, I think, to prove that the number three applies to the soul.

We have now added up the number relating to the body, to the old man, to the Old Law, and that relating to the soul, to the regenerated man, to the New Law, and have arrived at the number seven. Since all action in time has reference either to the number four assigned to the body, or to the number three assigned to the soul, the eighth day, the Day of Judgment, will follow afterwards and will pay to every man his due recompense. No longer to daily tasks will the saints proceed, but to life everlasting, whereas the wicked it will commit to eternal damnation.

3. Such is the punishment dreaded when the Church cries out in this Psalm: [V. 2] *O Lord, rebuke me not in thy indignation.* The Apostle also makes reference to the wrath of the judgment: *Thou treasurest up to thyself wrath against the day of wrath of the just judgment of God.*[10] No one who hopes to be cured of faults in this life has any desire to meet with rebuke on that day. *Nor chastise me in thy wrath. Chastise* seems a rather mild word, since it implies amendment, whereas the man who is rebuked, accused in other words, has reason to fear final condemnation. But *wrath* sounds stronger than *indignation*, and some may be surprised at the lenient term *chastisement* being coupled with the severe one, *wrath*. I presume, however, that both words mean the same thing, for in the first verse the Greek θυμός denotes the same as ὀργή in the second. When the Latins likewise wanted two separate words, they searched for something akin to *ira*, indignation, and used *furor*, wrath. Thus copies vary. In some, *ira* is placed before *furor*; in others, *furor* before *ira*; in others again, instead of *furor* the word *indignatio* or *bilis* is

substituted. But whatever the expression employed, it implies an impulse urging the soul to inflict punishment. We cannot, however, attribute this impulse to God as we may to a human soul, since it is said of Him: *But thou, O Lord of hosts, judgest with tranquility;*[11] tranquility is incompatible with agitation. God, then, in His judgment is incapable of disturbance; but in so far as His laws occasion such an emotion in His ministers it is termed God's anger. Now the soul at prayer in this Psalm dreads being rebuked in this indignation; it wishes even to escape the chastisement which would correct and instruct, for the Greek word used is παιδεύσῃς, meaning instruction. On the Day of Judgment indeed, rebuke awaits all those who are not built on the foundation which is Christ; but those who upon this foundation have built with wood, hay and stubble will receive correction and purification.[12] They shall suffer loss but shall be saved, yet so as by fire. Then what is the Psalmist praying for, when he wishes to be neither rebuked nor corrected in the Lord's indignation? Why, surely, for a perfect cure. For where there is sound health, there need be no fear of death, or of the surgeon's hand with its cautery and knife.

4. Accordingly he goes on to say: [V. 3] *Have mercy on me, O Lord, for I am weak; heal me, O Lord, for my bones are troubled.* The bones in this context signify "the very foundation of my soul or strength." Under the figure of bones, the soul here complains that its strength is undermined. But do not imagine that the soul has bones such as we see in the body. The Psalmist has therefore added the phrase: [V. 4] *My soul is troubled exceedingly* to make his meaning plain, for fear the mention of bones should be interpreted literally. *But thou, O Lord, how long?* Who does not see at once the picture of a soul struggling against

its disorders, while the physician makes no haste whatever to help, in order to make the man realize the evils into which sin has plunged him? A thing easily remedied is not so sedulously avoided, but a cure that is difficult makes us more careful to keep in good health after recovery. Far from thinking God cruel when He is asked: *But thou, O Lord, how long?* we should understand that in His kindness He is showing the soul the wound it has inflicted on itself. For such a soul does not yet pray with a perfection which calls forth the response: *As thou art yet speaking I will say, Lo, here I am.*[13] At the same time God would teach the soul the magnitude of the punishment laid up for evildoers who refuse to turn to Him, if those who do thus turn meet with so much difficulty. *If the just man shall scarcely be saved,* as the Scriptures say in another place, *where shall the ungodly and the sinner appear?*[14]

5. [V. 5] *Turn to me, O Lord, and deliver my soul.* In turning towards God, the soul begs Him to turn likewise towards itself. *Turn ye to me, saith the Lord of hosts,* so it is written, *and I will turn to you.*[15] Or are we to interpret *Turn to me* as a way of saying, "Help me in my return," by reason of the difficulty and toil it finds in so doing? For a perfect conversion on our part will find God always ready, exactly as the prophet tells us: *We shall find Him ready as the dawn.*[16] The truth is that we lost Him, not because He was absent who is everywhere present, but because we turned our backs upon Him. *He was in this world,* it is said, *and the world was made by Him, and the world knew Him not.*[17] If then He was in this world without the world recognizing Him, it is because our impurity cannot endure to look upon Him. But when we would turn round completely, and set to work to alter our old ways and fashion our souls anew, we find it hard and pain-

ful to extricate ourselves from the blindness of earthly desires and turn towards the calm serenity of the divine light. During this arduous task we cry out: *Turn to me, O Lord;* aid us so that ours may be that complete conversion which finds thee ready and offering thyself for the delight of them that love thee. Therefore, after having said *Turn to me, O Lord,* the Psalmist has added, *and deliver my soul,* still obsessed with the problems of this world; in the very act of returning to thee it finds itself torn to shreds by the thorns of desire. *O save me,* he says, *for thy mercy's sake.* He realizes that he is cured through no merit of his own, since a sinner, a violater of the law, can expect in justice only condemnation. Heal me then, he says, not for any merit of mine but for thy mercy's sake.

6. [V. 6] *For there is no one in death that is mindful of thee.* He is aware, moreover, that now is the time for turning towards God: when this life is over, there remains only the recompense of our deeds. *And who shall confess to thee in hell?* The rich man of whom our Lord speaks confessed to God in hell, seeing Lazarus in comfort while he bewailed his own torture; he confessed to the point of wanting to give his brethren a warning to sin no more, on account of the torments of a hell in which they did not believe.[18] It was to no purpose, it is true, yet he did confess that the sufferings meted out to him were deserved, since he longed to forewarn his brethren not to run the same risk.

Then what is the meaning of: *And who shall confess to thee in hell?* Does hell denote the place into which evil-doers will be cast after judgment, where their eyes will no longer pierce through the thick darkness to catch a glimmer of God's light so that they can make any sort of confession to Him? Notice that by raising his eyes, although a yawning gulf sundered them, the rich man was still able to see Lazarus dwelling in peace, and the contrast drove him to acknowledge his own deserts. A further possible interpretation is that by death the Psalmist signifies sin committed in defiance of the divine law. Thus we call the sting of death, death, in so far as it leads to death, for the sting of death is sin.[19] This death consists in ignoring God and despising His law and precepts; thus the Psalmist terms hell that blindness which descends upon and engulfs the soul slain by sin. *And as they liked not to have God in their knowledge,* says the Apostle, *God delivered them up to a reprobate sense.*[20] This is the death, this the hell from which the soul implores deliverance, when it meets with obstacles in its effort to return to God.

7. The Psalmist thereupon adds: [V. 7] *I have labored in my groanings.* And as if he had reaped but little profit from it, he continues: *Evey night I will wash my bed.* The bed here symbolizes all that an ailing and sickly soul rests in, namely, bodily gratification and every worldly pleasure. He that bedews such pleasure with tears is the man who tries to extricate himself from it. He realizes indeed that sensual desire is blameworthy, yet he is weak enough to be held captive by enjoyment, and unresisting settles down, powerless to rise from it unless his soul be healed. But in saying *every night,* the Psalmist wished perhaps to depict a man of good will who perceives a certain amount of the light of truth, but sometimes sinks back into worldly pleasures through the weakness of his flesh. As a result, he is compelled to undergo in mind an alternation of light and darkness. *With the mind I serve the law of God,* he says, as he rejoices in daylight; yet he slips back once more into the night with the words, *but with the flesh the law of sin.*[21] This will continue until at length night of

every kind passes away and that unique day dawns of which it is said: *In the morning I will stand before thee and will see.*[22] Then he will stand upright; meanwhile, however, he is stretched out on the bed he must bedew every night with such a flood of tears as to win from God's mercy infallible remedy.

I will water my couch with tears: the phrase is a repetition. *With tears* explains the Psalmist's previous use of *I will wash,* and *couch* is here synonymous with *bed* above. Nevertheless *I will water* goes further than *I will wash.* A thing may be washed merely on the surface, whereas a watering soaks right through, thus signifying the tears which drench the inmost heart. The Psalmist, moreover, has changed the tense of the verb. He has used the past tense in *I have labored in my groanings,* and the future in *I will wash my bed;* he repeats the future in *I will water my couch with my tears* in order to teach us what to say to ourselves when tired out with useless lamentation: This has done me no good; I will try something else.

8. [V. 8] *My eye is troubled through indignation.*[23] Is the Psalmist referring to his own, or to that indignation of God in which he has begged to be neither rebuked nor chastised? But if God's indignation signifies the Day of Judgment, how is it to be applied to the present life? Or does it begin here below in the anguish and woe men endure, and worst of all in their loss of comprehension of truth, as I have already explained when I quoted: *God delivered them up to a reprobate sense?*[24] This is the effect of blindness of heart: every man in such a state is shut out from God's interior light; yet while life lasts, the blindness is not absolute. For there is an exterior darkness[25] reserved more especially to the Day of Judgment which will utterly cast out from God the man who refused to amend while he

yet had time. To be completely deprived of God—what does that denote if not total blindness? For God indeed dwells in light inaccessible[26] and they enter into it whom He invites with the words: *Enter thou into the joy of thy Lord.*[27]

This indignation, then, from the very outset weighs heavily in this life upon every sinner. Dread of the final judgment draws from the Psalmist sighs and tears, for fear he should end by meeting with a wrath whose approach already causes him such pain. For this reason he has not said, "My eye is blinded," but, *My eye is troubled through indignation.* We need not be surprised if the Psalmist is alluding to his own indignation troubling his eye, for it is possibly in this sense that we are told: *Let not the sun go down upon your anger.*[28] A soul in that disturbed state which prevents it from seeing God fancies that divine Wisdom, its interior sun, has somehow been forced to set.

9. *I have grown old amongst all my enemies.*[29] The Psalmist has simply spoken of anger, assuming, that is, that he spoke of his own anger, but upon turning his attention to other vices he discovers that they beset him on every side. As these are the vices of the old life and the old self which we must strip off in order to be clothed with the new,[30] the phrase *I have grown old* is a suitable one. *Amongst all my enemies* may denote either the vices or the men who refuse to return to God. For the latter, albeit unconsciously, despite the consideration they show, despite the fact that they live in peace with us at the same board, under the same roof, in the same city, that they often talk to us with all the appearance of friendship, yet these men by aims directly contrary to ours are enemies of all whose faces are turned towards God. The one class is devoted to and hankers after this world, the other strives to be de-

livered from it: are they not obviously mutual adversaries?
If possible these worldlings will drag us into punishment
with themselves. And it is a great grace, when in daily contact with them, not to stray from the path of God's commandments. Often enough a soul doing its best to journey
resolutely to God becomes unsettled and panic-stricken on
the way, and frequently fails to fulfil its good intentions
because it is afraid of offending its neighbors who are
searching with eagerness after fleeting and perishable
goods. With such as these the soul in perfect health parts
company, separated not by space but by spirit. Physical
bodies occupy a given space; the soul's space is its desire.

10. That prayer made with such vehemence should be
unavailing before Him who is the source of all mercy is
impossible. When therefore the struggles, the sighs, the
floods of tears are over, the words *The Lord is nigh unto
them that are of a contrite heart*[31] are spoken with truth
indeed. When the difficulties are overcome, the loving
soul, or the Church if you like, bears witness that it has
been heard after its hard fight. Notice then what it adds:
[V. 9] *Depart from me, all ye workers of iniquity, for
the Lord hath heard the voice of my weeping.* Either the
prophet foretells that on the Day of Judgment the evildoers will depart, will be separated from the righteous, or
he tells them to separate now; for although both share the
same society, yet on the threshing floor the pure grains of
wheat have already been separated from the chaff, although apparently still hidden among it. They can exist
together, but they cannot be blown away together by the
wind.

11. [V. 10] *For the Lord hath heard the voice of my
weeping; the Lord hath heard my supplication; the Lord
hath received my prayer.* This frequent repetition of the

same idea shows not so much the speaker's need of words as his transport of joy, for when a man is full of gladness he repeats himself and is not satisfied with stating the cause of it once and for all. Here you see the outcome of the Psalmist's sorrowful toil, of those tears with which he washed his bed and bedewed his couch, for the man who sows in tears will reap in joy,[32] and blessed are the mourners, for they shall be comforted.[33]

12. [V. 11] *Let all my enemies be ashamed and be very much troubled.* A short time ago the Psalmist exclaimed: *Depart from me, all ye;* and I have already told you how this may be brought about even in our present life. But I do not see how the wish *Let all be ashamed and troubled* can be fulfilled until the day when the rewards of the just and the chastisement of sinners are made manifest. So far are evildoers from being ashamed in this life that they never cease to scoff at us, and so effectual is their mockery that they frequently cause the fainthearted to blush at Christ's name; hence the warning: *He that shall be ashamed of me before men, of him I shall be ashamed before my Father.*[34] Indeed, if any one is desirous of carrying out the sublime instructions to distribute his goods, to give to the poor so that his justice may remain for ever,[35] to sell all his earthly possessions and spend the money on the needy, saying in his wish to follow Christ: *We brought nothing into this world, and certainly we can carry nothing out; but having food and wherewith to be covered, with these we are content,*[36] such a man incurs the sarcasm of the impious, who call him a madman while themselves refusing to return to right reason. So it often happens that to avoid being so dubbed by incurable rogues, he fears to take action and is slow to obey what the most trustworthy and able of all physicians has prescribed. Not in this world, then, will

these folk be abashed. And we for our part must see to it that they do not abash us, do not make us turn tail, or obstruct or delay us on our intended course. The day will dawn when they will be put to confusion, when they will say in the words of Scripture: *These are they whom we had some time in derision and for a parable of reproach. We fools esteemed their life madness and their end without honor. How are they numbered among the children of God, and their lot is among the saints? Therefore we have erred from the way of truth, and the light of justice hath not shined unto us, nor the sun risen upon us. We have been filled with the way of iniquity and destruction, and have walked through rugged deserts, but the way of the Lord we have not known. What hath pride profited us? Or what advantage hath the boasting of riches brought us? All those things are passed away like a shadow.*[37]

13. The Psalmist continues: *Let them be turned back and ashamed.* Who would not consider it a perfectly fair chastisement that theirs should be the conversion that ends in confusion, since they refused that which ends in salvation? *Very speedily* adds the Psalmist; for since they are no longer reckoning on the Day of Judgment, as they cry, " Peace," then shall sudden destruction come upon them.[38] For when what was no longer expected to come does come, it comes quickly. It is only looking forward to the future which makes this life seem long. Nothing seems swifter than that which is already past. Therefore, when the Day of Judgment comes, sinners will realize that their past lives have been far from long; and they will find it difficult to persuade themselves that the day was slow in overtaking those who did not expect it, or rather did not believe it ever would come.

There is another possible interpretation of the same passage. Inasmuch as God has considered the speaker's anguish and his frequent and continued tears, we may infer that the soul is now delivered from sin and has brought every disordered impulse of sensual desire under control, saying: *Depart from me, all ye workers of iniquity, for the Lord hath heard the voice of my weeping.* Since this is the soul's happy lot, we need not wonder if it is now so perfect as to pray for its enemies. It is in this sense perhaps that the Psalmist has said: *Let all my enemies be ashamed and be very much troubled,* so that they may do penance for their sins; and this they cannot do without shame[39] and agitation. There is nothing to prevent our interpreting the succeeding verse, *Let them be turned back and ashamed,* in the sense of a return to God and confusion at having once gloried in the darkness of sin which was their former state. *What glory therefore had you then,* so the Apostle asks, *in those things of which you are now ashamed?*[40] The Psalmist's next phrase, *very speedily,* may refer either to his own fervent desire or to the power of Christ who, when the Gentiles were persecuting the Church in the cause of idolatry, brought them in so short a time to the faith of the Gospel.

DISCOURSE ON PSALM 7

1. [Verse 1] *A Psalm for David himself, which he sang to the Lord, because of the words of Chusi, son of Jemini.* The story which occasioned this prophecy can, in fact, be easily gathered from the second book of Kingdoms.[1] It tells us that David's son Absalom was waging war against his father. Chusi, a friend of David, went over to Absalom's headquarters to find out and report to David what plans Absalom was making at Achitophel's suggestion; for the

latter, who had deserted from David's friendship, was exerting all his powers to furnish the son with advice against his father.

However, in this Psalm we are not going to consider the actual story with which the prophet has veiled its inner meaning; but, assuming that we have been converted to Christ, let us draw the veil aside.[2] And first let us enquire into the significance of the names. There has been no lack of interpreters, indeed, who have searched for the spiritual rather than the literal and natural meaning of such names. They tell us that Chusi signifies "silence"; Jemini, "the propitious"; and Achitophel, "brother's ruin,"—names which bring once more before our eyes Judas the traitor, thus prefigured by Absalom, whose name signifies "peace of his father." David, in fact, was always ready to make peace with him, even though he, deceiver that he was, cherished war in his heart. All this I have dealt with in Psalm 3.[3] Now just as in the Gospels we find the disciples of our Lord Jesus Christ called His children,[4] so also in the Gospels we find them called His brethren. For when risen from the dead our Lord said: *Go, and say to my brethren.*[5] The Apostle also calls Him the first-born among many brethren.[6] Hence the fall of the disciple who betrayed Him is aptly designated a brother's ruin, the meaning, as we have said, of the name Achitophel. Chusi, signifying "silence," may very well denote the silence with which our Lord met the treachery of His enemies, in that deep mystery which struck Israel in part with blindness, when they persecuted our Lord and thus made entrance for the full complement of the Gentiles, that so all Israel might be saved.

The Apostle, then, approaching this profound mystery and this awful silence, exclaimed as though struck down by a kind of dread at its very profundity: *O the depth of the riches of the wisdom and of the knowledge of God! How inscrutable are His judgments, and how unsearchable His ways! For who hath known the mind of the Lord, or who hath been His counselor?*[7] Thus he does not so much find words for this great silence, as simply by his astonishment draw our attention to it. It was under cover of this silence that our Lord, hiding the secret purpose of His passion, made a brother's self-ruin, the detestable crime of the man who betrayed Him, part of the design of His own wisdom and pity, so that what the traitor in his perversity did to bring about one man's death. God by His guiding wisdom would turn to the salvation of all mankind.

This Psalm then is a song to the Lord of a perfect soul already worthy of knowing the secret of God. The Psalmist sings *for the words of Chusi,* words spoken in the silence which he has been given to understand. Among unbelievers and persecutors the silence is also a secret. But His own have been told: *I do not now call you servants, for the servant knoweth not what his Lord doth. But I have called you friends, because all things whatsoever I have heard of my Father, I have made known to you.*[8] For His friends, then, there is no silence but rather the words of silence, the explanation and manifest reason of that silence. Now this "silence," Chusi by name, is said to be the son of Jemini, son of "the Propitious." There could be no question of hiding from the saints what was being done for their benefit, even though our Lord says: *Let not thy left hand know what thy right hand doth.*[9] The perfect soul, then, who has penetrated the secret, is singing in prophecy, *for the words of Chusi,* or for the unveiling of this mystery. This is the hidden work wrought by the Propitious, by God in other words in His favor and mercy. Hence this silence is called "son of the Propitious," *Chusi, son of Jemini.*

2. [V. 2] *O Lord my God, in thee have I put my trust; save me from all them that persecute me, and deliver me.* The war against his vices is over and his battle won, and the soul now perfected has no enemy left but the devil in his envy. Therefore he cries: *Save me from all them that persecute me, and deliver me,* [V. 3] *lest at any time he seize upon my soul like a lion.* The Apostle warns us: *Your adversary the devil as a roaring lion goeth about seeking whom he may devour.*[10] So the speaker changes from the plural number, *Save me from all them that persecute me,* to the singular, *lest at any time he seize upon my soul like a lion.* He does not say "lest at any time they seize," knowing who the enemy is that remains to be conquered, the formidable foe of every perfect soul. *While there is no one to redeem me, nor to save*—for fear that the devil should pounce upon me whilst thou dost neither redeem nor save me. For if God should not redeem or save, the devil will seize upon his prey.

3. Notice how the words which follow show that all this is spoken by the perfect soul, by one who has nothing further to guard against except the devil with his insidious snares. [V. 4] *O Lord my God,* he says, *if I have done this thing.* What does he mean by *this thing?* Since he does not mention the offense by name, are we to understand sin in general? If this interpretation is not acceptable, we may take what follows as the soul's answer to our question: What do you mean by *this thing?* His reply is: *If there be iniquity in my hands.* Moreover, he is clearly speaking of sin in general when he declares; [V. 5] *If I have rendered to them that repaid me evils*—a statement that nobody but the perfect can make with truth. Our Lord does indeed

say: *Be you therefore perfect as your heavenly Father is
perfect, who maketh His sun to rise upon the good and
bad and raineth upon the just and unjust.*[11] Hence he who
has not repaid evil for evil is perfect. Now when the perfect soul prays *for the words of Chusi, the son of Jemini,*
he asks for understanding of the mystery, of the silence
which our Lord, in His mercy and bounty towards us,
guarded for our salvation in enduring with such supreme
patience the deceit of His betrayer. Then, as it were, our
Lord replies to this perfect soul, explaining the meaning of
the mystery thus: To wash away your sins, disloyal and
sinful as you were, by the shedding of my blood, I bore
with my betrayer in silence and in all patience for your
sake. Will you not imitate me in not rendering evil for
evil?

Considering, then, and understanding what our Lord
has done for him, and advancing towards perfection by following His example, the soul says: *If I have rendered to
them that repaid me evils;* in other words, if I have not followed what thy example has taught me, *let me deservedly
fall empty before my enemies.* He does well to say, not:
If I have rendered to them that "paid" me evils, but *repaid*
me; for one who repays has already received some benefac-
tion. Now it shows greater patience not to take vengeance
on him who receives benefits and then returns evil for good,
than not to take it on one who having received no previous
benefits had a mind to injure. Well then, *If,* he says, *I
have rendered to them that repaid me evils,* if I have not
imitated thee in that silence, that patience, which thou hast
shown forth for my sake, *let me deservedly fall empty
before my enemies.* It is baseless presumption, in fact, for
any one, mere man that he is, to wish to avenge himself on
another. Outwardly he strives to get the better of a human

being, and inwardly he is himself overcome by the devil; his own senseless, haughty elation in thinking himself invincible has brought him to nothing. The perfect soul, then, knows where the greater victory is to be obtained, and where the Father who sees in secret will repay.[12] And rather than render to them that repaid him evils, he prefers to take a lesson from the words of Scripture: *He that conquers his anger is better than he that takes a city;*[13] he prefers to master his own anger rather than another human being. *If I have rendered to them that repaid me evils, let me deservedly fall empty before my enemies.* He seems to take an oath by calling down evil upon himself; this is the most serious kind of swearing, when a man says, "If I have done so and so, may I suffer so and so." But swearing in a swearer's mouth is one thing, in the phraseology of the prophets quite another. For the prophet declares what evils really will befall men who repay evil with evil; but he does not invoke them either upon himself or upon others by his imprecations.

4. [V. 6] *Let the enemy pursue my soul and take it.* In speaking a second time of his enemy in the singular, the Psalmist indicates more and more clearly the one whom he has already referred to as a lion, this enemy who pursues and makes himself master of a soul once he has managed to ensnare it. Men in their rage can kill the body; once the body is dead they cannot hold the soul subject to their power. But the devil will pursue souls, capture them and possess them forthwith. *And tread down my life into earth.* Let the devil trample on my life like so much earth, to serve as his food. For he is called not only a lion but a serpent also, to whom God said: *Earth shalt thou eat.* Likewise when man sinned he was told: *Earth thou art and unto earth thou shalt return.*[14] *And bring down my glory to the*

dust. This is the dust that the wind drives from the face of the earth,[15] the useless and silly boasting of the proud, which has no solidity but resembles a puff carried away by the wind like a ball of dust. Rightly does the soul speak here of his glory, which he does not wish to be brought down to the dust. For he wants to have true glory in his conscience and in God's sight, where there is no room for boasting. *He that glorieth,* so it is written, *let him glory in the Lord.*[16] This true glory is reduced to dust, when through pride any one scorns the promptings of conscience (where alone God proves a man's worth) and desires instead the empty praise of his fellows. Hence we find elsewhere in the Scriptures: *God hath scattered the bones of them that please men.*[17] But he who knows by learning or experience the steps in overcoming vice will understand that this vice of empty boasting is, if not the only one, at least the chief one the perfect must avoid. That vice by which the soul first falls is the last it overcomes. Now *pride is the beginning of all sin;* and *The beginning of pride in man is to fall away from God.*[18]

5. [V. 7] *Rise up, O Lord, in thy anger.* Why does the man whom we term perfect insist upon calling down God's anger? Was not he to all appearances more perfect who exclaimed as he was being stoned: *Lord, lay not this sin to their charge?*[19] But surely in this Psalm the soul is praying not against men but against the devil and his angels, to whom the sinners and the ungodly belong? Hence it is a sign of pity, not of anger, when any one beseeches the Lord, who justifies the ungodly,[20] to rob the devil of his prey. For to justify the ungodly means to make him pass from impiety to holiness, and transform the property of the devil into the temple of God. Now since it is a punishment to lose a possession one wants to keep, the Psalmist

refers to this punishment as God's anger, directed against the devil to deprive him of the souls he possesses. *Rise up, O Lord, in thy anger. Rise up* here means, "Show thyself." He speaks in human fashion, using obscure terms, as though God were asleep when He lies hid and is not recognized in His secret workings. *And be thou exalted in the borders of my enemies.* By borders the speaker means that dominion in which he wishes God and not the devil to reign, to be honored and glorified. He means, in fact, the ungodly who are now to become justified and thereupon praise God. *And arise, O Lord my God, in the precept which thou hast commanded.* Since thou hast enjoined humility, show thyself lowly; do thou first fulfil thine own precept, that man, following thy example, may overcome pride and not pass into the power of the devil. For he tempted man to pride in opposition to thy commands, saying: *Eat, and your eyes shall be opened, and you shall be as gods.*[21]

6. [V. 8] *And a congregation of people shall surround thee.* This may be taken in two ways. The *congregation of people* may be understood either of believers or of persecutors, since our Lord's humility had this twofold result. The crowd of persecutors surrounded Him because they despised His humility; of these we read: *Why have the Gentiles raged, and the people devised vain things?*[22] But the crowd of those who believed in Him in virtue of His humility also flocked around Him, so much so that it was true to say: *Blindness in part hath happened to Israel, until the fulness of the Gentiles should come in:*[23] and again: *Ask of me, and I will give thee the Gentiles for thy inheritance, and the utmost parts of the earth for thy possession.*[24]

And for their sakes return thou on high. For the sake of this multitude of people, return thou on high. This, as we know, Christ did, by rising from the dead and ascending into heaven. Thus glorified, He sent the Holy Spirit; for before Christ was raised to glory the Spirit could not be given. The Gospel tells us so. *For as yet the Spirit was not given, because Jesus was not yet glorified.*[25] Thereupon, having returned to heaven for the sake of the multitude of the people, He sent the Holy Spirit, with whom the preachers of the Gospel were filled when in their turn they filled the whole world with churches.

7. This passage, *Rise up, O Lord, in thy anger, and be thou exalted in the borders of my enemies,* can also be interpreted thus: Rise up in thy anger, and do not let my enemies recognize thee. Then *Be thou exalted* would mean: Make thyself remote, so as to be incomprehensible. This bears upon that silence we have already discussed. Another Psalm speaks thus of this withdrawal on high: *And He ascended upon the cherubim, and He flew. And He made darkness His covert.*[26] But while this lifting up will hide thee from those whose sins rightly prevent them from recognizing thee as they crucify thee, it will also gather about thee a multitude of believers. For it is in His very humility that our Lord has been exalted, that is, goes unrecognized. This is implied in: *And arise, O Lord, in the precept which thou hast commanded.* When thou appearest lowly, be thou exalted, that my enemies may not recognize thee. For sinners are enemies of the upright, and the ungodly enemies of the godly. *And a congregation of people shall surround thee.* The very thing, in other words, which misleads those who crucify thee will lead the nations to believe in thee, and thus the people will surround thee in throngs. But if the interpretation of the verse which follows is sound, we should rather grieve over its consequence which we already feel here below, than rejoice in having

understood it. For the words which follow are these: *And for their sakes return thou on high*. For the sake of this multitude of the human race which fills the churches, return thou on high—once more cease to be recognized. What does *and for their sakes* imply, but that this multitude also will offend thee and thus justify thy prediction: *The Son of Man when He cometh, shall He find, think you, faith on earth?*[27] And again, referring to false prophets, another name for heretics: *Because of their iniquity the charity of many shall grow cold.*[28] Even in the churches, in that society of peoples and nations among whom the Christian name has been so widely spread, there will be a vast number of sinners, as is already too often our experience. Have we not here, indeed, a prophecy of that famine of God's word which has also been announced by another prophet?[29] Is it not also because of this multitude, who by their sins estrange themselves from the light of truth, that God returns on high? In other words, true faith, pure and free from any admixture of false opinions, will find support and understanding nowhere except in a very few of whom we are told: *Blessed is he that shall persevere unto the end, he shall be saved.*[30] Not without cause, then, are the words employed: *And for their sakes—*for the sake of this assembly—*return thou on high*, implying: Withdraw thyself again into the depths of thy secrecy, because of this assembly of people who bear thy name but do not perform thy deeds.

8. But whether we adopt the former explanation of this passage or the latter, the words which follow: [V. 9] *The Lord judgeth the people*, fit both interpretations without favoring either, whether one be better than the other or both equally acceptable.

If He returned on high when He ascended into heaven

after His resurrection, the words *The Lord judgeth the people* follow on well; for from thence He shall come to judge the living and the dead. On the other hand, if He was to return on high when Christians in their sinfulness had lost their understanding of the truth, the text is still suitable; for it was of His final coming that He said: *The Son of Man, when He cometh, shall He find, think you, faith on earth?*[31] *The Lord*, then, *judgeth the people.* Who is the Lord, but Jesus Christ? *For neither doth the Father judge any man, but hath given all judgment to the Son.*[32] Observe how this soul which prays perfectly is not afraid of the Day of Judgment, but indeed prays with a longing free from anxiety: *thy kingdom come.*[33]

Judge me, O Lord, says the Psalmist, *according to thy justice.* In the preceding Psalm it was a weak soul who prayed, rather imploring God's mercy than mentioning any deserts of his own; for the Son of God came to call sinners to repentance.[34] Hence on that former occasion he said: *O save me for thy mercy's sake*,[35] not, that is, for the sake of what I deserve. Here, however, obedient to God's call, he has kept and observed the commands received and so makes bold to say: *Judge me, O Lord, according to my justice and according to my innocence upon me.* This is the true innocence which does no harm even to an enemy. Rightly then does the speaker ask to be judged according to his innocence, since he could truthfully say: *If I have rendered to them that repaid me evils.* The phrase *upon me* may refer not only to the word innocence but also to justice, so that the sense would be: Judge me, O Lord, according to my justice and according to my innocence, since my justice and innocence are from on high. This addition shows clearly that the soul is upright and innocent not of its own accord, but through God the giver of clarity and light. This light is mentioned in another Psalm: *Thou lightest my lamp, O Lord.*[36] And of John we are told: *He was not the light, but was to give testimony of the light.*[37] *He was a burning and a shining lamp.*[38] But Truth itself, that light from which souls like lamps are enkindled, shines forth with no borrowed beam but with its own. Therefore, *According to my justice*, the soul affirms, *and according to my innocence upon me*, as if a burning and shining lamp were to say: Judge me according to the flame which is from on high, which does not originate in me but shines in me from thine enkindling.

9. [V. 10] *The wickedness of sinners shall be consummated.* It *shall be consummated*, shall be brought to completion, according to that text of the Apocalypse: *He that is just, let him be justified still, and he that is filthy, let him be filthy still.*[39] It might indeed seem that men's wickedness reached its consummation when they crucified the Son of God; but greater is the wickedness of those who refuse to live uprightly and hate the precepts of true doctrine—those for whom the Son of God was crucified. *The wickedness of sinners*, the Psalmist declares, *shall be consummated*. In other words, let it mount to the full sum of wickedness, that just judgment may come without delay. However, in the Apocalypse we have not only the words: *He that is filthy, let him be filthy still*, but also: *He that is just, let him be justified still;* hence the speaker adds: *And thou shalt direct the just; the searcher of hearts and reins is God.* How can the just man be directed, then, except in secret? For now that the Christian name has arrived at the zenith of its glory, the very actions men admired in the first ages of Christianity, when worldly powers crushed the saints beneath persecution, do but serve to foster the growth of hypocrisy and pretense in men who are Christian in name

but prefer to please men rather than God. Amid the confusion of such hypocrisy, how, I ask, is the just man to be directed except by the God who searches hearts and reins, who looks into our thoughts, here designated by the word "heart," and our pleasures, here called "reins"? The Psalmist correctly ascribes to our reins the pleasure we experience in temporal and earthly gifts, for they belong to the lower part of man's nature. There too dwells the instinct of carnal generation, through which the race is continued, human nature passed on, and man brought into this life of toil and deceptive joys. To resume: this God, who searches our heart and finds that it is where our treasure is,[40] namely, in heaven, who searches our reins and finds that we do not consent to flesh and blood[41] but take our delight in the Lord, this same God directs the just man in his conscience. No man can penetrate it; it lies open before God, who alone sees what each man thinks and what each man enjoys. The aim and object of our solicitude is enjoyment; by care and forethought every man endeavors to secure it for himself. He who searches the heart sees our cares; He who carefully searches the reins sees also what enjoyment is the object of our solicitude. And when He finds our solicitude not directed towards the concupiscence of the flesh, or the concupiscence of the eyes, or the pride of life, all of which pass away like a shadow,[42] but raised upwards to the joys of things eternal, which know neither change nor decay, then will God, who searches the hearts and reins, direct the just. For what we do by exterior word or deed may be known to men; but with what intention we do these things, or what purpose we hope to attain by means of them, is known only to God, who searches the hearts and reins.

10. [V. 11] *Just is my help from the Lord, who saveth the upright of heart.* Medicine has a twofold task: first to

cure sickness, then to preserve health. It was with the first aim in view that the Psalmist prayed in the previous Psalm: *Have mercy on me, O Lord, for I am weak;*[43] with the second he prays in the present Psalm: *If there be iniquity in my hands, if I have rendered to them that repaid me evils, let me deservedly fall empty before my enemies.* In the former instance a sick man begs for cure; in the latter a healthy one prays not to be laid low. The former cries: *O save me for thy mercy's sake;*[44] the latter: *Judge me, O Lord, according to my justice.* One asks for a remedy to rid him of disease, the other for protection against falling into it. One says: *Save me, O Lord, according to thy mercy;* the other: *Just is my help from the Lord, who saveth the upright of heart.* Both the one prayer and the other will save the soul; but the former restores it from sickness to health, whereas the latter preserves it in a healthy condition. Thus in the former instance the help is given in mercy, since the sinner deserves nothing, yet longs to be made just, believing in Him who justifies the ungodly;[45] in the latter it is given in justice, being bestowed upon one who is already righteous. Let the sinner who said: *I am weak,* add: *Save me, O Lord, for thy mercy's sake;* and let the just man who said: *If I have rendered to them that repaid me evils,* add: *Just is my help from the Lord, who saveth the upright of heart.* For if He proffers the medicine which will heal us in sickness, how much more that which will keep us in health? *For if, when as yet we were sinners, Christ died for us, how much more being now justified shall we be saved from wrath through Him?*[46]

11. *Just is my help from the Lord, who saveth the upright of heart.* God, who searches the hearts and reins, directs the just, but with just help He saves the upright of

heart. He is not said to save those who are upright of heart and reins in the same way as He is said to search hearts and reins. For this reason: thoughts reside in the heart: evil when it is depraved, good when upright; but to the reins belong those blameworthy pleasures which are part of our lower nature and of earthly origin, whereas pleasures that are pure pertain not to the reins but to the heart. Hence we cannot speak of the upright of reins as we can of the upright of heart, for where the thought is, there is the pleasure; we cannot be upright unless our thoughts are upon divine and eternal things. So the Psalmist cried out: *Thou hast given gladness in my heart*, after having said: *The light of thy countenance, O Lord, is signed upon us.*[47] It is not the heart, in fact, but the reins which find a certain delight in a mad and delirious joy caused by foolish imaginings, when the illusions of earthly things, conjured up by the mind, beguile it with vain and worldly ambition. All these illusions are drawn from things beneath us, in other words from things earthly and carnal. Thus it comes about that God, searching hearts and reins, and finding right thoughts in the heart and no concupiscence in the reins, affords help in justice to the upright of heart, in whom pure thoughts are coupled with heavenly delights. And therefore after having said in another Psalm: *Moreover my reins also have corrected me even till night*, the Psalmist spoke of the help given him: *I set the Lord always in my sight, for He is at my right hand, that I be not moved.*[48] Here he shows he has suffered suggestions from the reins but not been enticed; had he been enticed he would certainly have been disturbed. But *The Lord is at my right hand*, he said, *that I be not moved*, and added at once: *Therefore my heart hath been delighted.*[49] His reins might indeed torment him; they could not give him pleasure.

Thus the delight originated not in the reins but in the heart, where God took care to be at his right hand to protect him against the incitement of the reins.

12. [V. 12] *God is a just judge, strong and patient.* Who is God the judge, if not the Lord who judges the peoples? He is just who *will render to every man according to his works.*[50] He is strong who, all-powerful as He is, for our salvation bore even with ungodly persecutors. He is patient who did not hurry away His persecutors to punishment immediately after His resurrection, but bore with them so that at length they might turn from their disloyalty to the task of saving their souls. And even yet He bears with them, reserving the final punishment for the Last Judgment, but for the present still inviting sinners to repentance. *Not bringing down anger every day.*[51] Perhaps *bringing down anger*, as we find it in the Greek copies, is a more significant expression than "being angry." It implies that the anger by which God punishes is not in Himself but in the minds of those ministers who comply with the precepts of truth. By these ministers orders are given to the lower ministries, called angels of wrath, to punish sins. These angels in turn find satisfaction in punishing man, not out of justice, which affords them no joy, but out of malice. God, then, does not bring down anger every day; in other words, God does not summon His ministers of vengeance every day. For the present, God's patience invites to repentance; but at the end of time, when through their hardness and their impenitent hearts men have stored up wrath for themselves against the day of wrath and the revelation of the just judgment of God,[52] He will brandish His sword.

13. [V. 13] *Except you will be converted, He will brandish His sword.* The Man of the Lord[53] Himself may

be taken to be God's sword, His weapon that is, which at His first coming He did not brandish but hid, so to speak, within the sheath of humility. But He will brandish it when He appears at His second coming to judge the living and the dead, and in the manifest splendor of His glory flashes forth light upon the just and terror upon the wicked. For in other copies, instead of *He will brandish His sword*, we find *He will make His sword flash forth*. This latter phrase applies very appropriately, I think, to our Lord's coming in glory, seeing that "sword" stands for the Person of our Lord, as is evident from another Psalm: *Deliver my soul from the wicked one, thy sword from the enemies of thy hand.*[54] *He hath bent His bow and made it ready*. The tenses of the verbs are not to be disregarded, for in speaking of the sword the Psalmist has used the future tense, *He will brandish*, in speaking of the bow the past tense, *He has bent*, and finally the verbs which follow continue in the past tense.

14. [V. 14] *And in it He hath prepared the instruments of death; He hath made ready His arrows for them that burn.* This bow, then, I would readily assume to be the Holy Scriptures, in which the strength of the New Testament, like a bowstring, has bent and overcome the rigidity of the Old. This bow has shot forth the apostles like arrows, or has sent forth preachers of the divine word. These arrows He has made ready for those that burn, in other words for such as would be fired with the love of God when pierced by them. With what other arrow was the soul pierced who says: *Bring me into the wine cellar, set me amid perfumes, compass me about with honey, because I am wounded with love?*[55] What other arrows could set on fire the man who makes up his mind to return to God, who quits his wanderings, begs for help against

deceitful tongues, and is told: *What shall be given to thee, or what shall be added to thee, against a deceitful tongue? The sharp arrows of the mighty, with coals that lay waste.*[56] As if to say: If you are pierced by these arrows and set on fire by these coals, you will burn with so great a love of the kingdom of heaven as to despise the tongues of all who resist you and would turn you back from your purpose. Then you will deride their persecutions and answer: *Who shall separate me from the love of Christ? Shall tribulation, or distress, or famine, or nakedness, or danger, or persecution, or the sword? For I am sure*, the Apostle adds, *that neither death, nor life, nor angels, nor principalities, nor powers, nor things present, nor things to come, nor might, nor height, nor depth, nor any other creature shall be able to separate us from the love of God which is in Christ Jesus our Lord.*[57] In this way He has made ready His arrows for those that burn. But whereas the Greek copies give: *He hath made ready His arrows for those that burn*, in several Latin copies we find *burning arrows*. Still, whether the arrows themselves burn, or whether they set others alight (which, of course, they cannot do unless they themselves are burning), the sense is exactly the same.

15. Now since, according to the Psalmist, the Lord has prepared in His bow not only arrows but also *the instruments of death*, we may inquire: What are these instruments of death? Are they perhaps heretics? For these latter shoot forth at souls from the same bow, or the same Scriptures, not to set them on fire with charity but to destroy them with poison, a thing that happens only to such as deserve it. Even this course of events can be ascribed to divine providence; not that God causes men to sin, but that His providence deals with them after they have sinned. Sin makes them study the Scriptures with ill intent, and the

corrupt interpretation they are forced to give them becomes the chastisement of their wrong-doing; their evil fate acts as a kind of goad to rouse the children of the Catholic Church from slumber and incite them to progress in the true understanding of the Sacred Books. As the Apostle says: *There must be also heresies, that they also who are approved may be made manifest among you,*[58] among men, that is, since before God they are already manifest. Or possibly God has ordained these selfsame arrows, these instruments of death, both for the destruction of unbelievers and at the same time as shafts burning, or, if you like, aimed at those who burn, in order to arouse the faithful? The Apostle's words are not false: *To some we are the odor of life unto life, to others the odor of death unto death. And for these things who is so sufficient?*[59] No wonder, then, that these same apostles are both instruments of death to their persecutors and fiery arrows to enkindle the hearts of believers.

16. But after the present dispensation will come the just judgment. As to this, the Psalmist gives us to understand that each man's punishment is fashioned from his own sin; his offense becomes his penalty. Thus we are not to suppose that punishment for sins issues from the calm and ineffable light of God. No, but He so ordains the course of things that the very pleasure a man tasted in his sin becomes God's instrument for his punishment. [V. 15] *Behold,* says the Psalmist, *he hath been in labor with injustice.* What had he conceived, then, that he should be in labor with injustice? *He hath conceived toil,* that toil of which it is written: *In labor shalt thou eat thy bread;*[60] and elsewhere: *Come to me, all you that labor and are burdened. For my yoke is mild and my burden light.*[61] For toil cannot cease as long as the object of a man's love can be wrested

from him against his will. When we love things that can be lost against our will, we toil in misery; deep in worry over temporal cares, we scheme and plot to get what we want, each one endeavoring to snatch it for himself and forestall or extort it from another. In fact and in perfectly logical order, he who conceived toil has been in labor with injustice. But what is it he hatches? Why, what he has been incubating, of course. Not what he began with, for what is born is not precisely what has been conceived. The germ is conceived, but what is brought to birth is the offspring formed from the germ. Hence toil is the germ of iniquity; to conceive toil is to conceive sin, that initial sin which consists in falling away from God.[62] So he who conceived toil has been in labor with injustice *and brought forth iniquity*. Iniquity and injustice are one; he has brought forth what he has been developing in secret. With what result?

17. [V. 16] *He hath opened a pit and dug it.* To open a pit is to prepare a trap in mundane affairs, as if in the earth, to ensnare him whom the unjust man would delude. The sinner opens this pit when he opens his soul to the evil suggestions of worldly covetousness; he digs it when, having done so, he goes on to the actual deception. But how is it possible for injustice to harm the upright man it attacks, before it has first harmed the unprincipled heart which commits it? For example, if a man steals money, at the moment he desires to bring loss and ruin upon another he himself is stabbed with the wound of avarice. What madman even could not see what a vast distance separates these two men, when one suffers the loss of his money, the other of his integrity? And thus *he will fall into the hole he made*. Or as another Psalm puts it: *The Lord shall be*

known when He executeth judgments; the sinner hath been caught in the works of his own hands.[63]

18. [V. 17] *His sorrow shall be turned on his own head, and his iniquity shall come down upon his crown.* For he himself had no will to avoid sin, but became, so to speak, a slave to sin, according to our Lord's words: *Whosoever committeth sin is a slave.*[64] His iniquity, in fact, will come down upon him while he himself bends beneath it; and therefore he has been unable to say to the Lord with the blameless and upright: *My glory and the lifter up of my head.*[65] So low will he be brought that his iniquity will dominate him and descend upon him; for it weighs him down and burdens him, and prevents him from soaring upwards to take his rest with the saints. That is what happens to an evil man when his reason becomes a slave and his passions have the mastery.

19. [V. 18] *I will confess to the Lord according to His justice.* This is not a confession of sins, for it is made by that soul who has already said in all truthfulness: *If there be iniquity in my hands.* It is, then, an avowal of God's justice in which we address Him thus: Truly, Lord, thou art just when thou dost protect the upright by enlightening them with thine own light, and dost deal with sinners in such a way that they are punished by their own ill will and not by thine. This confession thus gives praise to God and brings to naught the blasphemies of the wicked, who, wishing to make excuse for their crimes, refuse to take the responsibility for their own misdeeds. In other words, they refuse to attribute their wrongdoing to their own fault. So they contrive to accuse fortune or fate, or else the devil to whom, by our Maker's will, we have the power to deny our consent. Or they fall back on some nature which does not originate from God; and so, poor wretches, they drift

and wander, rather than win God's pardon by a sincere confession. For pardon is only possible to the man who says: "I have sinned." He, then, who realizes that God in His wisdom gives to each soul its deserts without in any way impairing the beauty of the universe, praises God in all His works; and this is the confession not of sinners but of the upright. For it is no confession of sins when our Lord says: *I confess to thee, Father, Lord of heaven and earth, because thou hast hid these things from the wise and prudent and hast revealed them to little ones.*[66] In the same way we find in Ecclesiasticus: *Confess the Lord in all His works. And in confessing Him you shall say in this manner: All the works of the Lord are exceeding good.*[67] All this can be seen in our Psalm, if we attune our minds to God and with His help offset the punishments of sinners against the rewards of the just, observing in this twofold effect of His justice how God maintains every creature He has made and rules, with a beauty full of wonder but recognized by few. Hence the speaker cries out: *I will give glory to the Lord according to His justice,* as one does who sees that darkness was not made by God but merely set in order by Him. For God said: *Be light made, and light was made.*[68] He did not say: Be darkness made, and darkness was made. Yet He set it in order, since the Scripture tells us: *And He divided the light from the darkness; and He called the light Day and the darkness Night.*[69] There is this difference: the one He made and set in order, the other He did not make, though this also He set in order. Now darkness denotes sin, as we learn from the prophet: *And thy darkness shall be as the noonday,*[70] while the Apostle says: *He that hateth his brother is in darkness,*[71] and again, emphatically: *Let us cast off the works of darkness and put on the armor of light.*[72] Not that darkness possesses a nature of its own. Every nature, as such, must have existence; light has existence, darkness has no existence. He who forsakes his Maker and reverts to that from which he was made, in other words to nothingness, is enveloped in the darkness of his sin. Yet he does not perish utterly, but is placed in due order in the lowest depths. Thus, having said: *I will confess to the Lord*, for fear we should think he was referring to the confession of sins the Psalmist adds finally: *And will sing to the name of the Lord most high*. For singing is a mark of joy, whereas repentance for sin bespeaks sadness.

20. We may also apply this Psalm to the Man of the Lord, provided that we refer to our own weak nature which He took upon Himself anything which is said to our discredit.

Discourse on Psalm 8

1. [Verse 1] *Unto the end, for the presses. A Psalm for David himself.*[1] The text of this Psalm tells us nothing whatever about these wine presses from which it takes its title, thus showing that the Scriptures often convey one and the same idea under many and various symbols. The wine presses, then, we may take to mean the Church, on the same principle by which we also understand a threshing floor to represent the Church. In fact, both on the threshing floor and in the wine press, the produce is merely cleared of its coverings, necessary as they were for the formation, growth and ripening of the harvest or vintage. From this protective covering both the wheat and the wine are separated: the wheat from the chaff on the threshing floor and the wine from the grapeskins in the presses. Similarly in the Church the good are to be found in company

with a multitude of worldly people whose presence has been necessary to bring them into the world and prepare them for the word of God; and God's ministers work to separate them from this throng by means of a desire which is spiritual. For at this present time it so happens that the good are set apart from the bad not by space but by difference of aim, although as far as bodily presence goes they mingle together in the churches. The time will come, however, for the grain to be separated and stored in barns and the wine in cellars. *He will gather the wheat into his barns*, says the Evangelist, *but the chaff he will burn with unquenchable fire*.[2] The same thought can be expressed in another simile: He will store the wine in cellars, but the grapeskins he will cast out for the cattle; so that the maw of the cattle may be taken as representing the punishments of hell.

2. We may look at the wine presses from another angle, provided that we always regard them as a figure of the Church. The grapes can be viewed as a symbol of the divine Word; for our Lord was typified by the cluster of grapes which the spies sent ahead by the people of Israel carried, hung crucified as it were upon a pole, on their return from the Promised Land.[3] Accordingly, when the Word of God has need of borrowing the sound of a voice to reach the ears of His hearers, His meaning is enclosed in the utterance of the voice as wine in the skin that contains it. Thus this "cluster of grapes" comes to our ears to be trodden out as if in a wine press. There it is crushed, so that while the sound reaches as far as the ears, the meaning sinks into the memory of the hearers as into a sort of vat. Thence it passes into moral training and a habit of mind, as wine from the vat passes into the cellars, where, if it does not turn sour through carelessness, it will mature with age.

With the Jews it turned sour, and this vinegar of theirs they gave our Lord to drink.[4] On the contrary, that wine, the produce of the fruit of the New Testament,[5] which our Lord is to drink with His saints in the kingdom of His Father, must needs be very sweet and mellow.

3. Often enough, wine presses also denote martyrdom; for having been trampled beneath the weight of persecution, the mortal remains of the confessors of Christ's name have been flung on the ground like grapeskins, while their souls flowed forth into the repose of their heavenly dwelling place. But this figurative sense by no means departs from the idea of the Church's fruitfulness. Therefore the Psalmist sings *for the wine presses*, to celebrate the inauguration of the Church, when our Lord rose again in order to ascend into heaven. For then it was that He sent the Holy Spirit, who so filled the disciples that they preached the word of God with confidence and gathered together the members of the Church.

4. The Psalmist begins, then: [V. 2] *O Lord, how admirable is thy name in the whole earth.* How, I ask, is it that His name is wonderful throughout the earth? The answer comes: *For thy magnificence is elevated above the heavens.* The meaning, then, is this: O Lord, who art our Lord, how all the dwellers upon earth marvel at thee, since through thine abasement in this world, thy majesty has been exalted above the heavens. For those who witnessed and for those others who have believed in it, thine ascent on high has declared who thou wast that didst first descend.

5. [V. 3] *Out of the mouths of babes and of sucklings thou hast perfected praise because of thy enemies.* I cannot take babes and sucklings to mean any others but those to whom the Apostle says: *As unto little ones in Christ I gave you milk to drink, not meat.*[6] These little ones are symbol-

ized by the children who went before our Lord praising
Him. When the Jews told Him to rebuke them, our Lord
defended them with these words: *Have you never read:
"Out of the mouths of infants and of sucklings thou hast
perfected praise"?*[7] With good reason the Psalmist says not,
thou hast fashioned, but *thou hast perfected praise.* For in
the Church there are also those who are no longer given
milk to drink, but eat solid food; it is to these the same
Apostle refers when he says: *We speak wisdom among the
perfect.*[8] Yet the Church is not brought to its full stature
through these alone, for were these the only ones, no
allowance would have been made for the human race in
general. But out of regard for their weakness, those as yet
incapable of understanding things spiritual and eternal are
nurtured on faith in the historical events which have been
wrought for our salvation since the times of the patriarchs
and prophets, especially in the mystery of the Incarnation,
by Him who is the incomparable Power and Wisdom of
God. Whoever accepts it with faith finds in it salvation;
for every one who is inspired by our Lord's leadership will
submit to the ordinances which will purify him. Then,
rooted and founded in charity, he will be capable of running with the saints, no longer now a babe fed on milk, but
a youth who can take solid food, able to comprehend what
is the breadth and length and height and depth, to know
also the charity of Christ which surpasses all knowledge.[9]

6. *Out of the mouths of infants and of sucklings thou
hast perfected praise because of thy enemies.* In general
we should understand as enemies to the dispensation made
by Jesus Christ, and Him crucified, all those who forbid
belief in the unknown and who promise certitude. Such is
the conduct of all heretics and of those whom pagan super-
stition terms philosophers. Not that the promise of knowl-

edge is blameworthy in itself, but they think they can ignore faith, the sound and indispensable ladder by which we attain to a certitude whose object can only be the things of eternity. Obviously they cannot possess that knowledge they promise, since in despising faith they neglect so useful and necessary a means of acquiring it. Out of the mouth, then, of infants and sucklings our Lord has perfected praise. Firstly He enjoins through the prophet: *If you will not believe, you shall not understand,*[10] and then He Himself declares: *Blessed are they that have not seen and shall believe.*[11]

Because of thy enemies, because of these same men of whom thou didst also say: *I confess to thee, O Father, Lord of heaven and earth, because thou hast hid these things from the wise and prudent, and hast revealed them to little ones.*[12] The Lord calls them wise, not that they really are wise but that they think they are. *That thou mayest destroy the enemy and the defender.*[13] Whom but the heretic? For he is both enemy and defender, who while bent on attacking the Christian faith appears to be defending it. However, the philosophers of this world can also quite well be considered both enemies and defenders, since in truth the Son of God is the Power and Wisdom of God who enlightens all those, whoever they may be, that truth has rendered wise. Now these philosophers, thus called because they profess to love wisdom, appear to defend it whereas they are its enemies, since they never cease to advocate harmful superstitions, such as the worship and veneration of the elements of this world.

7. [V. 4] *For I will behold thy heavens, the works of thy fingers.* We read that the Law was written with the finger of God and given through Moses His holy servant.[14] Many consider the finger of God to be the Holy Spirit. If

we are right, then, in taking the fingers of God to signify those servants of His who were filled with the Holy Spirit, and through His working within them wrote for us the whole of the Sacred Scriptures, we may aptly interpret the heavens in this context as the books of both Testaments. Moreover, when King Pharaoh's magicians saw themselves outdone by Moses, they cried out: *This is the finger of God.*[15] Although the expression *The heavens shall be folded together as a book*[16] denotes the sky above, yet it may very well be interpreted also in an allegorical sense as referring to the sacred books. *For I will behold the heavens*, says the Psalmist, *the works of thy fingers:* in other words, I will study and understand the Scriptures which thou hast written by the hands of thy servants through the operation of the Holy Spirit.

8. Hence we may also see the sacred books in those heavens of which the Psalmist spoke previously: *For thy magnificence is elevated above the heavens.* Thus the meaning of the whole passage would be: Because thy magnificence is exalted above the heavens, for thy majesty surpasses all that the Scriptures have declared, therefore out of the mouths of infants and of sucklings thou hast perfected praise in obliging those who would come to a knowledge of thy majesty to begin by a faith in the Scriptures. This majesty is elevated above the Scriptures because it exceeds and surpasses all that words and tongues can utter. God, then, has bowed down the Scriptures to the comprehension of infants and sucklings, as we sing in another Psalm: *He bowed the heavens and came down.*[17] And this He has done because of His enemies, who detest the cross of Christ, and whose proud and fluent speech is unable to profit little ones and sucklings even when they say things that are true. In this way the enemy and defender is

destroyed, who, whether it is wisdom he appears to defend or even the name of Christ, yet attacks that very truth he so readily promises to teach, since he attacks faith which is its basis. He is convicted of not possessing the truth for this reason, because by attacking faith, which is a step on the ladder to truth, he shows that he has no idea how to mount up to it. Hence to destroy the foolhardy, blind promiser of the truth, who is at once its enemy and its defender, we must look at the heavens, the work of God's fingers. We must study, that is to say, the Scriptures, which adapt themselves to the backwardness of infants, whom they nourish in the first place by humble belief in the historical deeds accomplished in the temporal order for our salvation, and subsequently strengthen in order to lift them up to the sublime understanding of things eternal. These heavens then, or these sacred books, are the works of God's fingers, for they have been composed by the Holy Spirit working in the saints. But they who regarded their own glory rather than the salvation of men have spoken without the Holy Spirit in whom abides the tenderness of God's mercy.

9. *For I will behold the heavens, the works of thy fingers, the moon and stars which thou hast founded.* The moon and stars have been founded in the heavens because both the universal Church, frequently signified by the "moon," and the particular churches in various places, intimated I think by the word "stars," have been established upon those Scriptures, which we believe are denoted by the term "heavens." In another Psalm we shall see why the moon should be a correct symbol for the Church, when we deal with the words: *The wicked have bent their bow, to shoot in the dark moon the upright of heart.*[18]

10. [V. 5] *What is man that thou art mindful of him, or the son of man that thou visitest him?* What, it may be

asked, is the difference between man and the son of man?
If there were no difference, the disjunctive form, *man or
the son of man*, would not be employed. For instance, if
the wording had been: "What is man that thou art mindful
of him, and the son of man that thou visitest him?" it might
have seemed to be a mere repetition of the word "man."
But now, since the expression is *man or son of man*, clearly
some difference is intimated. It is worth remembering that
every son of man is a man, although not every man is a son
of man. Adam, for instance, was a man without being a son
of man. From considering this fact we may discover what
is the difference here between man and son of man. Those
who bear the image of the earthly man, like Adam who
was not a son of man, are termed men, whereas those who
bear the image of the heavenly man[19] should rather be
termed sons of men. The former class is also called the old
man and the latter the new man.[20] But the new is born of
the old, since spiritual rebirth begins with a change from an
earthly and worldly life; hence the new self is called son
of man. Man, therefore, in this connection represents the
earthly man, the son of man the heavenly; the former is far
removed from God, the latter stands before God. For this
reason God is mindful of the former as of one set at a great
distance; the latter, who is before Him, He visits and
illumines with the light of His countenace. *Salvation*, indeed, *is far from sinners*,[21] and *the light of thy countenance, O Lord, is signed upon us.*[22] Thus in another
Psalm the Psalmist associates men with the beasts and says
that God preserves them with the brute creation, not in
communicating inward light but through an extension of
His mercy by which His goodness reaches out even to the
lowest beings; for God preserves carnal men in the way
that He preserves the beasts. Here the Psalmist separates

the sons of men from those men whom he has classed with the beasts, and proclaims them to be blessed in a far nobler way, since they are enlightened with the truth, and flooded as it were by the fountain of life. These are his words: *Men and beasts thou wilt preserve, O Lord, even as thou hast multiplied thy mercy, O God. But the children of men shall put their trust in the protection of thy wings. They shall be inebriated with the plenty of thy house, and thou shalt make them drink of the torrent of thy pleasure. For with thee is the fountain of life, and in thy light we shall see light. Extend thy mercy to them that know thee.*[23] God is mindful of man, then, in His manifold mercy, as He is of the beasts, for His manifold mercy reaches even to those afar off. But the son of man He visits, overshadowing and sheltering him with the wings of His mercy, enlightening him with His own light, giving him to drink of His delights and inebriating him with the plenty of His house, making him forget the woes and wanderings of his former life. This son of man, this new man, is brought forth with pain and groaning through the penance inflicted upon the old. Yet new as he is, he is still called carnal as long as he is fed on milk. *I could not speak to you as unto spiritual*, says the Apostle, *but as unto carnal;* and to show that he refers to those already reborn, he adds: *As unto little ones in Christ, I gave you milk to drink, not meat.* And when, as often happens, this son of man relapses into his former way of life, he hears in reproof that he is only a man: *Are you not men, and do you not walk according to man?*[24]

11. This son of man, then, was first visited in the person of the Man of the Lord[25] Himself, born of the Virgin Mary. The frailty of human nature which the Wisdom of God deigned to take upon Himself, and the humiliation of the passion, make the Psalmist declare with truth: [V. 6]

Thou hast made him a little less than the angels. But he hastens to proclaim the glory of His resurrection and ascension into heaven: *Thou hast crowned him,* he adds, *with glory and honor,* [V. 7] *and hast set him over the works of thy hands.* Now since the angels too are works of God's hands, we believe that the only-begotten Son has been set on high even above the angels, just as we hear and believe that He was made a little lower than the angels in the humiliation of His bodily nativity and passion.

12. [V. 8] *Thou hast subjected all things under his feet.* In saying *all things* the Psalmist excepts nothing. And for fear there might be room for understanding him otherwise, the Apostle commands us to believe it in this sense, saying: *He is excepted who put all things under Him.*[26] To the Hebrews[27] also he adduces the testimony of this very Psalm, wishing it to be understood that all things are so subjected to our Lord Jesus Christ that nothing is excluded.

Yet the Psalmist does not seem to mention anything very important when he enumerates: *All sheep and oxen, moreover the beasts also of the fields.* [V. 8] *The birds of the air and the fishes of the sea, that pass through the paths of the sea.* He seems to ignore the heavenly virtues and powers and all the hosts of angels, to leave aside even human beings and mention only the cattle as subject to Him. Perhaps, however, we should understand the sheep and oxen as holy souls yielding the fruit of innocence or laboring that the earth may bring forth fruit, in other words that earthly men may be regenerated into the rich life of the spirit. But if we would interpret this text to mean that all things are subject to our Lord Jesus Christ, we must understand these holy souls to include not men only but all the angels also. For if the prince-spirits, so to call them, are subject to Him, there is not a single creature but will thus be subject. Now how are we to prove that the term *sheep* can be taken to include not only men but those blessed spirits, the angels on high? May we do so from our Lord's saying that He left the ninety-nine sheep on the mountains, or the heights of heaven, in order to come down for the sake of one?[28] For if we are to take the one sheep as the human soul fallen in Adam (Eve, after all, was made from his side,[29] but this is not the time to treat of and consider the spiritual significance of all that), then the ninety-nine left on the mountains must mean not human but angelic spirits.

As to the oxen, we can easily determine their meaning from the words: *Thou shalt not muzzle the ox that thresheth the corn;*[30] men are called oxen for no other reason than this, that by preaching the Gospel of God's word they imitate the angels. How much easier is it not for us to denote under the figure of oxen those messengers of truth, the angels, when they who preach the Gospel and share their office are termed oxen? Hence we are told: *Thou hast subjected all sheep and oxen*—every holy spiritual being; and among them we must include men who lead holy lives in the Church, or in that wine press, now referred to under the further simile of moon and stars.

13. *Moreover the beasts also of the fields*. The addition of *moreover* is far from meaningless. Firstly, because the beasts of the fields could include both sheep and oxen, so that if goats are the beasts of rocks and mountainous regions, then sheep may well be called beasts of the fields. Thus, even had the phrase run, "All sheep and oxen and the beasts of the field," we might well have inquired the meaning of beasts of the fields, since in fact sheep and oxen could be understood as such; but the addition of the word *moreover* forces us to recognize some sort of distinction.

Now this *moreover* covers not only the beasts of the field but the birds of the air and the fishes of the sea, that pass through the paths of the sea. What is this distinction, then? Let us recall the wine presses, containing grapeskins as well as wine, the threshing floor covered with both chaff and grain,[31] the nets in which were enclosed good fish and bad,[32] Noe's ark, which held both clean and unclean animals;[33] and you will see that for all time until the final judgment the Church will contain not only sheep and oxen, in other words both laymen and clerics of holy life, but also *the beasts of the fields, the birds of the air, and the fishes of the sea, that pass through the paths of the sea.* The beasts of the field may appropriately be taken as those human beings who delight in mere bodily pleasures and climb no steep and difficult road. The field also stands for the broad way which leads to destruction;[34] thus it was in the field that Abel was put to death.[35] We have reason to fear, then, that in coming down from the mountains of God's justice (*Thy justice*, says the Psalmist, *is as the mountains of God*[36]), and making choice of the broad and easy ways of bodily gratification, we may end by being butchered by the devil. Now look too at the birds of the air, the proud, of whom we are told: *They have set their mouth against heaven.*[37] See how they are borne aloft on the wind, these men who say: *We will magnify our tongues; our lips are our own, who is Lord over us?*[38] Look also upon the fishes of the sea, the eager seekers who pass through the paths of the sea, those who delve deep into the affairs of this world for temporal gains which vanish and perish, like paths in the sea the moment the waters meet together again after parting to make way for passing ships or for anything that ploughs the waves or walks the waters. And the Psalmist says not merely "pass" but *pass through,* to show the intense determination with which such men pursue their futile and fleeting aims.

Now these three types of vices, gratification of the flesh, pride, and curiosity, comprise all kinds of sin. These, it seems to me, the Apostle John enumerates when he says: *Love not the world. For all that is in the world is the concupiscence of the flesh, and the concupiscence of the eyes, and the pride of life.*[39] The eyes above all minister to curiosity; the rest of the quotation is clear enough. The temptation of the Man of the Lord was threefold: through food, that is through the concupiscence of the flesh, when it was suggested to Him: *Command that these stones be made bread;*[40] through vainglory, when He was set down upon a mountaintop and all the kingdoms of the earth were shown Him and promised Him if He would render adoration; through curiosity, when He was advised to cast Himself down from the pinnacle of the Temple, to see whether the angels would uphold Him. Accordingly, when the enemy could not prevail against Him with any of these attempts, this is what is written about him: *When the devil had ended every temptation.*

To return to the metaphor of the wine presses, not only the wine but the grapeskins too are put under His feet. Not only sheep and oxen, in other words saintly souls among the faithful, are His, whether in the body of the Church or among its ministers, but also the beasts of sensuality, the birds of pride, the fishes of curiosity. All these classes of sinners, as we ourselves witness, are mingled with the upright and holy in the Church. May God work in His Church, then; may He separate the pure wine from the skins. Let us, on our part, strive to become the wine and to rank with the sheep or oxen, not the grapeskins or the beasts of the field, the birds of the air or the fishes that pass through the paths of the sea. Not that this is the only way of interpreting and explaining these creatures; it depends on the context; elsewhere they may have a different signification. This rule is to be observed in all allegorical interpretation, namely, that the meaning given should look to the context. Such is the teaching of our Lord and His apostles. To conclude, let us repeat the last verse, with which the Psalmist opened his song, and let us praise God with the words: [V. 16] *O Lord our God, how admirable is thy name in all the earth.* After the body of the treatise it is fitting, indeed, to return to the head, which sums up the whole discourse.

DISCOURSE ON PSALM 9

1. The title of this Psalm runs: [Verse 1] *Unto the end, for the hidden things of the Son, a Psalm for David himself.* We may inquire what the hidden things of the Son are, but since this Son is not defined, we must infer that it is the only-begotten Son of God Himself. In fact, when David's son is mentioned in the title of a Psalm, the words used are: *When he fled from the face of his son Absalom.*[1] To name him leaves no doubt about the son's identity, yet Scripture not merely says *from the face of son Absalom* but adds the word *his.* Here, however, both because the Psalmist has omitted *his,* and also because he says a good deal about the Gentiles, it cannot denote Absalom. Nor can the war which that abandoned youth waged against his father have any reference to the Gentiles, since in it the people of Israel alone were divided against themselves. Obviously, then, this Psalm is a hymn celebrating the mysteries of God's only-begotten Son. In fact, when our Lord refers simply to the Son, He wishes to signify that

He Himself is the only-begotten Son, as when He says: *If therefore the Son shall make you free, you shall be free indeed.*[2] He did not say, "the Son of God," but by merely saying, *the Son,* He gave His hearers to understand whose Son He was. This manner of speaking is due to the dignity of the one thus spoken of, so that even though we do not name Him, our meaning is clear. In the same way we say: "It rains," "it is fine," "it thunders," and suchlike expressions, without specifying who does it, because the high dignity of the doer arises spontaneously in the minds of all without need of words.

What, then, are these mysteries of the Son? To begin with, we may understand from this expression that there are some things regarding the Son that are manifest; and from them we distinguish those which are termed hidden. Now we believe in two comings of our Lord, the one already past, which the Jews did not recognize, the other, which both we and they await; and since the first coming, ignored by the Jews, has been of benefit to the Gentiles, one may well interpret the phrase *for the hidden things of the Son* as this first coming, when *blindness struck Israel in part, so that the fulness of the Gentiles should come in.*[3] If one does but look, two judgments are also hinted at in the Scriptures, the one hidden, the other manifest. The hidden one, of which the Apostle Peter declares: *The time is that judgment should begin at the house of God,*[4] is taking place now. This hidden judgment is the affliction in this life which prompts a man to make use of it to purify himself, or warns him to turn to God, or strikes him with a blindness which will destroy him if he despises God's voice and chastisement. The manifest judgment, on the other hand, is that in which the Lord will come to judge the living and the dead, when all will confess that it is He who dispenses reward to the good and punishment to the wicked. But the confession then made, far from healing the wicked, will but heap up their condemnation. It seems to me that our Lord was speaking of those two judgments, the one secret and the other manifest, when He said: *He that believeth me is passed from death to life and shall not come into judgment*,[5] that is to say, into the visible judgment. This passing over from death to life through some suffering or other, by which God scourges every son whom He receives, is the secret judgment: *He that believeth not*, our Lord declares, *is already judged*.[6] In other words, this secret judgment has already prepared him for the one which will be manifest. Of these two judgments we also read in the Book of Wisdom: *Therefore thou hast sent a judgment upon them, as senseless children, to mock them. But they that were not amended by mockeries and reprehensions experienced the worthy judgment of God*.[7] Those, in fact, who are not corrected by God's hidden judgment are most deservedly punished by His manifest one. This Psalm, therefore, speaks to us of the mysteries of the Son, that is to say, of His coming in humility, so profitable for the nations while the Jews remained blind, and of the afflictions which God now uses in secret, not to destroy sinners, but either to exercise the faith of those already turned to Him, or to urge others to conversion, or finally by blinding them to prepare for damnation those who persist in their impenitence.

2. [V. 2] *I will give praise to thee, O Lord, with my whole heart*. It is not he who doubts of God's providence in any matter that praises God with his whole heart, but rather he who beholds in the mysterious designs of God's wisdom the greatness of the unseen reward in store for us, the man who can say: *We glory in tribulation*.[8] Such a man

recognizes how all sufferings in this body of ours serve either to discipline those already converted to God, to persuade others to repent so that they may be converted, or to prepare the obdurate for their just and final condemnation; and thus he refers all things to the government of God's providence, whereas the unwise suppose that everything happens by chance or accident, not by any divine ordering.

I will relate all thy wonders. To relate all God's wonders is to reveal God's workings, not only in what is wrought visibly upon the body, but in His invisible and far more sublime and marvelous action in souls. For men who are worldly-minded and addicted to secret sins are more struck by the bodily resurrection of the dead Lazarus than by the spiritual resurrection of Paul the persecutor. Now the visible miracle is a call to the soul to be enlightened, while the invisible miracle enlightens the soul which has already responded to that call; and thus he who believes in the visible marvels and passes on to the understanding of invisible ones is he who relates all the wonders of God.

3. [V. 3] *I will be glad and rejoice in thee.* Not henceforth in the things of this world, not in pleasure arising from physical contacts, nor in delicacies for tongue and palate, not in sweet odors nor in the delight of transient melodies, not in the shape and color of material things, nor in the hollowness of human praise, not in wedlock and mortal offspring, nor in a superabundance of worldly wealth, not in the researches of profane science, whether it scans the wide spaces or considers the ages of time. No, *I will be glad and rejoice in thee,* or rather in the mysteries of the Son, where *the light of thy countenance, O Lord, is sealed upon us;*[9] for *Thou shalt hide them,* says the Psalmist, *in the secret of thy face.*[10] It is thyself, therefore, who art

the joy and gladness of those that recount all thy wonders. And He whom the prophets now foretell, He above all will recount thy wondrous doings who comes not to do His own will but the will of Him who sent Him.[11]

4. Already the Person of our Lord begins to emerge as the speaker in this Psalm. Listen to what follows: *I will sing to thy name, O thou most high*, [V. 4] *when my enemy shall be turned back*. Now when was His enemy turned back? Was it not when Christ told him: *Go behind me, Satan?*[12] For then the tempter who wished to put himself forward was put behind, since his seductions came to nothing and he failed to win the slightest advantage. The earthly man indeed must remain in the background, whereas the heavenly man although last is nevertheless first; for the first man was from the earth, earthly, the second man from heaven, heavenly.[13] It was from the race of the first that he came who said: *He that shall come after me is preferred before me*.[14] The Apostle too, forgetting what lies behind, reaches out to what lies ahead.[15] The enemy was turned backward then, when he failed to deceive the heavenly Man whom he had tempted, and directed his attention to the men of the earth whom he could dominate. For this reason, no man can get the start of this enemy and turn him back unless he has exchanged the image of the earthly man for that of the heavenly one.[16]

We can, however, without any absurdity apply the phrase *my enemy* to sinners or pagans in a general way. In that case, the words *When my enemy shall be turned back* imply not punishment, but rather a benefit, and a benefit so great that nothing can be compared to it. What indeed could be a greater blessing than to destroy pride and renounce all desire to precede Christ, as though we were in sound health and in need of no physician, but rather to be content to follow after Christ, who called His disciple to a more perfect life with the words: *Follow me?*[17] Still, *When my enemy shall be turned back* does apply more appropriately to the devil. For in truth the devil has been forced back even in the act of persecuting the upright, since he is far more useful to them when he pursues them than he would be were he to go before them as their prince and leader. Let us, then, sing praise to the name of the Most High, since He has repulsed our enemy, whose pursuit we should prefer to his leadership. The Lord has become our refuge;[18] we have a refuge and hiding place in the mysteries of the Son.

They shall be weakened and perish before thy face. Who are they that shall faint and melt away but the wicked and impious? *They shall be weakened,* in that they will be robbed of strength; *and perish,* for the impious shall cease to exist; *before* God's *face,* at the sight of God, as that man melted away who said: *I live, now not I, but Christ liveth in me.*[19] But why are the impious to *be weakened and perish before thy face?* The answer comes: [V. 5] *For thou hast maintained my judgment and my cause.* Thou hast turned to my advantage both the judgment which seemed likely to go against me, and the condemnation men pronounced against me, just and innocent as I was. In fact, these vicissitudes have served Him for our deliverance; just as sailors call "theirs" the wind of which they have taken advantage for a prosperous run.

6. *Thou hast sat on the throne, who judgest justice.* This perhaps is the language of the Son towards the Father, in the same sense that He said: *Thou shouldst not have any power against me, unless it were given thee from above,*[20] ascribing to the Father's equity and to His own secret designs the very fact that the Judge of mankind has been

judged for the benefit of men. Or we may suppose that man is saying to God: *Thou hast sat on the throne, who judgest justice*, and calling his own soul God's throne. In that case perhaps his body would be represented by the earth, which has been termed God's footstool;[21] for God indeed was in Christ reconciling the world to Himself.[22] Or again the words may be addressed to her Bridegroom by the soul of the Church, now made perfect and without spot or wrinkle,[23] worthy in short of the mysteries of the Son because the King has brought her into His chamber.[24] *Thou hast sat on the throne, who judgest justice*, she would say, because thou hast risen from the dead and ascended into heaven and sittest at the Father's right hand. Whichever of these opinions as to the speaker of this verse may be preferred, none of them goes beyond the measure of the faith.

7. [V. 6] *Thou hast rebuked the Gentiles, and the wicked one hath perished*. It seems more appropriate to take these words as spoken to, than actually by, our Lord Jesus Christ. Who else indeed rebuked the Gentiles and brought the wicked one to nothing as He did after His ascension into heaven? For He sent the Holy Spirit to fill the apostles so that they preached the word of God with confidence and freely reproved the sins of men. Their rebukes made the wicked vanish; for the evildoer was made just and became a devoted disciple.

Thou hast blotted out their name forever to the age of ages. The name of the wicked has been blotted out; for they who have come to believe in the true God can no longer be called the wicked. Their name is blotted out *forever*: as long, that is, as this world shall last. *To the age of ages*. Now what is this *age of ages*? Is it not that of which this world is, as it were, an image and shadow? The course of the seasons following one another, the waning and wax-

ing of the moon, the sun returning to the same position
year by year, spring, summer, autumn and winter each
passing away only to come round again—all this is a kind of
imitation of eternity. But the duration underlying an immutable continuity is termed the age of ages. It may be
compared with a line of poetry, first conceived in the mind
and then uttered by the tongue. The mind gives form to
the spoken word; the one fashions an abiding work of art,
the other resounds in the air and dies away. Thus, too, the
age which passes takes its pattern from that unchangeable
age which is termed the age of ages. The latter abides in the
divine workmanship, that is to say, in the Wisdom and
Power of God, whereas the former is worked out in the
government of creation. Perhaps, however, in this word
forever we have mere repetition, so that after saying *forever*
the Psalmist adds *to the age of ages,* in case the phrase
might be taken to refer to this passing world. The Greek
copies run thus: εἰς τὸν αἰῶνα, καὶ εἰς τὸν αἰῶνα τοῦ αἰῶνος,
translated by most Latin writers not as *forever to the age
of ages* but as "endlessly and for all time," so that "for all
time" explains "endlessly." *Thou hast blotted out the name
of the wicked forever;* for henceforth the wicked are
no more. And if the name of wicked can no more be given
to them in this world, still less will it be in eternity.

8. [V. 7] *The swords of the enemy have failed unto
the end.* The enemy spoken of is in the singular, not the
plural. Now this enemy whose swords have lost their edge,
who is he if not the devil, whose weapons are the thousand
erroneous theories he employs like sword blades to put
souls to death? To overcome these swords, however, and
bring them to naught, that sword is at hand which is
spoken of in Psalm 7: *Except you be converted, He will
brandish His sword.*[25] And perhaps He, God's sword, is the

end upon which the enemy swords come to grief; until they reach Him they are to some degree effective. At present He works in secret, but at the Last Judgment He will burst forth in visible splendor. With this sword, as the Psalmist goes on to relate, cities are destroyed: *The swords of the enemy have failed unto the end; and their cities thou hast destroyed.* These cities are places where the devil holds sway, where insidious and deceitful suggestions hold, as it were, a royal court. Before this overlordship the members of the body are ranged in attendance as satellites and ministers. There are the eyes for curiosity, the ears for wanton talk, eager to catch every whisper of dissolute tittle-tattle, the hands practised in robbery and every criminal violence; and so on with the rest of the members, all serving this mighty tyrant with his evil suggestions. The populace of this city would consist of the sensual appetites and disturbing emotions of mind which stir up daily discord within a man. For where there is a king, a court, ministers and populace, there we have a city; and such misdeeds would not be found in evil cities unless they first existed in individual human beings, the elements and germ, as it were, of the city. These cities our Lord destroys when He casts out their prince as He has told us: *The prince of this world has been cast out.*[26] The word of truth works havoc in these kingdoms; it silences dangerous suggestions, subdues impure affections, takes captive bodily members and senses and gives them over to the service of justice and good deeds. In this way is fulfilled the Apostle's saying *that sin may no longer reign in our mortal body*,[27] and so forth. Then the soul is tranquilized and made ready to enter upon rest and happiness.

Their memory hath perished with a noise; the memory, that is, of the wicked. *With a noise* may be added because when wickedness is overthrown there is an uproar; a man does not return to the depths of peace, where the most profound silence dwells, unless amid much turmoil he has waged war upon his vices. Or else *with a noise* implies that the memory of the ungodly perishes along with the tumult in which their wickedness involved them.

9. [V. 8, 9] *But the Lord remaineth forever.* To what purpose, then, have the nations raged and the peoples devised vain projects against the Lord and against His Christ,[28] seeing that *the Lord remaineth forever? He hath prepared His throne in judgment* [V. 9] *and He will judge the world in equity.* He prepared His throne when He was judged; His endurance merited heaven for us men, and God clothed in human nature brought blessings to believers. This, then, is the hidden judgment of the Son. But because He is to come again openly and in all men's sight to judge the living and the dead, He was preparing His throne in His hidden judgment. And, moreover, *He will* openly *judge the world in equity;* in other words, He will give to each his deserts, setting the lambs on His right hand and the goats on His left.[29] *He shall judge the people in justice.* This is a repetition of the former sentence, *He shall judge the world in equity.* He will judge, not as human beings judge, who cannot see the heart, and in whose verdicts those that are acquitted are very often more guilty than those that are condemned. But the Lord will judge fairly and justly, according as a man's conscience bears witness and his own mind either accuses or defends him.[30]

10. [V. 10] *And the Lord is become a refuge for the poor.* However much that enemy who has been turned back may persecute, what harm will come to those for whom the Lord is become a refuge? And so it will be if they have chosen to be poor in this world, of which the

enemy is ruler, not setting their heart on the things that elude a man even while he lives and loves them, and when he dies must be left behind. Such are the poor for whom the Lord has become a refuge. *A helper in due time, in tribulation.* Thus He makes them poor, since He scourges every son whom He receives.[31] What a helper in due time is, the Psalmist explains by adding *in tribulation;* for a soul does not turn towards God except when it turns away from this world, and there is nothing better calculated to turn it away from this world than to find its frivolous, harmful, soul-destroying pleasures mingled with toil and suffering.

11. [V. 11] *And let them trust in thee who know thy name:* because they have ceased to trust in riches and the other attractions of this world. When the soul tears itself away from this world and seeks an object for its trust, the knowledge of God's name comes opportunely to the rescue. The actual name of God has been published everywhere nowadays; but the knowledge of the name implies the knowledge of Him whose name it is, for a name does not exist for its own sake but for what it signifies. Now we have been told: *The Lord is His name.*[32] Hence he knows this name who willingly devotes himself to God's service. *And let them trust in thee who know thy name.* Again, the Lord says to Moses: *I am who am; and thou shalt say to the children of Israel: He who is hath sent me.*[33] *Let them trust in thee,* then, *who know thy name,* so that they may not trust in the things that flow by on the rapid stream of time, possessing nothing but the future "will be" and the past "has been." For the future, when it comes, at once becomes the past; with longing we await it, with sorrow we see it pass away. But in God's nature there will be nothing future, as if not yet existing, nor yet past as if existing no

longer, but only that which is; and this is what we mean by eternity. Those, then, who know the name of Him who said: *I am who am,* and of whom it was said, *He who is hath sent me,* must cease to trust in and set their hearts upon the things of time, and must betake themselves to the hope of things eternal. *For thou hast not forsaken them that seek thee, O Lord.* Those who seek Him no longer seek for passing and perishing things, for no man can serve two masters.[34]

12. [V. 12] *Sing ye to the Lord, who dwelleth in Sion.* The words are addressed to those whom the Lord has not forsaken when they sought Him. He dwells in Sion, which signifies contemplation, and typifies the Church in this world, even as Jerusalem typifies the Church to come, the city of the saints already enjoying the life of angels, since Jerusalem signifies "vision of peace." Now contemplation comes first and vision follows, just as this Church precedes that promised city which is imperishable and eternal. Its precedence, however, is one of time, not of dignity, for the place we are striving to gain is more honorable than anything we can do to reach it. Now we watch, so that afterwards we may enjoy the vision. But unless God were dwelling in this His Church on earth, even the most careful observation might well end in some kind of error; and therefore the Church is warned: *The temple of God is holy, which you are,*[35] and: *That Christ may dwell by faith in the inward man in your hearts.*[36] Hence we are bidden to sing to the Lord who dwells in Sion, so that with one heart we may praise the Lord who dwells in the Church. *Declare His wonders among the Gentiles.* It has been done already and will never cease to be done.

13. [V. 13] *For requiring their blood He hath remembered them.* It is as though those who had been sent to

preach the Gospel were replying to the command: *Declare His wonders among the Gentiles*, and saying: *O Lord, who hath believed our report?*[37] and: *For thy sake we are killed all the day long.*[38] The Psalmist rejoins aptly that for the persecuted Christians the fruit of death will be nothing less than the acquisition of eternity: *For requiring their blood He hath remembered them.* But why has he expressly mentioned *their blood?* Perhaps it is in case somebody with imperfect knowledge and little faith should inquire: How are they to proclaim His wonders, seeing that the unbelief of the Gentiles will be raging against them? Such a person receives the reply: *For requiring their blood He hath remembered them.* In other words, the Last Judgment is to come, and in it both the glory of the slain and the punishment of the slayers will be made manifest. Nobody must imagine from these words that God is subject to forgetfulness. It is merely that the judgment is a long way ahead and the words are accommodated to the feelings of weak persons who think that God has, as it were, forgotten, when He does not act with the speed they would like. To such people are also addressed the words which follow: *He hath not forgotten the cry of the poor.* He has not forgotten, as you suppose. You heard the words, *He hath remembered,* and forthwith exclaimed: Then He had forgotten; but no, says the Psalmist, *He hath not forgotten the cry of the poor.*

14. However, I should like to know what is this cry of the poor which God does not forget. Is it the cry that follows: [V. 14] *Have mercy on me, O Lord, see my humiliation which I suffer from my enemies?* Then why did not the Psalmist say: "Have mercy on us, O Lord, see our humiliation which we suffer from our enemies," as though many poor men were crying out: *Have mercy on*

me, O Lord, and not merely one? Is it because there is but One who, rich as He was, first became poor for our sakes[39] and now would plead for His saints? Is it not He who goes on to say: [V. 15] *Thou that liftest me up from the gates of death, that I may declare all thy praises in the gates of the daughter of Sion?* For it is our Lord who uplifts man, not only the manhood in which He is clothed and which is Head of the Church, but every one of us who is counted among His members; He lifts us up above all evil desires, which are gates of death because through them we go to death. Death, indeed, already lurks in the very exhilaration of our enjoyment when we secure what it was iniquitous to covet. Covetousness is the root of all evils;[40] and it is moreover the gate of death, for a widow who lives a luxurious life is dead.[41] Now it is by unholy desires that we come to such luxury, as if through the gates of death. But all noble endeavors are the gates of the daughter of Sion, through which we come to the vision of peace in Holy Church. Within these gates it is proper to declare all God's praises, so that what is holy shall not be given to dogs, nor pearls be cast before swine. The dogs, in fact, find it more to their liking to bark persistently than to search with care, while the swine neither bark nor search but wallow in the mire of their own sensuality. But when the praises of God are proclaimed with holy zeal, those who ask receive, those who seek find, to those who knock the door is opened.[42]

Or possibly the gates of death stand for man's bodily senses, and his eyes which were opened when he tasted the fruit of the forbidden tree?[43] Above these senses are those exalted who are bidden to seek not the things that are seen but those that are not seen, for things seen are temporal but those not seen are eternal.[44] The gates of the daughter of Sion, then, would signify the sacraments and the rudiments of faith, which are opened to those who knock, to enable them to attain to the mysteries of the Son. For eye has not seen, nor ear heard, nor has there entered into the heart of man, what God has prepared for them that love Him.[45] Even thus far does the cry of the poor prevail, which the Lord has not forgotten.

15. [V. 16] *I will rejoice,* the Psalm continues, *in thy salvation;* in other words, I shall be encompassed with blessedness by thy salvation, which is our Lord Jesus Christ, the Power and Wisdom of God.[46] Obviously it is the Church speaking. Afflicted here on earth, yet saved by hope, as long as the judgment of the Son remains hidden she cries out with confidence: *I will rejoice in thy salvation.* For the present she is worn out by the roar of violence and pagan errors all round her. *The Gentiles have stuck fast in the deadly devices which they have prepared.* Notice how the punishment reserved for the sinner arises from his own deeds, and how those bent on persecuting the Church have been caught in that very degradation they thought they were inflicting. For while eager to butcher bodies they were inflicting death upon their own souls.

Their foot hath been taken in the very trap[47] which they hid. The hidden trap represents their crafty plotting. The foot typifies the soul's affection, which when depraved is termed cupidity or lust, but when upright, love or charity. Love is the magnet which draws the soul towards its goal. This goal is not in any kind of space such as is occupied by the body, but consists in fruition, to which the soul rejoices that love has led it. Cupidity is followed by an enjoyment which brings ruin, love by one which brings profit. Hence cupidity is called a root,[48] the root being like the foot to a tree. Love is also called a root in the passage where our Lord speaks of the seeds fallen on stony places, which

wither away when the sun blazes forth because they have
no depth of root.[49] By these He means those who receive
the word of truth gladly, but give way under persecution,
which can be resisted only by love. The Apostle too enjoins: *That being rooted and founded in charity, you may
be able to comprehend.*[50] Hence the sinners' foot, that is to
say their affection, gets caught in the trap they have
secretly laid. When the deception is followed by pleasure,
and God gives them over to the desire of their hearts,[51]
then that pleasure holds them fast so that they dare not tear
away their affection and set it upon something worth
while. For when they attempt to do so, they suffer pain of
mind as a man would in trying to free his foot from a
fetter; so yielding to the pain they prefer not to sever themselves from their harmful pleasures. Thus, *in the very trap
which they hid,* or in their evil designs, *their foot has been
taken;* in other words, by deceit their affections have
achieved a worthless enjoyment which they must pay for
with suffering.

16. [V. 17] *The Lord is known when He executeth
judgments.* Such is the manner of God's judgment, that it
is not from the calm of His own happiness, nor from the
hidden depths of His wisdom, to which the souls of the
blessed are admitted, that He brings forth sword or fire or
wild beast or any such thing to torment sinners. Then in
what way are they tormented, and by what means does the
Lord execute judgment? *In the works of his own hands,*
says the Psalmist, *the sinner hath been caught.*

17. Here the words, *Song for the diapsalma,*[52] are inter-
posed, to express as best we can the secret joy caused by
the present separation, not indeed of space but of the
heart's affections, between sinners and the just, like the
separation of the chaff from the grain as yet on the thresh-

ing floor. The Psalmist continues: [V. 18] *The wicked shall be turned into hell;* that is to say: Let them, as long as God spares them, be handed over to their own devices and entrapped in their own deadly pleasures.[53] *All the nations that forget God;* for since they have refused to reckon with God, God has delivered them over to a reprobate mind.

18. [V. 19] *For the poor man shall not be forgotten to the end.* In this life he seems to be forgotten, for sinners appear to be prospering in this world's happiness, while the just suffer affliction; but *the patience of the poor,* declares the Psalmist, *shall not perish forever.* Certainly they need patience at present to put up with the wicked, already separated from them by the bent of their wills, until the final separation of the day of judgment.

19. [V. 20] *Arise, O Lord, let not man prevail.* The Psalmist sighs for the coming of the judgment, but before it does come, *Let the Gentiles,* he asks, *be judged in thy sight.* In secret, that is, under the eye of God, since the judgment is pronounced in God's sight and only the handful of saints and just men are aware of it. [V. 21] *Appoint, O Lord, a lawgiver over them.* This, if I am not mistaken, will be the Antichrist to whom the Apostle refers in the words: *When the man of sin shall be revealed.*[54] *Let the Gentiles know themselves to be but men;* and since they refuse to be set free by the Son of God, to belong to the Son of Man and become sons of men, in other words new men, let them be slaves to a human being, in fact to their own sinful self, since they are themselves but men.

ON THE SECOND PART OF PSALM 9

20. And because Antichrist will attain to such a pitch of empty glory and be allowed to take such action against

all men, and especially against God's saints, that at length some of the weak will indeed suppose God does not trouble about human affairs, the Psalmist interposes a *diapsalma* and goes on to express the groaning, so to speak, of those who ask why the judgment is delayed: [2 Ps. 9, V. 1] *Why, O Lord*, he asks, *hast thou retired afar off?* Then, as though he had suddenly understood, or perhaps had known all along and asked for the sake of giving the answer, the questioner continues: *Thou dost slight us in due season, in tribulations.* Thou dost slight us for our advantage and send troubles to stir up our minds with desire for thy coming. The more burning the thirst, the more welcome is the life-giving fountain. Hence the Psalmist hints at the cause of the delay in the words: [V. 2] *Whilst the wicked man is proud, the poor is set on fire.* It is truly wonderful to see with what earnestness and what firm hope God's little ones are enkindled to upright living when in contest with sinners. Even heresies are allowed to exist for the same hidden reason; not, of course, that this is the intention of the heretics, but God's providence knows how to draw good out of their perversity. For just as God creates light and sets it in order, whereas darkness He merely sets in order,[55] so that in comparison with darkness light shall be the more pleasing, so too in the face of heresy the discovery of truth becomes all the more acceptable. By this contrast those who have been known to God alone are tested and made manifest also among men.

21. *They are caught in their schemes which they devise.* Their evil schemes become their bonds. Now how do they become their bonds? [V. 3] *For the sinner*, declares the Psalmist, *is praised in the desires of his soul.* The tongues of flatterers bind souls fast in their sins; the sinner enjoys doing things for which he not only fears no reproof but

draws forth approval. *And he who acts knavishly is blessed.* Hence *they are caught in their schemes which they devise.*

22. [V. 4] *The sinner hath provoked the Lord.* Let nobody congratulate the man who prospers in his doings, whose sins have an approver at hand and not an avenger. This very fact is a proof of the Lord's greater anger. The sinner has provoked the Lord, and this is the penalty he suffers—that he does not undergo the chastisement which corrects. *The sinner hath provoked the Lord; according to the multitude of His wrath He will not seek him.* God's wrath is at its height when He does not seek out the sinner but apparently forgets him, paying no attention to his sins, while the offender attains by trickery and crime to riches and honors. This will happen very notably to Antichrist, who will appear so blessed in the sight of men as actually to be mistaken for God. But the greatness of this divine anger we shall learn from what follows.

23. [V. 5] *God is not before his eyes; his ways are filthy at all times.* Anybody who has tasted true spiritual joy and gladness will also know how grave an evil it is to be deprived of the light of truth. If men regard the privation of bodily sight which robs the eyes of daylight as a grievous calamity, how terrible will be the penalty of a man who so prospers in his sins as to lose sight of God entirely, who walks perpetually in filthy paths, whose thoughts and designs, in other words, are stained with guilt! *Thy judgments are removed from his sight.* For the mind conscious of its wrongdoing and so far as it can see suffering no chastisement, supposes that God is not judging, and thus His judgments are removed from the man's sight. This in itself is a very serious punishment. *And he will rule over all his enemies.* Tradition has it that the man of sin will overcome all kings and become sole ruler, and

then, according to the Apostle who prophesies about him, *He will sit in the temple of God, shewing himself above all that is worshiped and that is called God.*[56]

24. And since he has been abandoned to the unholy desires of his own heart and destined for final condemnation, he is going to rise by his evil cunning to the very summit of worthless and ostentatious dominion. Hence the Psalmist continues: [V. 6] *For he hath said in his heart: I shall not be moved from generation to generation without evil.* In other words, my fame and name will not pass down from this generation to a future one unless I attain by evil deeds to such a height of power that posterity cannot be silent concerning it. For a soul which is thoroughly corrupt, devoid of good practices and blind to the light of justice, carves out for itself by villainy a career leading to such notoriety that even future generations must needs speak of it. And they who cannot achieve a reputation by good means, crave for men even to speak ill of them, provided only that their renown is spread far and wide. This, I think, is the meaning of the words: *I shall not be moved from generation to generation without evil.*

There is also another interpretation. Some unthinking and misguided person may suppose that he cannot pass from this mortal generation to the generation of eternity except by means of evil practices. So Simon[57] is reported to have done: he thought to gain heaven by his wicked arts and pass from the human to the divine generation by his skill in magic. What wonder, then, if that man of sin, who will personify in himself all the villainy and impiety begun by every false prophet, and show signs and wonders so great as to deceive, were it possible, the very elect, should say in his heart: *I shall not be moved from generation to generation without evil?*

25. [V. 7] *His mouth is full of cursing, and of bitterness and of deceit.* It is a horrible blasphemy, indeed, to seek heaven by these abominable practices and expect an eternal prize in return for getting together such earnings. But his mouth is crammed full of this blasphemy. Those pretensions of his will come to naught; they will merely remain in his mouth to destroy the man who has dared to promise himself such a reward by means of his bitterness and deceit, by means, that is, of the violence and artifice through which he will gain over the multitude to his side.

Under his tongue are labor and sorrow. No work is more laborious than injustice and ungodliness; and such labor is followed by misery, for it is not only fruitless but disastrous. This labor and misery characterize the words already discussed which the sinner has uttered in his heart: *I shall not be moved from generation to generation without evil.* The Psalmist adds, *under his tongue,* and not "on" his tongue, because he will ruminate in silence, while he speaks to other men in quite a different tone, so as to appear the champion of goodness and justice, yea the very son of God.

26. [V. 8] *He sitteth in ambush with the rich.* Who are these rich, but those upon whom he will heap the riches of this world? And he is said to sit in ambush with them for this reason, because he will parade their counterfeit happiness to deceive men; and these, seized with a fatal desire to resemble them rather than to seek the good things of eternity, will fall into his snares. *In private places, that he may kill the innocent. In private places* refers, I think, to a state of mind in which it is not easy to see what should be sought and what shunned. To kill the innocent is to take an innocent man and pervert him.

27. [V. 9] *His eyes are upon the poor man.* He will principally dog the upright of whom we are told: *Blessed*

are the poor in spirit, for theirs is the kingdom of heaven.[58]
He lieth in wait in secret, like a lion in his den. By the lion
in his den the Psalmist means one who will use both violence and craft. The first persecution of the Church was
by violence, when the Christians were compelled to sacrifice by dint of proscriptions, torture and bloodshed. The
second persecution is by means of trickery, practised in
these days by heretics of all sorts and false brethren. There
still remains a third to come through Antichrist, and this
will be the most dangerous of all, because it will comprise
both violence and deception. Violence he will exert in his
power as ruler, evil devices in his wonder-working. *Lion*
refers to his violence, *in his den* to his evil ruses. This is
now repeated in reverse order. *He lieth in ambush*, declares
the Psalmist, *that he may catch the poor.* Here you have
the trickery. What follows: *To catch the poor whilst he
draweth him to him*, indicates the violence; he dominates
him by inflicting every kind of torture.

28. The same idea is expressed in the next two phrases.
[V. 10] *In his trap he will bring him down* shows you the
deception; *he will crouch and fall, when he shall have
power over the poor* implies violence. For the trap well
enough suggests trickery, while power clearly hints at in-
timidation. And the Psalmist aptly says: *He will bring him
down in his trap*, for when he, Antichrist, begins to perform his marvels, the more wonderful they appear to men,
the more will the saints then living be despised and set at
naught, while he whom they resist by persevering in justice
and innocence will appear to overcome by dint of the
prodigies he works. But *he will crouch and fall, when he
shall have power over the poor*, when he inflicts all kinds
of punishments, that is, upon the servants of God who
resist him.

29. Now what will cause him to crouch and fall?
[V. 11] *For he hath said in his heart: God hath forgotten,
He hath turned away His face not to see to the end.* In
this consists the crouching and the fatal fall—when a
human soul, apparently prospering amid its sins, supposes
it is to be left unpunished, whereas in reality it is being
blinded and reserved for just and final vengeance. With
this in mind, the Psalmist now cries: [V. 12] *Arise, O
Lord God, let thy hand be exalted;* let thy power be made
manifest. Previously he had said: *Arise, O Lord, let not
man prevail; let the Gentiles be judged in thy sight;* in
secret, that is, where God alone beholds. This happens
when the wicked appear to men to have attained to great
prosperity and a lawgiver such as they deserve is set over
them, as has been related in the words: *Appoint, O Lord, a
lawgiver over them; let the Gentiles know themselves to be
but men.* Now, however, after that secret punishment and
vengeance, comes the appeal: *Arise, O Lord God, let thy
hand be exalted,* no longer in secret but in the full display
of thy glory. *Forget not the poor unto the end,* as the
wicked imagine when they say: *God hath forgotten, He
hath turned away His face not to see to the end.* Those
who declare that God has no concern for human and
earthly affairs deny that He sees to the end. For earth is as
it were the end of all things, being the last of the elements;
there men toil in their appointed way, but they cannot see
what part their labors play in the plan, for that more
especially belongs to the mysteries of the Son. The Church,
then, struggling with the circumstances of these times like
a ship laboring amid high seas and heavy weather, would
arouse the Lord as from sleep and beg Him to command
the winds and restore calm.[59] Accordingly she cries: *Arise,*

O Lord God, let thy hand be exalted, forget not the poor unto the end.

30. And now men begin to discern the visible judgment and rejoice, saying: [V. 13] *Wherefore hath the wicked provoked God?* What has he gained by doing so much evil? *For he hath said in his heart, He will not require it.* The Psalmist continues: *Thou seest it, for thou considerest labor and wrath, that thou mayest deliver them into thy hands.* In dealing with this passage we must bring out the sense, which will be obscure unless it is rightly explained. What the impious man has said in his heart is this: God will not exact an account; as if God, weighing the trouble and anger involved in delivering them into His hands, and fearing the labor as well as the anger, pardons these evildoers in order not to go to the trouble of chastising them, or disturbing Himself by an outburst of anger. This is how mortal men often act; they neglect to punish merely in order to spare themselves trouble and vexation.

31. *To thee is the poor man left.* He is poor in that he has despised all this world's temporal goods in order to put his trust in thee alone. *Thou wilt be a helper to the orphan,* to him to whom the world which fathered him, so to say, is dead, that world which begot him and of which he can now say: *The world is crucified to me, and I to the world.*[60] To such orphans God becomes a father. Our Lord, indeed, teaches His disciples that they must become orphans, telling them: *Call none your father upon earth.*[61] He Himself was the first to set an example of this when He asked: *Who is my mother, and who are my brethren?*[62] Hence certain poisonous heretics[63] would assert that He had no mother. It does not strike them that if they take these words in this way, then logically His disciples must have had no fathers; for just as He asked: *Who is my*

mother?, so He taught them, saying: *Call none your father upon earth.*

32. *Break thou the arm of the sinner and of the malignant;* that man's arm, of course, of whom it was previously said: *He shall rule over all his enemies.* Thus his arm is another name for his power, opposed by the power of Christ, in regard to which the Psalmist exclaims: *Arise, O Lord God, let thy hand be exalted.*

His sin shall be sought, and he shall not be found because of it. Judgment shall be passed upon his sin, and because of it he himself shall perish. After that, what wonder at the sequel: [V. 16] *The Lord shall reign to eternity, yea, forever and ever: ye Gentiles shall perish from His land?* The name *Gentiles* signifies the sinners and the ungodly.

33. [V. 17] *The Lord hath heard the desire of the poor:* that desire which consumed them when amid the distress and affliction of this world they longed for the day of the Lord. *Thy ear hath heard the preparation of their heart:* that preparation of heart of which another Psalm sings: *My heart is ready, O God, my heart is ready,*[64] and of which the Apostle declares: *But if we hope for that which we see not, we wait for it with patience.*[65] As usual we must take God's ear to mean not a bodily faculty but the power by which He gives heed to us. In like manner, to run the risk of repetition, when other members are attributed to God which in us are visible and belonging to the body, they denote in Him the powers by which He works. For we must not suppose it is by any bodily faculty when the Lord God hears, not the sound of the voice but the preparation of the heart.

34. [V. 18] *To judge for the fatherless and for the humble:* in other words, not for those who conform to this world, nor for the proud. For it is one thing to judge the

fatherless, and quite another to judge for the fatherless. He
who condemns the fatherless judges him; he who gives
sentence in his favor judges for the fatherless. *That man
may no more presume to magnify himself upon earth.* Men,
in this context, are those referred to in the words: *Set, O
Lord, a lawgiver over them, let the Gentiles know themselves to be but men.* But the man in question here to be set
over them will be a human being, and of him the Psalmist
now says: *That man may no more presume to magnify
himself upon earth.* This will come to pass when the Son
of Man comes to judge in favor of the orphan who has rid
himself of the old man and thus, as it were, buried his
earthly father and proclaimed his heavenly one.[66]

35. The secrets of the Son, of which much has been said
in this Psalm, will be followed by the manifestations of this
same Son which are mentioned a little towards its conclusion. But the subject indicated by the title occupies the
greater part of it. One can, indeed, count among the hidden
things of the Son the day of our Lord's coming, even
though the actual appearance of the Lord is to be manifest
before all, since we are told that it is known to nobody,
neither angels, nor powers, nor even the Son of Man.[67]
What could be so hidden as that which is declared to be
secret from the very Judge Himself, not of course as regards the knowledge of it, but as regards the commission to
reveal it? If, however, any one should wish to refer *the
hidden things of the Son* not to the Son of God but to
David's own son, inasmuch as the whole Psalter is attributed to him since they are called the Psalms of David,
let such a person listen to the cry addressed to our Lord:
Son of David, have mercy on us.[68] In this way also he will
recognize the same Christ our Lord, whose hidden things
have given the Psalm its title. So too the angel said: *God*

shall give unto Him the throne of David His father.[69] Nor is there any conflict between these texts and our Lord's question to the Jews: *If Christ is the Son of David, how then doth David in spirit call Him Lord, saying: "The Lord said to my Lord: Sit on my right hand, until I make thy enemies thy footstool"?*[70] That was said to the unenlightened, who in the Christ whose coming they awaited saw a mere man and not the Power and Wisdom of God. Accordingly He there teaches them the true and pure faith, that inasmuch as He is the Word from the beginning, God dwelling with God, through whom all things were made,[71] He is King David's Lord; and inasmuch as He was made to him of the seed of David according to the flesh,[72] He is his Son. He does not say, Christ is not the Son of David, but: If you already hold that He is his Son, now learn how He must also be his Lord. Nor, while you hold that Christ is the Son of Man and so the Son of David, must you refuse to believe that He is the Son of God and therefore David's Lord.

DISCOURSE ON PSALM 10

1. [Verse 1] *Unto the end, a Psalm for David himself.* This title needs no fresh discussion; we have already sufficiently explained the meaning of *unto the end.* Let us then turn to the text of the Psalm, which to my mind is a hymn against the heretics.[1] These men, by raking up and exaggerating the misdeeds of many members of the Church, as though in their own camp the majority, if not all, were blameless, strive to turn us away and snatch us from the bosom of the Church, our only true Mother. They claim that Christ is in their midst; they would advise us as if from charity and pure kindness to pass over to them in order to

find the Christ whom they falsely declare they possess. Now it is noteworthy that among the many other allegorical titles given to Christ, He is also called a mountain. We must therefore meet these gentry with the words: [V. 2] *In the Lord I put my trust. How then do you say to my soul: Get thee away from hence to the mountain like a sparrow?* I maintain there is only one mountain; in Him I steadfastly trust: why do you tell me to cross over to you as if there were many Christs? Or if, through pride, you call yourselves mountains, then I must be the sparrow winged with the virtues and precepts of God; but these wings prevent me from flying towards counterfeit mountains or putting my trust in the proud. I have a home to rest in, since my trust is in the Lord. For the sparrow hath found herself a house.[2] And the Lord is become a refuge for the poor.[3] Thus, for fear that we should lose Christ by seeking Him among the heretics, we must say with entire confidence: *In the Lord I put my trust. How then do you say to my soul: Get thee away from hence to the mountains like a sparrow?*

2. [V. 3] *For lo, the wicked have bent their bow; they have prepared their arrows in the quiver, to shoot in the dark moon*[4] *the upright of heart.* These are the threats of those who menace us with the anger of the wicked to induce us to join their party. *Lo,* they cry, *the wicked have bent their bow.* This bow, I suppose, is Holy Scripture, which since they interpret it in their own coarse fashion, thus furnishes them with nothing but poisoned maxims. *They have prepared their arrows in the quiver:* they have made ready in the hiding place of their heart these sayings which they will shoot at us with the authority of Scripture. *To shoot in the dark moon the upright of heart:* they believe that a crowd of ignorant men of rude understanding

has dimmed the light of the Church, whereas their own position is unassailable; thus they corrupt good manners by their evil company.[5] But in the teeth of all their terrors we must reply: *In the Lord I put my trust.*

3. I promised, I remember, to consider in this Psalm how the moon is an appropriate symbol of the Church.[6] There are two probable opinions about the moon: which of these is true it is impossible, or very difficult I think, for man to ascertain. If you ask whence the moon derives its light, some say that it has its own light, but that half its sphere is luminous and the other half is in darkness. Hence when it revolves on its own axis the luminous half turns gradually to the earth and becomes visible to us; that is why it appears at first crescent-shaped. For supposing you take a ball half white and half black and place the black half before your eyes, you can see nothing white; but if you begin to turn the white face towards you, doing so by degrees, you will notice at first a white crescent which will increase little by little until the whole thing appears to you completely white, leaving nothing of the black side visible. If you continue to turn it gradually, the black begins to show itself, and the white diminishes until it becomes crescent-shaped once more and finally disappears out of sight, leaving only the black part visible. This is what happens, they say, when the light of the moon is seen to increase up to the fifteenth day and then to wane until the thirtieth day, resuming its crescent shape until it finally conceals its light altogether. According to this theory the moon is an allegorical figure of the Church. When she shines forth on her spiritual side, her human side is in darkness. Often enough her spiritual character is made conspicuous to men by her noble deeds, but often enough also this spiritual side is hidden away in the conscience where

God alone can see it, while men are left to see only her human aspect. This occurs, for example, when we pray interiorly and seem outwardly to be doing nothing, yet our hearts are no longer on earth but, as we are bidden, are uplifted towards the Lord.[7]

Others however say that the moon has no light of its own but is illumined by the sun. When in the face of the sun, therefore, the moon presents to us its shadowy side and thus seems devoid of light; but in proportion as it turns away from the sun, that part which it presents to the earth becomes bright and of necessity begins by appearing crescent-shaped, until on the fifteenth day the moon is completely opposite the sun. It is then that the moon rises as the sun sets, a fact that anyone may verify by watching the sun go down and disappear from view; if he then turns towards the east he will behold the rising of the moon. On the other hand, in the measure in which the moon tends to approach the sun it gradually shows us its dark face, assumes a crescent shape once more only to disappear completely; for then its illuminated portion is turned entirely towards the heavens, whereas it is showing the earth the face to which the sun cannot communicate its light.

According to this second theory also, the moon symbolizes the Church, which possesses no light of her own but derives her light from the only-begotten Son of God, who in many places in Holy Scripture is allegorically termed the sun. Incapable of understanding and seeing this invisible sun, certain heretics[8] make every effort to turn the minds of simple folk to the cult of this visible material sun which gives light equally to the eyes of flies and men. They sometimes succeed in enticing those who being as yet unable to open the eyes of their mind to the interior light of truth, are not satisfied with the simple Catholic faith, the sole salvation for little ones, the only milk which can strengthen them with certainty and prepare them for the support of more solid food. In these two theories, then, no matter which is correct, the figure of the moon perfectly symbolizes the Church. Nevertheless if we are not disposed to occupy ourselves with these puzzles, which are more trouble than they are worth, or if we lack the leisure or the ability, it is sufficient to consider the moon from a popular angle, and without entering into abstruse arguments, to notice as everyone does, that the moon waxes, comes to the full and finally wanes. In so far as she wanes only to rise again she becomes, even for the most unlettered multitude, a figure of the Church with its faith in the resurrection of the dead.

4. Next we must examine the signification in this Psalm of *the dark moon* in which the wicked have prepared to shoot their arrows at the upright of heart. The moon can be called dark in more senses than one: it is dark at the end of its monthly course, and dark when a cloud obscures its light, or when it disappears completely. We can therefore apply the expression to the persecutors of the martyrs whose desire was to shoot at the upright of heart while the moon was dark. That may denote the newborn Church which had not yet cast her brightness over the earth and dissipated the darkness of pagan superstitions; or possibly the blasphemies and calumnies of the evil-tongued against the Christian name, which had enwrapped the earth as in a cloud, so as to render invisible the clear light of the moon, that is to say, the Church; or again the slaughter of so many martyrs accompanied with so much bloodshed which had alienated weak souls from the Christian name, by covering it with a bloodstained veil like that which sometimes appears on the moon during an eclipse. Amid all

this terror the wicked shot forth their crafty and sacrilegious words like so many arrows to pervert even the upright of heart.

This passage can also be applied to the sinners within the
Church's fold, inasmuch as they seized the opportunity of
an eclipse of this moon to commit the crimes which the
heretics in reproach now cast in our teeth, whereas their
own founders are said to have perpetrated them.[9] But whatever the origin of the deeds committed while the moon was
dark, now that the Catholic name is spread and honored
throughout the whole world, why should I trouble myself
about things I know nothing about? *In the Lord* indeed
I put my trust, and I turn a deaf ear to those who say to my
soul: *Get thee away from hence to the mountains like a
sparrow*.

*For lo, the wicked have bent their bow to shoot in the
dark moon the upright of heart*. And the moon appears
dark to these men even today, since they try to cast doubt
over the true Catholic Church by making the sins of her
many unspiritual members a reason for confuting her
claim. But even so, what does that matter to the man who
says in all sincerity: *In the Lord I put my trust?* Such
language proves a man to be wheat; he can endure the chaff
with patience until the time of winnowing is come.

5. *In the Lord*, therefore, *I put my trust*. Let those
tremble who put their trust in a man and who cannot deny
that they follow him, since they swear by his grey hairs.[10]
If you ask them in conversation to what communion they
belong, unless they admit they are of his faction, they can
find no name to describe themselves. Tell me, what answer
can they make when you enumerate to them the countless
misdeeds and crimes which daily abound in that sect of
theirs? I ask you, can they reply: *In the Lord I put my*

trust. How then do you say to my soul: Get thee away from hence to the mountains like a sparrow? Surely it is not in the Lord they trust, these men who say that the sacraments are holy only if administered by holy men? Furthermore, if you ask them who these saints are, they will be ashamed to answer: "We are"; yet if they can say so without blushing for themselves, those who are listening will blush for them. Such men, therefore, force those who receive the sacraments to put their trust in a man whose heart is hidden from their eyes. And cursed is every one who puts his trust in man.[11] To say in effect: "What is administered by me is holy" surely amounts to saying: "Put your trust in me." And what if you are no saint? Very well; show me your heart. And if you cannot, how am I to know whether you are holy? Or perhaps you will quote Scripture: *By their works you shall know them?*[12] To be sure, I see your marvelous works; I see the daily deeds of violence of your Circumcellions[13] as they rush hither and thither under the leadership of bishops and priests and give the name of Israels to their terrifying clubs. Men alive in our days see and experience these things only too well. As for the days of Macarius which rouse such antagonism, few have witnessed them, and to all they are now a thing of the past.[14] Any Catholic who did see them could nonetheless declare, if he wished to be a servant of God: *In the Lord I put my trust.* He can repeat the words now when he notices many things in the Church of which he disapproves, for he must realize that he is swimming inside a net full of fish both good and bad,[15] and this will continue until the shore is reached where the good will be separated from the bad.

On the other hand, what can these heretics reply if their candidate for baptism should ask: How can you command me to trust? For if the validity depends on the giver and the recipient, let it depend on God who gives, and my conscience which receives: both are terms of which I am certain, His goodness and my own good faith. Why interpose yourself, you of whom I can have no certain knowledge? Allow me to sing: *In the Lord I put my trust.* For if I put my trust in you, what guarantee have I that you committed no fault last night? Finally, if you insist that I take your word, can I do more than believe what you tell me about yourself? How can I feel sure, for instance, that those who were in communion with you yesterday, in communion with you today and in communion with you tomorrow, have committed no sin during these three days? But if neither you nor I are defiled because we do not know, what reason have you for rebaptizing those who know nothing of the treachery and reproach of the days of Macarius? As for the Christians hailing from Mesopotamia who have never so much as heard the names of Caecilian and Donatus, how can you dare to rebaptize them on the plea that they are not Christians? Surely if they are defiled by the unknown sins of others, you also, you stand convicted of the crimes committed every day without your knowledge in your own faction; in vain do you cast up the imperial edicts[16] against the Catholics when in your own camp, unsupported by authority, men maltreat others with bludgeon and flame. See to what depths they have fallen who when they saw disorders in the Catholic Church could not say: *In the Lord I put my trust,* but placed their hope in man instead. They would doubtless have said it, had they not been themselves, or even had they been such as they supposed those men to be from whom in their sacrilegious pride they pretended to seek separation.

6. Let the Catholic soul cry out therefore: *In the Lord*

I put my trust. How then do you say to my soul: Get thee away from hence to the mountains like a sparrow? For lo, the wicked have bent their bow; they have prepared their arrows in the quiver, to shoot in the dark moon the upright of heart. Then turning away from such men towards the Lord, let it add: [V. 4] *For they have destroyed the things which thou hast made perfect.* This charge may be leveled not only against the sinners already mentioned but against all heretics. For all, so far as they are able, have destroyed that praise which God has perfected out of the mouths of infants and babes at the breast,[17] when by their idle and subtle questioning they disturb the little ones and will not allow them to draw sustenance from the milk of faith. And as if one had said to such a soul: "Why do these men bid you: *Get thee away from hence to the mountains like a sparrow?* Why do they terrify you with the threat of sinners who have bent their bow to shoot in the dark moon the upright of heart?" it makes reply: "They terrify me for this reason, because *they have destroyed the things which thou hast made perfect.*" Where? Why, in their meeting places, where far from feeding on milk the little ones and those who have no experience of interior light, they kill them with their poison. *But what has the just man done?* If Macarius, if Caecilian are both culprits, what has Christ done to you? *Peace I leave with you,* He said, *my peace I give unto you;*[18] and you have violated that peace by the most iniquitous dissension. What has Christ done to you, the Christ who bore with His betrayer with such patience that He admitted him like the other apostles to the first Holy Eucharist consecrated by His own hands and set before them by His own word?[19] What has Christ done to you, who gave the mission to preach the kingdom of heaven to this same traitor whom He had already called a devil,[20] who even before the betrayal of his Lord could not so much as be trusted with His purse,[21] and whom He nevertheless sent forth with the other disciples[22] in order to teach us that the gifts of God reach those who receive them with faith, even though the minister who distributes them is a man like Judas?[23]

7. [V. 5] *The Lord is in His holy temple.* It is in this sense that the Apostle tells us: *For the temple of God is holy, which you are. But if any man violate the temple of God, him shall God destroy.*[24] He violates the temple of God who violates its unity. For he is no longer dependent upon the Head[25] from whom the whole Body is organized and unified by each contact with the source which supplies it, and thus, each limb receiving the active power it needs, achieves its natural growth, building itself up through charity.[26] The Lord, then, is in this His holy temple formed out of many members, each one having its own function and cemented by charity to form a single edifice.[27] To separate from Catholic fellowship for the sake of one's own independent rule[28] is to violate this temple. *The Lord is in His holy temple. The Lord's throne is in heaven.* If we take heaven to signify the just man as earth signifies the sinner who was told: *Earth thou art and into earth thou shalt return,*[29] then the words: *The Lord's throne is in heaven* are a repetition of the preceding phrase: *The Lord is in His holy temple.*

8. *His eyes look on the poor man.* It is to Him indeed that the poor man has been abandoned; it is He who acts as a refuge for the poor.[30] That is why all the revolts and disturbances provoked within this net until the shore is reached are caused by men who refuse to be Christ's poor; and it is to their own ruin but for our amendment that the heretics avail themselves of these troubles to insult us. But

can they turn away God's eyes from such as would be Christ's poor? No, for *His eyes look on the poor man*. Are we to fear that among the crowd of rich He cannot discern the handful of poor in order to bring them up safely in the bosom of the Catholic Church? *His eyelids examine the sons of men*. Here, according to our former rule,[31] I should not hesitate to interpret as *sons of men* those who have passed from their old self to the regenerated life of faith. For God's eyes seem to close upon them when certain difficult passages of Scripture stimulate them to discover their sense, just as the eyes seem to open again when they rejoice in receiving light from the clear language of other passages. Now these truths of the sacred writings, sometimes clear and sometimes veiled, are as it were the eyelids of God which scrutinize, which probe these sons of men, stimulated rather than wearied by the obscurities, strengthened rather than elevated by the knowledge they acquire.

9. [V. 6] *The Lord trieth the just and the wicked*. And since He thus reads the hearts of both innocent and sinful, why need we fear that the wicked will do us harm when they happen to share our sacraments, even though in bad faith? *But he that loveth iniquity hateth his own soul*.[32] In other words, it is not to the man who trusts God and places no hope in man, but simply to his own soul that the friend of wrongdoing proves an enemy.

10. [V. 7] *He shall rain snares upon sinners*. If clouds signify the prophets in general, whether good or bad (these latter are also termed false prophets), then the false prophets are destined by the Lord God to become the snares which He rains down upon sinners. For no one would follow them and so be entrapped except the sinner, who may thereby prepare the way for final torment if he choose to persist in wrongdoing, or else abandon his pride

and sooner or later seek God with greater zeal and sincerity. If, however, clouds denote none but good and true prophets, it is evident that God can use these also to rain snares upon sinners while using them at the same time to bedew the godly and make them bring forth fruit. *To some*, says the Apostle, *we are the odor of life unto life, to some the odor of death unto death.*[33] For not only the prophets, but all who refresh souls with the word of God may be called clouds. When His word is interpreted falsely, God rains snares upon sinners; but when interpreted in its true sense, He makes fruitful the hearts of His loyal and faithful ones. That text of Scripture, for example, *And they shall be two in one flesh*[34] can become a snare rained upon the sinner for the man who interprets it as an incentive to deeds of impurity. If, however, you interpret it as he did who cried out: *But I speak in Christ and in the Church,*[35] it becomes a shower on fertile ground. It is the same cloud, namely Holy Scripture, which produces these two results. In the same way our Lord tells us: *Not that which goeth into your mouth defileth you, but that which cometh out.*[36] At these words the sinner prepares to cram his belly, whereas the same words guard the upright man from making superstitious discriminations between foods. This same cloud of Scripture lets fall, therefore, according to the merits of each, a shower of snares upon the sinner, and upon the righteous a shower of fruitful rain.

11. *Fire and brimstone and storms of winds shall be the portion of their cup.* Such is the chastisement and doom of those who blaspheme the name of the Lord. First they are consumed by the fire of their own passions, then the stench of their corrupt deeds cuts them off from the company of the blessed, and finally, swept away and drowned, they undergo unspeakable torments. This indeed is the portion

of their cup; but as for thy chalice which inebriateth the just, how goodly it is![37] They shall indeed be ravished with the plenty of thy house.[38] I think, moreover, that the Psalmist has used the word "cup" to prevent our imagining that, even in the punishment of evildoers, Divine Providence ever goes beyond the bounds of moderation and equity. So he has added, as if adducing the reason for their chastisement: [V. 8] *The Lord is just and hath loved justices.* Not without reason has he used *justices* in the plural, in order to show us that by them he denotes human beings, just men. For in a number of just men there would seem to be, so to speak, a number of justices, whereas in God there is only one, the source of all the rest; as when a single face gazes into many mirrors which reflect and repeat it many times over, while in itself it is but one. And so the Psalmist returns to the singular number with the words: *His face hath beheld righteousness.* Perhaps he has said *His face hath beheld righteousness* in the sense: It is in His face that we see righteousness, when, that is to say, we know His face; for God's face is the power by which He makes Himself known to those worthy of it. Or else *His face hath beheld righteousness* because He does not bestow the knowledge of Himself on evildoers but on the upright: this constitutes true righteousness.

12. If anyone wishes to interpret the moon as the synagogue, he may apply the Psalm to the passion of our Lord and say of the Jews that *they have destroyed the things which thou hast made perfect,* and of our Lord Himself: *But what has the just man done?* They accused Him of destroying the law while they themselves destroyed its precepts by their evil lives, by despising them and by substituting their own traditions. Then our Lord would speak, as He so often did, in His humanity, and would say:

In the Lord I put my trust. How then do you say to my soul: Get thee away from hence to the mountains like a sparrow?, thus making answer to the threats of those who sought to seize and crucify Him. In this case the wicked who wished to shoot *the upright of heart*, those namely who believed in Christ, *in the dark moon*, may very well signify the synagogue filled with evildoers. This would agree with the next passage: *The Lord is in His holy temple; the Lord's throne is in heaven.* The Word, that is to say, or the Son of Man Himself who is in heaven, dwells also in a man. *His eyes look on the poor man*, either the man with whom, as God, He has clothed Himself,[39] or mankind for whom He has suffered in His human nature. *His eyelids examine the sons of men.* To shut the eyes and then open them, an action which the word "eyelids" probably denotes, symbolizes, we may suppose, our Lord's death and resurrection; for then He scrutinized the sons of men, His disciples, whom His passion had filled with terror and His resurrection with joy. *The Lord trieth the just and the wicked* from the heights of heaven whence He now governs the Church. *But he that loveth iniquity hateth his own soul:* the succeeding verse gives the reason. *He shall rain snares*, it assures us, *upon sinners*. From this passage to the end the Psalm should be interpreted in the way already indicated.

DISCOURSE ON PSALM 11

1. [Verse 1] *Unto the end, for the octave, a Psalm for David.* We have said, in Psalm 6,[1] that the octave may denote the Day of Judgment. The phrase *for the octave* may also denote the day of eternity which is to be awarded

to the saints when time with its rotation of seven days is no more.

2. [V. 2] *Save me, O Lord, for there is now no saint:* in other words, none is to be found. We speak in this sense when we say, "There is no wheat," or, "There is no money." *Truths are decayed among the children of men.* Without doubt there is only one truth which enlightens holy souls; but as souls are many, so we may speak of their many truths, in the same way as a single face is reflected in many mirrors.

3. [V. 3] *They have spoken vain things every one to his neighbor.* The word *neighbor* embraces every human being, for we are allowed to injure no man, and the love of our neighbor worketh no evil.[2] *With deceitful lips, with a heart and a heart they have spoken evils.* This repetition *with a heart and a heart* signifies their duplicity.

4. [V. 4] *May the Lord destroy all deceitful lips. All,* says the Psalmist, for fear any one should think himself exempt. *Upon every soul of man that worketh evil,* so the Apostle tells us, *of the Jew first, and of the Greek.*[3] *The tongue that speaketh proud things* is a tongue full of pride.

5. [V. 5] *Who have said: We will magnify our tongue; our lips are our own; who is Lord over us?* This is the language of proud men and hypocrites, who rely on their words to seduce men and who refuse to submit to God.

6. [V. 6] *By reason of the misery of the needy and the groans of the poor, now will I arise, saith the Lord.*[4] Thus indeed it was our Lord Himself, according to the Gospel, who took pity on His people because they had no leader even though they were prepared to obey. Furthermore, the Gospels tell us: *The harvest is great, but the laborers are few.*[5]

We may attribute these words, on the other hand, to

God the Father who has deigned to send His Son on behalf of the needy and poor, for the sake of the poverty and indigence of those who lack spiritual possessions. That is why our Lord opens His sermon on the mount in Matthew with the words: *Blessed are the poor in spirit, for theirs is the kingdom of heaven.*[6]

I will set in salvation. God has not specified what He will set, but *in salvation* must surely refer to Christ, according to those words: *Because mine eyes have seen thy salvation.*[7] We must therefore conclude that God has constituted in Christ whatever is necessary to put an end to the misery of the needy and to console the bitter cries of the poor. *I will deal confidently in his regard;* thus the Gospel tells us: *For He was teaching them as one having power, not as their scribes.*[8]

7. [V. 7] *The words of the Lord are pure words.* It is the prophet in his own person who observes: *The words of the Lord are pure words. Pure,* he says; they contain no admixture of insincerity. Many preach the truth impurely: they barter it for the bribe of this world's advantages. It is these whom the Apostle accuses of preaching Christ impurely.[9] *Silver tried by the fire from the earth.* The tribulations of evildoers have put those words of the Lord to the test. *Refined seven times,* by the fear of the Lord, by godliness, by knowledge, by fortitude, by counsel, by understanding, by wisdom.[10] The degrees of the Beatitudes are also seven in number, and our Lord enumerates them in the same sermon preached on the mount, reported by Matthew: *Blessed are the poor in spirit, blessed are the meek, blessed are they that mourn, blessed are they that hunger and thirst after justice, blessed are the merciful, blessed are the clean of heart, blessed are the peacemakers.*[11] The whole sermon can be regarded as a development of

these seven points. For the eighth, which runs: *Blessed are they that suffer persecution for justice' sake* denotes the fire itself which has refined the silver seven times over. At the conclusion of this sermon we are told of our Lord: *For He was teaching them as one having power, not as their scribes,*[12] which is in keeping with the words of this Psalm: *I will deal confidently in his regard.*

8. [V. 8] *Thou, O Lord, wilt preserve us, and keep us from this generation and forever:* here below in need and poverty; hereafter in wealth and plenty.

9. [V. 9] *The wicked walk round about;*[13] they are insatiable, in other words, for this world's goods, and this thirst of theirs is like a wheel which repeats its circle every seven days and consequently never arrives at that eighth day or the day of eternity, which forms the title of the Psalm. We meet the same idea in the words of Solomon: *A wise king is a winnower of the wicked and bringeth over them the wheel of their evil deeds.*[14]

According to thy highness thou hast multiplied the children of men. For in things of time there is that multiplicity which separates us from God's unity, since the corruptible body is a load upon the soul; and the earthly habitation presseth down the mind that museth upon many things.[15] The righteous, on the other hand, are given increase according to the depths of God's wisdom; He will make them go from strength to strength.[16]

DISCOURSE ON PSALM 12

1. [Verse 1] *Unto the end, a Psalm for David. For the end of the law is Christ, unto justice to everyone that believeth.*[1] *How long, O Lord, wilt thou forget me unto the end?* How long wilt thou hold me back from understand-

ing in a spiritual manner this Christ who is the Wisdom of God and the true end of the soul's every aspiration? *How long dost thou turn away thy face from me?* God does not turn away His face any more than He forgets: Holy Scripture speaks in human fashion. To say that God turns away His face means that He no longer imparts knowledge of Himself to the soul whose mind's eye is as yet insufficiently cleansed.

2. [V. 2] *How long shall I take counsel in my soul?* It is only in adversity that we need counsel. Thus, *How long shall I take counsel in my soul* signifies: How long shall I suffer adversity? Or else these words may actually be a response signifying: Until I make the resolution in my soul, just so long wilt thou forget me as regards my end, just so long wilt thou turn away thy face from me. Unless a man has purposed in his soul to practise mercy in its perfection, then God will not direct him towards his goal; He will withhold that complete knowledge of Himself which only comes when face to face. *Sorrow in my heart all the day?* The words, "How long shall I have," are to be understood. *All the day* denotes prolongation, *day* here signifying time; whoever would be delivered from it has sorrow of heart and prays that he may ascend to the things of eternity in order to escape this day of mortal man.

3. [V. 3] *How long shall my enemy be exalted over me?* The enemy may be either the devil or sensual habits of life.

4. [V. 4] *Look*[2] *and hear me, O Lord my God. Look* follows from the cry: *How long dost thou turn away thy face from me?* and *Hear me* follows from that other cry: *How long, O Lord, wilt thou forget me unto the end?*

Enlighten my eyes that I never sleep in death. These

eyes, we must realize, are the eyes of the heart; may they not be blinded by the death-dealing delight of sin.

5. [V. 5] *Lest at any time my enemy say: I have prevailed against him.* The devil's invective is a thing to be dreaded. *They that trouble me,* the devil and his angels, *will rejoice when I am moved.* They failed to triumph over Job when they launched their attack; just man that he was, he stood undaunted, and wavered not in his unchangeable faith.[8]

6. [V. 6] *But I have trusted in thy mercy.* No man who stands unshaken and remains steadfast in the Lord must attribute it to himself, for fear that pride should undo him in the very act of preening himself on his own constancy. *My heart shall rejoice in thy salvation,* in Christ, in the Wisdom of God. *I will sing to the Lord who giveth me good things:* spiritual good things unconnected with man's mortal day. *Yea I will chant to the name of the Lord most high:* in other words, I joyfully render thanks, and I treat my body in strict accordance with His precepts; this it is which constitutes the spiritual harmony of the soul. If one wishes to draw a distinction, then *cantabo, I will sing,* would express the praise of the heart, *psallam, I will chant,* the praise of good deeds; *to the Lord* in so far as He alone has knowledge of them, but *to the name of the Lord* in so far as He communicates to men that knowledge of Himself which is beneficial not to Him but solely to ourselves.

DISCOURSE ON PSALM 13

1. [Verse 1] *Unto the end, a Psalm for David himself.* The meaning of *Unto the end* need not be explained too often, since the Apostle tells us that *the end of the law is Christ, unto justice to every one that believeth.*[1] We be-

lieve in Him when we begin to take the right road; and we shall behold Him when we reach our destination. Thus Christ is the end of the way.

2. *The fool hath said in his heart: There is no God.* Not even those philosophers whose impiety and false and perverse theories concerning the Godhead are to be detested have dared to say: "There is no God." This assertion is therefore made merely *in his heart;* even if he dare to think such a thing, he dares not proclaim it. *They are corrupt, and are become abominable in their affections,* because they have given their hearts to the world and not to God: these are the affections which cause such corruption and blindness of soul that the fool can go so far as to say in his heart: *There is no God.* For as they liked not to have God in their knowledge, God delivered them up to a reprobate sense.[2] *There is none that doth good, there is none even to one.* This expression *even to one* may include the one so as to signify every man without exception, or it may exclude the one, in order to signify the Lord Christ. Thus we say: "That field goes as far as the sea," without meaning to include the sea as well. It is better to take the text as meaning: No man has really practised virtue until the coming of Christ, because unless Christ has first instructed him, no man is able to practise virtue, since it is a fact that the practice of virtue is impossible until a man comes to the knowledge of the one God.

3. [V. 2] *The Lord hath looked down from heaven upon the children of men, to see if there be any that understand and seek God.* This may denote the Jews, to whom the Psalmist gives the more honorable title of children of men because they adored only the one God, in contrast with the Gentiles to whom he has previously referred, it seems to me, in the verse: *The fool hath said in his heart:*

There is no God, and so forth. The Lord casts His glance by means of His holy ones, here designated by the phrase *from heaven;*[3] as for God Himself, nothing escapes Him.

4. [V. 3] *They are all gone aside, they are become unprofitable together.* The Jews, in other words, have become like the Gentiles of whom it has just been said: *There is none that doth good, there is none even to one.* We should interpret these expressions as explained above. *Their throat is an open sepulcher.* These words imply either the excess of insatiable gluttony or, symbolically, those who kill and then as it were devour the slain whom they have drawn into their own dissolute way of life. It is thus, but in a contrary sense, that Peter was told: *Kill and eat,*[4] in order that he should draw the Gentiles into his own faith and holy manner of living. *With their tongues they acted deceitfully.* Flattery is invariably the boon companion of the glutton and evildoer. *The poison of asps is under their lips.* *Poison* indicates deceit, and the *asps* those who remain deaf to the precepts of the law, like asps deaf to the voice of the charmer, as we are told more explicitly in another Psalm.[5] *Their mouth is full of cursing and bitterness:* there you have the poison of asps. *Their feet are swift to shed blood:* a reference to their inveterate habit of sin. *Destruction and unhappiness in their ways.* For every road trodden by wicked men is full of nothing but toil and misery. Therefore our Lord cries aloud: *Come to me, all you that labor and are burdened, and I will refresh you. Take up my yoke and learn of me, because I am meek and humble of heart. For my yoke is mild and my burden light.*[6]

And the way of peace they have not known, that peace which our Lord symbolizes, as I have said, by the mildness of His yoke and the lightness of His burden. *There is no fear of God before their eyes.* Without asserting "There is no God," they nevertheless have no fear of God.

5. [V. 4] *Shall not all they know that work iniquity?* Judgment looms ahead. *Who devour my people as the food of bread,* that is, every day; for bread is our daily food. Now they who turn their ministry to self-profit, instead of referring it to God's glory and the salvation of the souls in their charge, such men as these devour the people.

6. [V. 5] *They have not called upon the Lord.* For no man truly calls upon Him if he goes after what is displeasing to Him. *There they have trembled for fear, where there was no fear:* they have trembled before temporal losses. They said in fact: *If we let Him alone so, all will believe in Him; and the Romans will come and take away our place and nation.*⁷ They feared what they had no need to fear, the loss of an earthly kingdom, and so they lost the kingdom of heaven, a loss they should have dreaded. So it is with all worldly advantages: whenever men fear their loss, they fail to arrive at eternal possessions.

7. [V. 6] *For God is in the just generation:* He is not to be found among those who love the world. For it is an injustice to forsake the Maker of worlds and fix one's heart on the world itself, to serve the creature rather than the Creator.⁸ *You have confounded the counsel of the poor man, but the Lord is his hope.* In other words, you despised the humble advent of the Son of God because He did not flaunt in your eyes the pomp of this world: thus would He force those whom He called, to put their trust not in transitory things but in God alone.

8. [V. 7] *Who shall give out of Sion the salvation of Israel?* Supply: "Who but He whose humility you have despised!" For He shall come in glory to judge the living and the dead, and to put the just in possession of His king-

dom, in such a way that if the lowliness of His first coming struck Israel in part with blindness in order that they might make entrance for the full complement of the Gentiles, yet in His second coming all Israel will be saved according to St. Paul's prediction immediately afterwards.[9] It is in favor of the Jews again that the Apostle also appeals to the testimony of Isaias' words: *There shall come out of Sion He that shall turn away ungodliness from Jacob.*[10] In the same sense we read in this Psalm: *Who shall give out of Sion the salvation of Israel? When the Lord shall have turned away the captivity of His people, Jacob shall rejoice and Israel shall be glad.* There is a repetition here, as so frequently happens; for I assume that *Israel shall be glad* and *Jacob shall rejoice* are identical in meaning.

DISCOURSE ON PSALM 14

1. [Verse 1] *A Psalm for David himself.* This title offers no difficulty. *Lord, who shall sojourn*[1] *in thy tabernacle?* Sometimes we speak of a tabernacle or tent to symbolize our eternal dwelling place, but properly speaking a tent is a thing used in war. Hence soldiers are called tent fellows, because they share the same tents. This interpretation is supported by the phrase, *who shall sojourn.* At present indeed we are warring against the devil, and so we have need of a tent in which to renew our strength. This tent denotes above all our faith in the temporal economy of the Incarnation which our Lord accomplished in this life for our salvation. *Or who shall rest on thy holy hill?* Here perhaps our everlasting dwelling is indicated, so that we should interpret the hill as the surpassing grandeur of Christ's love in life eternal.[2]

2. [V. 2] *He that walketh without blemish and work-*

eth justice. This verse states the theme which the rest of the Psalm develops.

3. [V. 3] *He that speaketh truth in his heart.* Some people, to be sure, present the truth on their lips although it is absent from their hearts. Thus, suppose some one points out a road which he knows to be infested with robbers, and blandly assures you: "If you go this way, you will have nothing to fear from thieves." Now it may happen that you do not in fact encounter any. He spoke the truth right enough, but it was not in his heart. He thought the contrary and uttered the truth unwittingly. Speaking the truth matters little, therefore, unless our words correspond with our hearts as well. *Who hath not used deceit in his tongue.* The tongue utters deceit when the lips say one thing and the heart hides quite another. *Nor hath done evil to his neighbor.* This title of neighbor, notice, must include every human being. *Nor taken up a reproach against his neighbor:* who has not lent a ready or imprudent ear, in other words, to evil gossip.

4. [V. 4] *In his sight the malignant one has been brought to nothing.* Perfection consists in this: that the malignant one establish no hold over a man, and this actually *in his sight.* He must be fully conscious, that is to say, that the evil one is at a loss unless the rational soul[3] turn away from the eternal, immutable beauty of its Creator to attach itself to the beauty of a creature drawn out of nothingness. *But he glorifieth them that fear the Lord:* our Lord Himself without doubt glorifies them. For the fear of the Lord is the beginning of wisdom.[4] And as all the preceding refers to the perfect, so all that now follows refers to beginners.

5. *He that sweareth to his neighbor and deceiveth not;* [V. 5] *he that hath not put out his money to usury, nor*

taken bribes against the innocent.[5] These are hardly noble virtues; but if a man is unable to practise even these, much less is he able to tell the truth in his own heart and to say aloud what he inwardly believes to be true without being double-tongued, having a simple *Yea, yea: No, no*[6] on his lips. Nor will he avoid doing injury to his neighbor whoever he may be, or casting a slur upon his fellow men. These are the deeds of the perfect in whose sight the malignant one has been brought to nothing. Yet the Psalmist rounds off even these lesser virtues with the words: *He that doth these things shall not be moved forever.* He will attain, that is to say, to the higher virtues which confer on us this great and unshakable security. Observe that it is probably not without reason that the Psalmist has passed from one tense to another, so that whereas his first conclusion was in the past, this is in the future. In the first he declared: *In his sight the malignant one has been brought to nothing;* and here: *He shall not be moved forever.*

DISCOURSE ON PSALM 15

1. [Verse 1] *The inscription of a title:*[1] *to David himself.* This Psalm is the song of our King in His human nature, that King whose royal title was proclaimed on the inscription during His passion.

2. His words are these: *Preserve me, O Lord, for I have put my trust in thee.* [V. 2] *I have said to the Lord: Thou art my God, for thou hast no need of my goods.*[2] Thou dost ask nothing of mine to complete thy happiness.

3. [V. 3] *To the saints who are in this land:* to the holy ones who have placed their hope in the land of the living, to the citizens of the heavenly Jerusalem, whose spiritual life is moored by the anchor of hope to that coun-

try which is rightly called God's land, although their bodies still inhabit the world below. *He hath made wonderful all my desires in them.* God has revealed to these holy souls the wonders of all my plans for their progress; they have thereby realized what benefits they reap from a God whose manhood enables Him to die, and from a Man whose Godhead enables Him to rise from the dead.

4. [V. 4]. *Their infirmities were multiplied,*[3] not to destroy them but to make them cry out for the physician. *Afterwards they made haste.* In view of their numberless ills, they hastened to seek a remedy. *I will not gather together their meetings for blood offerings.* Their assemblies will no longer be unspiritual, nor shall I gather them together, because I am appeased by the blood offerings of cattle. *Nor will I be mindful of their names by my lips.* By a change in spirit they will forget what they have been; and I, by the gift of my peace, shall henceforth look upon them, not as sinners, or foes, or even as men, but I shall call them just, my brethren, children of God.

5. [V. 5] *The Lord is the portion of my inheritance and of my cup.*[4] For they also shall possess, as I do, the inheritance which is the Lord Himself. Let those who will, choose to enjoy an inheritance which is earthly and fleeting: the portion of the saints is the Lord eternal. Let others drink deep of deadly desire: the Lord is the portion of my cup. In saying *my* cup, I include the Church with me, for where the Head is, there is the Body also. Therefore I shall gather together their assemblies for my inheritance, and in the inebriation of my cup I shall forget their former names. *It is thou that wilt restore my inheritance to me,* so that those whom I set free may know the glory which I had with thee before the world was made.[5] Not to me, indeed, wilt thou restore what I have never lost, but to

those who have lost the knowledge of this glory; and since I am in them, *thou wilt restore to me.*

6. [V. 6] *The lines are fallen unto me in goodly places.* Just as the property of priests and Levites is God Himself,[6] so the boundaries of my heritage have fallen as by lot in the splendor of thy glory. *For my inheritance is goodly to me.* My inheritance is glorious, not to all, but to those who comprehend it; and since I am in them, it *is goodly to me.*

7. [V. 7] *I will bless the Lord who hath given me understanding:* the understanding necessary to appreciate and possess this inheritance. *Moreover my reins also have admonished[7] me even till night.* Apart from the intellect, this lower part of my nature, the body I have assumed, has taught me even to meet death, to pass through the shadows of human mortality, an experience of which the intellect knows nothing.[8]

8. [V. 8] *I set the Lord always in my sight.*[9] In coming into a world which passes away, I have never lost sight of Him who abides forever, always foreseeing my return to Him at the completion of my life on earth. *For He is at my right hand, that I be not moved.* He graciously helps me to remain steadfast in Himself.

9. [V. 9] *Therefore my heart hath been merry, and my tongue hath rejoiced.* Joy in consequence has filled my thoughts, gladness has burst forth in my speech. *Moreover my flesh also shall rest in hope.* My flesh also will not be entirely consumed by death, but will sleep in hope of the resurrection.

10. [V. 10] *Because thou wilt not leave my soul in hell.* Thou wilt not deliver my soul as a prey to hell, *nor wilt thou give thy holy one to see corruption.* Thou wilt not abandon to corruption a hallowed body which is to sanctify others also. [V. 11] *Thou hast made known to me*

the ways of life. It is through me that thou hast taught the paths of humility so that men may return to the life which they had lost through pride; and since I am in them, *to me thou hast made known. Thou shalt fill me with joy with thy countenance.* When they see thee face to face, their joy will exclude every other desire; and since I am in them, *thou shalt fill me. At thy right hand is delight even to the end.* Thy favor and thy bounty are our delights on this life's journey; they will lead us to the height of glory in thine own presence.

Discourse on Psalm 16

1. [Verse 1] *The prayer of David himself.* We must ascribe this Psalm to the Person of our Lord united to the Church which is His Body.

2. *Hear, O Lord, my justice, attend to my supplication. Give ear unto my prayers from lips without deceit.* Not from lips that dissemble does this prayer rise to thee. [V. 2] *Let my judgment come forth from thy countenance.* May thy knowledge enlighten me and make me judge by the standard of truth. Or else, may my judgment never issue from treacherous lips but from thy light, so that I pronounce nothing contrary to what I discover in thee. *Let my eyes*—the eyes, of course, of the heart—*behold the things that are equitable.*

3. [V. 3] *Thou hast proved my heart, and visited it by night.* This heart of mine has been put to the proof when trials have befallen me. *Thou hast tried me by fire, and iniquity hath not been found in me.* The affliction which has tested and demonstrated my justice may be called not merely "night" from its wonted distress but "fire" from its burning pain.

4. [V. 4] *That my mouth may not speak the works of men:* that nothing may escape my lips but what redounds to thy glory and praise, rather than to men's works performed in opposition to thy will. *For the sake of the words of thy lips,* words of thine own peace or those of thy prophets; *I have kept hard ways,* the painful road of human mortality and suffering.

5. [V. 5] *To perfect my goings in thy paths,* so that the Church may reach the perfection of charity in the narrow ways which lead to thy rest. *That my footsteps be not moved,* in order that the traces of my journeying, imprinted like footsteps in the sacraments and in the writings of my apostles, may never be effaced, but may be marked and observed by all who would follow me. Or else perhaps: that after having trodden rough ways and completed my course along thy arduous paths, I may dwell forevermore in life everlasting.

6. [V. 6] *I have cried to thee, for thou, O God, hast heard me.* I have sent up my cry to thee with a fervor unhindered and strong, since thou didst hear me when I besought thee from my weakness to grant me this strength. *O incline thy ear unto me and hear my words.* Turn not a deaf ear to my humble pleading.

7. [V. 7] *Make wonderful thy mercies,* for fear they appear contemptible and of small value.

8. *Thou who savest them that trust in thee,* [V. 8] *from them that resist thy right hand,* who refuse the favor thou dost accord to me. *Keep me, O Lord, as the apple of thy eye,* which appears tiny and contracted; it is the pupil nevertheless which directs the sight and enables us to distinguish light from darkness, just as it is through Christ's humanity at the Judgment that the divine power distinguishes the just man from the evildoer. *Protect me under*

the shadow of thy wings. May thy love and gracious mercy serve me as shield [V. 9] *from the face of the wicked who have afflicted me.*

9. *My enemies have surrounded my soul;* [V. 10] *they have shut up their fat.* They have glutted their greed with deeds of darkness and have become entirely wrapped up in their own gross pleasures. *Their mouth hath spoken proudly.* Thus they gave tongue to the insolent sneer: *Hail, King of the Jews,*[1] with suchlike abuse.

10. [V. 11] *They have cast me forth and now they have surrounded me.* They have thrust me out of their city and now surround me on the cross. *They have set their eyes bowing down to the earth.* It was the bent of their heart that they lowered, fixing it on base things of earth, while they considered that He whom they put to death was enduring a mighty punishment, whereas they His executioners went scot-free.

11. [V. 12] *They have taken me, as a lion prepared for the prey.* They have closed in on me like that enemy who goes about to find his prey.[2] *And as a young lion dwelling in secret places.* And they are his offspring, that race of men who were told: *You are of your father the devil,*[3] as they hatched their plots to steal upon the Just One and destroy Him.

12. [V. 13] *Arise, O Lord, forestall them and overthrow them.* Arise, O Lord, thou whom they imagine to be asleep and unconscious of men's evil-doing. Let their own malice blind them beforehand so that vengeance may overtake their crime and thus bring them to destruction.

13. *Deliver my soul from the wicked ones.* Deliver my soul by making me rise victorious from that death which impious men have inflicted upon me. [V. 14] *Thy sword*[4] *from the enemies of thy hand.* That sword of thine is my

soul, a sword which thy hand, or thine eternal strength, has grasped in order to lay waste the kingdoms of iniquity and separate the just from the unrighteous. This sword, therefore, thou must *deliver from the enemies of thy hand;* thy hand is thy power, and the enemies are mine. *In destroying them, O Lord, from the earth, scatter them in their life.* Clear them away, Lord, from the soil on which they live; scatter them far and wide throughout this life of theirs which they claim to be the only one, since they hold no belief in life eternal. *Their belly is filled with thy hidden things.* Their punishment will not confine itself to sensible pain; in addition, like dark clouds obscuring the light of thy truth, their sins so occupy their minds as to efface God. *They are full of swine's flesh.* They are surfeited with impurity, these men who trample underfoot the pearls of God's word.[5] And with the cry: *His blood be upon us and upon our children,*[6] forthwith *They have left to their little ones the rest of their substance.*

14. [V. 15] *But as for me, I will appear before thy sight in thy justice.* As for me, who have never been recognized by men that are unclean, darkened of heart and powerless to perceive the light of wisdom, I shall stand before thee on the day of thy justice. *I shall be satisfied when thy glory dawns.* Whereas, saturated with impurity, such men are unable to recognize me, I shall be filled with thy glory when it bursts forth in those who understand me aright. With reference to the verse which reads: *They are full of swine's flesh,* we find in some copies: *They are full of children.* The two readings are due to the ambiguity of the Greek original.[7] The children signify works; the fruit of the good will be good works, that of the evil in like manner will be evil.

DISCOURSE ON PSALM 17

1. [Verse 1] *Unto the end, for David himself, the servant of the Lord:* in other words, for Christ, who in His human nature is the mighty of hand. *Who spoke to the Lord the words of this canticle, in the day that the Lord delivered him from the hands of all his enemies, and from the hand of Saul.*[1] This Saul was the king of the Jews whom they themselves had demanded as ruler. Just as David signifies the mighty of hand, so Saul signifies a demand. Now we know how that people demanded a king, and he was given to them not according to God's will, but according to their own.[2]

2. Here then Christ united to the Church, the whole Christ Head and Body, cries aloud: [V. 2] *I will love thee, O Lord, my strength.* Thee will I love, O Lord, who makest me strong.

3. [V. 3] *The Lord is my firmament, my refuge and my deliverer.* Lord, thou hast established me because I have fled to thee for refuge; and to thee have I fled because thou hast rescued me. *My God is my helper, and in Him will I put my trust.* Thou, my God, first granted me the help of thy call in order to give me confidence in thee. *My protector and the horn of my salvation and my redeemer.* My protector, because I have never relied upon myself, never thrown up against thee as it were a rampart of pride, but in thyself I have found the bulwark, the steep and solid fortress of my safety. It was for this thou didst redeem me.

4. [V. 4] *Praising, I will call upon the Lord, and I shall be saved from my enemies.* In search not of my own but rather of the Lord's glory, I shall call upon Him; and then I need fear no harm from the folly of impiety.

5. [V. 5] *The sorrows of death,* death of the body,

surrounded me. And the torrents of iniquity troubled me. Hostile multitudes, seething for the moment like rain-swollen rivers that will soon subside, have swept down to afflict me.

6. [V. 6] *The sorrows of hell encompassed me.* Among those who stood around plotting my destruction were the tortures of jealousy which make for death and are the high-road to the hell of sin. *And the snares of death prevented me.* They anticipated me, wanting to wreak on me before-hand the retribution afterwards to befall themselves. They ensnare in order to ruin such men as they have wickedly led astray with a show of justice. This justice of theirs, a mere name devoid of reality, they flaunt before the Gen-tiles.

7. [V. 7] *And in my distress I called upon the Lord, and I cried to my God. And He heard my voice from His holy temple.* He listened to my voice from His dwelling place in my own heart. *And my cry before Him,* that cry of mine which no ear of man can catch but which I utter inwardly in His presence, *shall come into His ears.*

8. [V. 8] *The earth shook and trembled.* Thus when the Son of Man was glorified, sinners shivered and trem-bled. *The foundations of the mountains were troubled.* The hopes that the proud had set on this world were over-turned. *And they were moved, because God was angry with them,* in order that confidence in earthly possessions should henceforth be prevented from striking root in men's hearts.

9. [V. 9] *There went up a smoke in His wrath.* Filled with repentance in the face of God's threats against the un-godly, men sent up tears and supplications. *And a fire flamed from His face.* Penance was followed by burning charity set aflame by the knowledge of God. *Coals were*

kindled by it. Those who were already dead, insensible to the flame of holy desire or the light of justice and plunged in frozen darkness, have received warmth and light, and come to life again.

10. [V. 10] *He bowed heaven and came down.* He humbled the Just One who thereupon stooped down to men's weakness. *And darkness was under His feet.* Blinded by their own wickedness, those evildoers who appreciate nothing but earthly things failed to recognize Him, for earth lay at His feet as a kind of footstool.

11.[V. 11] *And He ascended upon the cherubim, and He flew.* He rode far above the plenitude of knowledge to show that no one could approach Him except by love. For love is the fulfilling of the law.[3] And immediately He showed those who love Him that He is incomprehensible, for fear they should suppose that He is to be grasped by mere images. *He flew upon the wings of the winds.* God's swift flight, which shows that He is incomprehensible, surpasses those powers by which souls mount as though winged, above earthly anxieties into realms of freedom.[4]

12. [V. 12] *And He made darkness His covert.* He chose the darkness of the sacraments, the hidden hope in the heart of believers where He might shroud Himself without abandoning them. He hides also in that darkness where as yet we walk by faith and not by sight,[5] while we hope for something still unseen and wait for it with patience.[6] *His pavilion round about Him.* His followers who believe in Him surround Him on every side; He is in their midst, equally the friend of all, and while this world lasts He dwells in them as in a tent. *Dark waters in the clouds of the air.* Let no one imagine that a deep understanding of the Scriptures will put him in possession here and now of that light which will be ours when faith passes

into vision. There remain difficulties in the teaching of the prophets and in every preacher of God's word.

13. [V. 13] *Compared with the brightness that was before Him:* in comparison with His dazzling splendor when He reveals himself to our sight. *His clouds passed:* the heralds of His doctrine are no longer restricted to the boundaries of Judea, but have carried it to all nations. *Hail and coals of fire:* symbols of the reproaches which beat like hailstones against insensate hearts. Should it however fall upon well-tilled and genial soil, or rather upon a well-intentioned mind, this brittle hail will melt into water; in other words, these reproofs, hard as ice and terrifying as lightning, will dissolve into an invigorating lesson as hearts revive under the warmth of the fire of love. This has been the precise effect of God's clouds upon the Gentiles.

14. [V. 14] *And the Lord thundered from heaven:* the Lord made His voice heard from the heart of the just man as he boldly proclaimed the Gospel. *And the Highest gave His voice:* so that it might reach even to us, that while engulfed in human cares, we should catch something of the sounds of heaven.

15. [V. 15] *And He sent forth His arrows, and He scattered them.* He sent forth the preachers of the Gospel on mighty wings, and in their flight they traced the paths of rectitude, not by dint of their own powers but in the strength of Him who sent them. He has scattered those among whom He sent them, inasmuch as His messengers proved to some an odor of life unto life, but to others an odor of death unto death.[8] *He multiplied lightnings and troubled them.* He heaped miracle upon miracle and so threw them into consternation.

16. [V. 16] *Then the fountains of water appeared.* Then appeared the men whom the preaching of the Gospel

had transformed into fountains of living water springing up into life everlasting.[9] *And the foundations of the world were discovered.* Then was laid bare what had not been understood in the prophets, who form the foundation of this world which by faith attains to God. *At thy rebuke, O Lord:* when thou didst cry aloud: *The kingdom of God is come nigh unto you.*[10] *At the blast of the spirit of thy wrath*, with the words: *Except you do penance, you shall all likewise perish.*[11]

17. [V. 17] *He sent from on high and took me*, by summoning from the midst of the Gentiles this glorious Church as an inheritance, having neither spot nor wrinkle.[12] *He received me out of many waters:* He has drawn me from many nations.

18. [V. 18] *He saved me from my strongest enemies.* He delivered me from enemies powerful enough to inflict injury upon me and mar the peace of my life here below. *And from them that hated me; for they were too strong for me*, as long as I was subservient to their domination and blind to God's existence.

19. [V. 19] *They prevented me in the day of my affliction.* They were the first to do me harm while I was worn out enduring this mortal body of mine. *And the Lord became my support.* Since the bitterness of my misfortunes has loosened or rather torn up earthly pleasure by the root, the Lord Himself has become my strong stay.

20. [V. 20] *And He brought me forth into a large place.* Whereas I was constricted by earthly bonds, He led me into the spiritual spaciousness of the faith. Before I had even chosen Him, *He saved me from my most powerful enemies*, who bore me a grudge for loving Him, *and from them that hated me* because my desire was set on Him.

21. [V. 21] *And the Lord will reward me according to*

my justice. Our Lord will reward me for the uprightness of my good will, although He first had to show me His mercy before I could even exercise that will. *And will repay me according to the cleanness of my hands.* He will recompense me according to the purity of my actions, yet it was He who gave me the power to do good, by leading me into the spacious freedom of the faith.

22. [V. 22] *Because I have kept the ways of the Lord,* and found in them ample scope for the good works which are the fruit of faith, and consequent courage to persevere.

23. *And have not done wickedly against my God.* [V. 23] *For all His judgments are in my sight. All His judgments,* the reward of the righteous, the chastisement of the sinner, the afflictions which correct, the trials which test a man, all these I keep continually before my eyes. *And His justices I have not put away from me,* as they do who sink under the burden of His law and return to their own vomit.

24. [V. 24] *And I shall be spotless with Him, and shall keep myself from my iniquity.*

25. [V. 25] *And the Lord will reward me according to my justice.* Not only on account of the fulness of faith which works through charity,¹³ but also on account of my long perseverance, the Lord will reward me according to my uprightness. *And according to the cleanness of my hands before His eyes:* not as men see, but as things are in His sight. What we can see, lasts but for a moment, whereas what is unseen is eternal.¹⁴ This is the height to which hope rises.

26. [V. 26] *With the holy thou wilt be holy.* There is a mystery locked up in the words which explain how thou art holy with the holy, because it is thou who dost sanctify. *And with the innocent man thou wilt be innocent.* God

indeed injures no man, but every sinner is caught in the toils of his own wrongdoing.[15]

27. [V. 27] *And with the elect thou wilt be elect*, for the man of thy choice will choose thee in his turn. *And with the perverse thou wilt be perverted.*[16] To the man who turns his back on thee, thou dost seem perverse. *The way of the Lord is not right*,[17] such men cry, whereas it is their own which is crooked.

28. [V. 28] *For thou wilt save the humble people.* To the perverse, it seems perverse in thee to grant salvation to those who confess their wrongdoing. *But thou wilt bring down the eyes of the proud:* thou wilt humiliate those who do not recognize God's way of justification and who seek to establish their own.[18]

29. [V. 29] *For thou wilt light my lamp, O Lord:* our light does not originate in ourselves; it is thou, Lord, who wilt light my lamp. *O my God, thou wilt enlighten my darkness.* We are in the night of sin, but *O my God, thou wilt enlighten my darkness.*

30. [V. 30] *For by thee I shall be delivered from temptation.* Not by my own strength, but by thine alone I shall triumph over temptation. *And through my God I shall go over the wall.* Nor in my own power but by the help of God shall I leap over the wall which sins have reared between men and the heavenly Jerusalem.

31. [V. 31] *As for my God, His way is undefiled.* My God does not come to men unless they first clear the road of faith so that He whose ways are unsullied may enter. *The words of the Lord are fire-tried*, tested in the furnace of tribulation. *He is the protector of all that trust in Him.* All who trust not in themselves but in Him shall pass unscathed through that tribulation, for faith gives birth to hope.

32. [V. 32] *For who is God but the Lord* whom we serve? *Or who is God but our God?* Who is God if not our Lord whom we, His children, hope to possess as our inheritance after our lifetime of loyal obedience?

33. [V. 33] *God who hath girt me with strength:* God who has bound me with a girdle to make me strong, so that the fluttering robes of covetous desire may impede neither my actions nor my steps. *And made my way blameless.* He has prepared the road of charity so that I may go to Him, as I have had to prepare the road of faith by which He comes to me.

34. [V. 34] *Who hath made my feet like the feet of harts.* He has perfected my love to enable me to leap over the thorny and sinister entanglements of this world. *And who will set me upon high places.* He will fix my gaze upon our heavenly abode, so that I may be filled with God's plenitude.[19]

35. [V. 35] *Who teacheth my hands to war.* He trains me to skill in battling with the foes whose aim it is to bar against us the kingdom of heaven. *And thou hast made my arms like a brazen bow,* since thou hast given me untiring zeal to persevere in good deeds.

36. [V. 36] *And thou hast given me the protection of my salvation,*[20] *and thy right hand hath held me up.* The favor of thy grace has supported me. *And thy discipline hath directed me unto the end.* Thy chastisements prevent me from straying; they keep me on the straight path so that I refer all my actions to their proper end, which is union with thyself. *And thy discipline, the same shall teach me.* Those reproofs of thine are to instruct me how to reach the goal to which they point.

37. [V. 37] *Thou hast enlarged my steps under me,* and the constricting bonds of the flesh will not hamper my

course; for thou hast made me grow in that charity which works good with joy, and to which even my members and all that is mortal in me serve as instruments. *And my footprints are not weakened.* There is no uncertainty regarding either the road I have trodden or the traces I have left for those who wish to follow in my footsteps.

38. [V. 38] *I will pursue after my enemies and overtake them.* I shall root out in myself all unspiritual desires for fear they should master me. Indeed, I shall master them and make an end of them. *And I will not turn again till they are consumed.* I shall press on and give myself no respite until I have crushed every obstacle.

39. [V. 39] *I will break them, and they shall not be able to stand.* They will not hold out against me. *They shall fall under my feet.* When I have hurled them down, I shall set in their place the twofold feet of love on which to travel heavenwards.[21]

40. [V. 40] *And thou hast girded me with strength unto battle.* Thou hast girded up with strength the flowing garments of my earthborn desires, so that nothing should encumber me in such a fight. *And hast tripped up under me them that rose up against me.* Thou hast put in the wrong those that harassed me, so that they who aimed at establishing dominion over me find themselves under my feet.

41. [V. 41] *And thou hast put my enemies behind me.* Thou hast converted my foes and hast placed them behind my back in order to follow me. *And hast destroyed them that hated me.* Those, however, who persisted in their hatred thou hast brought to ruin.

42. [V. 42] *They cried, but there was none to save them.* Who could save them when thou didst not? *To the Lord, but He heard them not.* They cried out, not to some

man or other, but to the Lord; yet He deemed them unworthy of an answer, since they would not give over
their disorderly lives.

43. [V. 43] *And I shall beat them as small as dust
before the wind.* I shall reduce them to dust, for they
are dried up, having refused the shower of God's mercy.
Elated and inflated by pride, they are swept away from
the unshakable solidity of hope, like dust driven off the
firm and stable earth. *I shall bring them to naught, like the
dirt in the streets.* As they tread with the throng the broad
road of perdition,[22] these men of dissolute lives will slip
and stumble, and I shall make an end of them.

44. [V. 44] *Thou wilt deliver me from the contradic-
tions of the people.* Thou wilt deliver me from the con-
tradictions of those who said: *If we let Him alone, the
whole world will go after Him.*[23]

45. *Thou wilt make me head of the Gentiles.* [V. 45]
A people which I knew not hath served me. The people
of the Gentiles, whom I never visited with my bodily
presence, have worshiped me. *At the hearing of the ear
they have obeyed me.* Their eyes never beheld me; but in
welcoming my preachers, they have obeyed the first call
of my voice.

46. [V. 46] *The children that are strangers have lied
to me.* Children unworthy of being called mine, nay,
aliens who were rightly told: *You are of your father the
devil,*[24] have lied to me. *Stranger children are become old
men.* These sons become strangers, whom I wished to
make young by the provision of the New Testament,
have remained their old selves. *And they have halted from
their paths.* Lamed in one foot, since they were satisfied
simply with the Old Testament, they have rejected the
New Testament with scorn and consequently have become

cripples; moreover, even in the Old Law they followed their own traditions rather than God's. Unwashed hands, for instance, were a crime;[25] such being the paths that they themselves had traced and usage had well trodden, far from the path of God's precepts.

47. [V. 47] *The Lord liveth, and blessed be my God.* Now the wisdom of the flesh is death,[26] whereas my Lord is living, and blessed is my God. *And let the God of my salvation be exalted.* I must not reflect in terms of earth upon the God who saves me, nor is the salvation I look for temporal; I await it from God on high.

48. [V. 48] *O God, who avengest me and subduest the people under me.* God who dost avenge me by subjecting people to my yoke. *My deliverer from my raging enemies:* from the Jews who cried: *Crucify Him, crucify Him!*[27]

49. [V. 49] *Thou wilt lift me up above them that rise up against me.* Thou wilt exalt me in my resurrection above these Jews who jeer at me in my passion. *From the unjust man thou wilt deliver me.* Thou wilt deliver me from the domination of the wicked.

50. [V. 50] *Therefore will I give glory to thee, O Lord, among the nations.* It is through me, O Lord, that the nations will render praise to thee. *And I will sing a psalm to thy name.* My good works will spread thy name far and wide.

51. [V. 51] *Giving great deliverance to his king.* It is God who grants victory, who makes so wonderful the ways of salvation which His Son bestows on those who believe in Him. *And showing mercy to His anointed.* It is God again who shows mercy to Him who has received the anointing. *To David and to his seed forever:* to the Deliverer whose mighty hand has conquered this world,

and to all whom He has begotten unto eternal life through their faith in the Gospel.

Whatever words in this Psalm cannot be adapted to the Person of our Lord Himself as Head of the Church must be applied to the Church herself. For the words spoken are those of the whole Christ, of Christ united to all His members.

FIRST DISCOURSE ON PSALM 18

1. [Verse 1] *Unto the end, a Psalm for David himself.* The title is a familiar one, but our Lord Jesus Christ is not the speaker of the Psalm; He is rather the subject of it.

2. [V. 2] *The heavens show forth the glory of God.* The holy Evangelists, in whom God dwells as in the heavens, proclaim the glory of our Lord Jesus Christ, or perhaps the glory which the Son during His earthly life rendered to His Father. *And the firmament declareth the work of His hands.* It publishes the Lord's mighty deeds, this firmament which the power of the Holy Spirit has transformed into the dome of heaven, whereas under the influence of fear it was formerly mere earth.[1]

3. [V. 3] *Day unto day uttereth the word.* The Spirit reveals to the spiritual the unchangeable Wisdom of God in all His fulness, that Word which in the beginning was with God and was God.[2] *And night unto night proclaimeth knowledge:* and this mortal flesh which introduces the faith to unspiritual men cries out to them, as if they stood afar off, of the knowledge which follows upon faith.

4. [V. 4] *There are no speeches nor languages where their voices are not heard.* Who has not heard the voices of the Evangelists preaching the Gospel in every tongue?

5. [V. 5] *Their sound hath gone forth into all the earth, and their words unto the ends of the world.*

6. [V. 6] *He hath set His tabernacle in the sun.*[3] Now in order to wage war against the powers of temporal error, the Lord, who came to bring upon earth not peace but the sword,[4] pitched His army tent so to speak, that is, the mystery of His Incarnation, thus making Himself known in this temporal dispensation. *And He as a bridegroom coming out of his bridechamber.* He came forth from the Virgin's womb, where God contracted with human nature as it were the union of bridegroom and bride. *He hath rejoiced as a giant to run the way.* He has exulted like a powerful athlete outstripping all others in His incomparable strength, His aim being not to loiter but to cover the course. For He did not linger where sinners walk.[5]

7. [V. 7] *His going out is from the end of heaven.*[6] His starting place is from the Father; He is born of the Father not by a temporal but by an eternal generation. *And His circuit even to the height of heaven.* And in the fulness of His Godhead He reaches in His course equality with the Father. *And there is no one that can hide himself from His heat,* for when the Word was made flesh and clothed Himself with our mortality to dwell amongst us,[7] He would not allow any mortal man to hide behind the excuse of the shadows of death, since the burning heat of the Word has penetrated even death itself.

8. [V. 8] *The law of the Lord is unspotted, converting souls.* The law of the Lord is none but Himself, who came to fulfil the law, not to destroy it.[8] He is the immaculate law, He who did no wrong, on whose lips no treachery was found,[9] who did not oppress souls with a yoke of slavery but led them in all freedom to follow in His own steps. *The testimony of the Lord is faithful, giving wisdom*

to little ones. The testimony of the Lord is faithful because none knows the Father except the Son, and he to whom it shall please the Son to reveal Him.[10] This knowledge has been hidden from the wise and revealed to little ones,[11] since God resists the proud and gives grace to the humble.[12]

9. [V. 9] *The justices of the Lord are right, rejoicing hearts.* All the ordinances of the Lord are plain in Him who taught nothing which He had not Himself performed, so that those who were to model themselves on Him should do so in joy of heart, doing what they did with the freedom of love, not with the servility of fear. *The commandment of the Lord is lightsome, enlightening the eyes.* This clear commandment undimmed by the veil of corporal observances is the enlightenment of a man's interior sight.

10. [V. 10] *The fear of the Lord is chaste, enduring forever and ever.* This fear of the Lord is not that which was a penalty under the Old Law, one that dreaded the loss of those perishable good things, the desire for which is a form of spiritual fornication; but it is a chaste fear which leads the Church to avoid what may offend her Bridegroom with a care that equals her burning love for Him. Now perfect love does not cast out this fear[13] which abides forever.

11. *The judgments of the Lord are true, justified in themselves.* The judgments of Him who judges no man but has left all judgment to the Son[14] are true with an immutable justice. For God deceives neither in His threats nor in His promises, and none can withdraw the evildoer from punishment or the upright man from his reward. [V. 11] *More to be desired than gold and precious stone, much though it be.* The word *much* may qualify the gold and precious stones as being either much, or much to be prized or much more desirable; in any event, God's

judgments are to be set above the display of this world; those who value the latter, far from desiring God's judgments, end by fearing, despising or even ceasing to believe in them. But if a man in his turn is both gold and a precious stone, impervious to fire but rather reserved for God's treasure hoard, then he loves God's judgments more than himself and prefers God's will to his own.

And sweeter than honey and the honeycomb. Should a soul be pure honey, already freed from the bonds of mortal life and waiting simply to grace God's banquet, or should it be merely in the honeycomb, enveloped still in this life as in the waxen cells which it fills without becoming one with them, needing the pressure of God's hand, not to crush it but to make it drip like honey and so pass from life in time to eternity, then to such a soul God's judgments will be sweeter than it is to itself, for they are sweeter than honey and the honeycomb.

12. [V. 12] *For thy servant keepeth them.* The day of the Lord will be bitter indeed for the man who does not keep thy judgments. *And in keeping them there is a great reward.* This rich reward consists in no outward advantage but in the simple observance of God's law; rich it is, because its very exercise is joy.

13. [V. 13] *Who can understand sins?* Now how can anyone find sins delightful, since they are not subordinated to the intellect? How can the understanding play its part, when sins cloud the eye of the soul which makes truth its delight and finds God's judgments both desirable and sweet? As darkness blinds the eyes, so sins blind the soul and rob it both of light and of self-knowledge.

14. *From my secret sins cleanse me, O Lord.* Lord, cleanse me from the impure desires which lurk within me. [V. 14] *And from those of others spare thy servant,*[15] for

fear others lead me astray. The man purified from his own faults should not fall a prey to those of others. Preserve, then, from the sinful desires of others, not the proud man who would be his own master, but me thy servant. *If they shall have no dominion over me, then shall I be without spot.* So long as neither my own secret frailties nor those of others lord it over me, I shall be without fault. There is no third source of sin: there is simply the temptation from within which brought the devil low, and there is the temptation from without which seduced man and became his sin when he gave his consent to it. *And I shall be cleansed from a great sin.* Which sin? Surely, pride. There is no greater sin than to break away from God, which is pride's beginning in man.[16] That man is truly without fault who is innocent of even this sin, which is the last to depart when we return to God, as it was the first to enter when we turned our backs upon Him.

15. [V. 15] *And the words of my mouth shall be such as may please, and the meditation of my heart always in thy sight.* The thoughts of my heart will no longer seek after the vainglory of pleasing men, since I am now guiltless of pride, but they will ever abide in thy presence, for thou dost look with favor upon the heart which is pure. *O Lord my helper and my Redeemer.* Thou art my helper, O Lord, when I make my way back to thee, for to this end thou didst become my Redeemer. Whoever would attribute his return to thyself to his own wisdom, or his attainment of thee to his own powers, will only be rejected the more emphatically, since thou dost resist the proud.[17] Such a man is by no means innocent of the great sin, nor is he acceptable in thy sight, O Lord, who dost redeem us that we may return to thee, and grant us grace that we may attain at the last even unto thine own self.

SECOND DISCOURSE ON PSALM 18[1]

1. Having implored the Lord to cleanse us from our secret sins and spare His servants from those of others, we ought to understand the meaning of this petition, so as to sing like reasonable beings and not like birds. For blackbirds, parrots, ravens, magpies and suchlike birds are often taught by men to utter sounds they cannot understand; but to sing with intelligence is a God-given endowment of human nature. And we know to our sorrow how many evil men of dissolute lives thus sing ditties in keeping with their ears and hearts. They are all the more blameworthy in that they cannot help being aware of what they are singing. They know perfectly well they are singing obscene songs, yet the lewder the songs the more lustily they sing, for the murkier their souls the merrier they suppose themselves. But we, who have learnt in the Church to chant the oracles of God, should at the same time do our best to fulfil the words: *Blessed is the people that knoweth jubilation.*[2] Therefore, dearly beloved, we ought to study and examine with calm of heart what we have been singing in unison of voice. Each one of us has been beseeching our Lord in this canticle and saying to God: *From my secret sins cleanse me, O Lord, and from those of others spare thy servant. If they shall have no dominion over me, then I shall be without spot, and I shall be cleansed from the great sin.* Now to understand clearly the sense and implication of these words, let us briefly run through the text of this Psalm and see what the Lord shows us.

2. The canticle is an allegory of Christ. This is obvious from the passage in it which runs: *He, as a bridegroom coming out of his bridechamber.* Who is this bridegroom, then, if not He to whom the Apostle has espoused the

virgin? In his noble solicitude this faithful friend of the bridegroom fears that as Eve was seduced by the serpent's cunning, so too the mind of this virgin bride of Christ may be corrupted and fall from the purity which is in Christ.[3] In Him, indeed, in our Lord and Saviour Jesus Christ, resides full and abundant grace, of which the Apostle John declares: *And we saw His glory, the glory as it were of the only-begotten of the Father, full of grace and truth.*[4]

[Verse 1] This *glory the heavens show forth.* The heavens are the saints, poised above the earth, bearing the Lord. Yet the sky, too, after its fashion, has proclaimed the glory of Christ. When? When at the birth of this same Lord there appeared a new star never seen before. However, there are truer and loftier heavens, of which the following verses tell us: *There are no speeches nor languages where their voices are not heard. Their sound hath gone forth into all the earth, and their words unto the ends of the world.* Whose words, but those of the heavens? Whose, then, but those of the apostles? It is they who proclaim to us the glory of God, residing in Christ Jesus and manifested through His grace for the remission of sins. For all have sinned and do need the glory of God, being justified gratuitously by His blood.[5] Because gratuitously, therefore by grace; for grace is no grace unless it is gratuitous. Because we had done nothing good beforehand to deserve such great gifts and all the more because punishment, by no means undeserved, was to be inflicted, the favor was granted freely. There was nothing in our preceding merits that would earn anything but our condemnation. But He, not because of our own justice, but in accordance with His own mercy, saved us with the cleansing power[6] which gives us new birth. This, I say, is the glory of God; this it is that the heavens have shown forth. This, I repeat, is God's glory, not yours: you have done nothing good, and yet you have received such an immense benefit. If therefore you share in the glory that the heavens proclaim, say to the Lord your God: *My God, His mercy shall prevent me.*[7] Truly He forestalled you; He had to forestall you, because He found not an atom of virtue in you. You had forestalled His chastisement by your pride; He has forestalled your punishment by wiping out your sins. As a sinner made just, then, an ungodly man made godly, a condemned criminal received into a kingdom, send up your cry to the Lord your God: *Not to us, O Lord, not to us, but to thy name give glory.*[8] We may well say: *Not to us.* For what if it were *to us?* We may well say, I repeat, *Not to us,* because if He had dealt with us as our deeds deserve, He could only mete out punishment. Not unto us but unto His own name let Him give the glory, because He has not dealt with us according to our iniquities.[9] *Not to us,* then, *O Lord, not to us;* to repeat is to strengthen it. *Not to us, O Lord, but to thy name give glory:* this those heavens understood who declared the glory of God.

3. [V. 2] *And the firmament declareth the work of His hands.* The phrase, *the glory of God,* is repeated as *the work of His hands.* What works of His hands? It is not, as some people think, that God made all things by a word, and made man with His own hands as being more excellent than all the rest. We must not think thus: such a notion is weak and inexact; in fact He made all things by the Word. For although various works of God are mentioned, and among them His making of man to His own image,[10] yet all things were made by Him, and without Him was made nothing.[11] As for God's hands, we are told of the heavens too: *And the heavens are the works*

of thy hands;[12] and lest you might here confuse the saints with the heavens, the Psalmist has added: *They shall perish but thou remainest.*[13] Therefore God, to whom the words *The heavens are the works of thy hands* are addressed, has made with His own hands not only man but also the heavens which are to perish. And the same thing is said about the earth: *For the sea is His, and He made it, and His hands founded the dry land.*[14] Hence if He made the heavens with His hands and the earth with His hands, it was not man alone He made with His hands: and if He made the heavens by the Word and the earth by the Word, then He made man too by the Word. What He did by the Word, that He did with the hand, and what He did with the hand He did by the Word. For God has not limbs like ours to delineate His stature, since He is wholly everywhere and is contained in no place. Thus what He made by His Word, He made by His wisdom, and what He made by His hand, He made by His power. But Christ is the Power of God and the Wisdom of God;[15] all things were made by Him, and without Him was made nothing. The heavens have shown forth, do show forth and will show forth the glory of God.

The heavens, I tell you, will show forth the glory of God; in other words, the saints, who are poised aloft above the earth, bearing God, thundering forth precepts, flashing forth wisdom; this glory of God, as I have said, by which we have been saved, in spite of our unworthiness. This unworthiness, this glory we do not deserve, the younger son acknowledges when constrained by want. The younger son, I repeat, acknowledges this unworthiness when wandering far from his father's home, when he is a worshiper of demons, as though a keeper of swine; he acknowledges God's glory, but only when constrained by want. And because through that glory of God we have been made what we were not worthy to be, he says to his father: *I am not worthy to be called thy son.*[16] Unhappy as he is, he obtains happiness through humility and shows himself worthy by the confession of his unworthiness. This *glory of God the heavens show forth, and the firmament declareth the work of His hands.* The sky, the firmament, betokens a firm and fearless heart. All this has been proclaimed among the impious, among God's enemies, among the lovers of this world and the persecutors of the upright: all this has been proclaimed in the midst of a world of violence. But what could the violence of the world effect when the firmament proclaimed these things? *The firmament declareth*—what? *The works of His hands.* What are the works of His hands? That glory of God by which we have been saved, by which we have been created in good works. For we are His workmanship, created in Christ Jesus, in good works;[17] indeed, He made us, and not we ourselves,[18] not merely men but also just men, if so we be.

4. [V. 3] *Day unto day uttereth the word, and night unto night proclaimeth knowledge.* What does this mean? Perhaps *Day unto day uttereth the word* is plain and clear, plain and clear as the day itself; but *night unto night proclaimeth knowledge* is mysterious as the night itself. *Day unto day* would be the saints to the saints, the apostles to the faithful, Christ Himself to the apostles, whom He told: *You are the light of the world.*[19] That seems plain and easy to grasp. But how does *night unto night proclaim knowledge*? Some have understood these words quite simply, and this may be true enough. They take the sentence to mean that what the apostles heard in the days of our Lord Jesus Christ, while He dwelt on earth, has been

transmitted to posterity, from age to age, so to speak: day to day, night to night, from one day to another, from one night to another, for this doctrine is proclaimed day and night. This simple explanation may suffice for any one who is satisfied with it. Some passages of Scripture, however, have from their very obscurity this advantage, that they are capable of many interpretations. Accordingly, if these words were plain you would hear only one, but since they are obscure you are likely to hear several. Here is another interpretation: *Day unto day, night unto night*, spirit to spirit, flesh to flesh. Here is another: spiritual matters to the spiritually-minded, earthly matters to the earthly-minded. For both hear, though both do not equally understand. The former hear it as a word uttered, the latter as knowledge proclaimed. What is uttered, is uttered to those present, whereas what is proclaimed, is proclaimed to those at a distance. Several meanings can be found for the word *heavens*, but because of the pressure of time we must observe a limit. Yet we can mention one more idea which some have brought forward in explanation. When our Lord Christ was speaking to the apostles, they say, day unto day was uttering speech; when Judas betrayed Christ our Lord, night unto night was proclaiming knowledge.

5. [V. 4] *There are no speeches nor languages where their voices are not heard.* Whose voices, except those of the heavens that show forth the glory of God? *There are no speeches nor languages where their voices are not heard.* Read, in the Acts of the Apostles, how they were all filled with the Holy Spirit who came upon them, and how they spoke with the tongues of all nations, as the Spirit gave them utterance.[20] See then, *there are no speeches nor languages where their voices are not heard.* But not only

where they were filled with the Spirit did their voice resound, but [V. 5] *Their sound hath gone forth into all the earth, and their words unto the ends of the world.* That is why we are speaking here. For that sound has reached even as far as us, that sound which has gone forth into the whole earth, and yet the heretic does not enter the Church. The sound has gone forth into all the earth on purpose that you may find entrance into heaven. You baneful pest, you wicked creature, fond of strife and persistent in your love of error; you upstart son, listen to your Father's testament. See, what could be plainer or clearer? *Their sound hath gone forth into all the earth, and their words unto the ends of the world.* Does it need explaining? Why are you striving against your own interest? Would you quarrel to retain a fragment, when peace could put you in possession of the whole?

6. [V. 6] *He hath set His tabernacle in the sun*, by establishing His Church in broad daylight, not in obscurity, not in mystery and under a veil, for fear it should escape observation among the assemblies of the heretics. So too, a certain man was told in Holy Scripture: Since *thou didst it secretly, thou shalt suffer in the sun*;[21] in other words, you committed the evil in secret, you shall suffer the punishment in all men's sight. He has set His tabernacle, then, in the sun. Why, you heretic, do you flee into darkness? Are you a Christian? Then listen to Christ. Are you His servant? Listen to your Lord. Are you His son? Listen to your Father, mend your ways and come to life again. Of you too let us say: *He was dead and is come to life again; he was lost and is found.*[22] Do not say to me: "Why do you look for me, if I am lost?" I look for you for that very reason, just because you are lost. "Do not seek me," he says. Now this is the precise aim of the wickedness

which divides us, but not of the love which makes us brothers. I should not be a criminal were I to go in search of my servant; and must I be accused of crime because I go in search of my brother? Let anyone think so in whom brotherly love does not exist; but I will go in search of my brother for all that. Let him be angry, what matters it so long as he is sought for? He will be appeased when he has been found. I will seek out my brother, I repeat, and will appeal to my Lord, not against him but on his behalf. And my prayer will not be: "Lord, speak to my brother that he divide the inheritance with me";[23] but: "Speak to my brother that he may enjoy the inheritance with me." Why do you go astray, brother? Why run away in and out of corners? Why do you try to hide? *He hath set His tabernacle in the sun.*

And He, as a bridegroom coming out of his bridechamber: no doubt so that you may recognize Him. As a bridegroom coming out of his bridechamber, He *hath rejoiced as a giant to run the way. He* Himself *hath set His tabernacle in the sun.* In other terms, when the Word was made flesh, He found as a bridegroom His nuptial chamber in the Virgin's womb. Thence He came forth, united to a human nature, as from a chamber of surpassing purity, humble below all in His mercy, strong above all in His majesty. This is how the giant has rejoiced to run His way: He was born, grew up, taught, suffered, rose again, ascended; He ran His course, He did not loiter upon it. This same bridegroom who accomplished all these things, He it is who has set His tabernacle, the Church, in the sun, in full view of all men.

7. Would you hear about the course He ran so swiftly? [V. 7] *His going out is from the end of heaven, and His circuit even to the end thereof.* But after He had run forth

and returned whence He came, He sent His Spirit. There appeared upon those who received Him parted tongues as it were of fire.²⁴ Like fire the Holy Spirit came to burn up the grass of what was merely natural, to smelt and refine the gold. As fire He came; hence the Psalm continues: *and there is none that can hide* himself from His heat.

8. [V. 8] *The law of the Lord is unspotted, converting souls.* This is the work of the Holy Spirit. *The testimony of the Lord is faithful, giving wisdom to little ones:* not to the proud. This again is the Holy Spirit.

9. [V. 9] *The justices of the Lord are right,* not intimidating but *rejoicing hearts.* This is the work of the Holy Spirit. *The commandment of the Lord is lightsome, enlightening,* not dulling, *the eyes,* those eyes not of the flesh but of the heart, not of the outer but of the inner man. This again is the effect of the Holy Spirit.

10. [V. 10] *The fear of the Lord* is not a slavish but a *chaste* fear. It loves and looks for no recompense; it fears, not punishment from Him before whom it trembles, but separation from Him whom it loves. This is a chaste fear, not that fear which perfect charity casts out,²⁵ but *enduring forever and ever.* Here indeed is the Holy Spirit; or rather, this fear is bestowed, conferred, implanted by the Holy Spirit. *The judgments of the Lord are true, justified unto the selfsame.* So far from stirring up division and strife, they are a source of unity; this is the force of the phrase *unto the selfsame.* This is the work of the Holy Spirit. For this reason those upon whom He first descended received from Him the gift of tongues, to show us thereby that He would gather together the tongues of all nations into unity. What a single man did in those days upon receiving the Holy Spirit, namely to speak in the tongues of all his hearers, unity itself does now, for it speaks in all

tongues. Today it is still one man who speaks to all nations and in all tongues, one man, Head and Body, one man who is Christ and the Church, the perfect man; He the bridegroom, she the bride. For, He says: *They shall be two in one flesh.*[26] *The judgments of God are true, justified unto the selfsame,* by reason of this unity.

11. [V. 11] *More to be desired than gold and precious stone, much though it be.* Whether it be much gold, or of much price or much to be desired, at any rate it is much, though little to the heretics. They do not love that selfsame unity as we do, yet they confess Christ as we do. This Christ whom you confess with me, will you not also love with me? And he who does not desire that unity, refuses, spurns and rejects it. Not for him is it more desirable than gold and much precious stone. Listen again. *And sweeter,* says the Psalmist, *than honey and the honeycomb.* But that condemns the man who goes astray; honey is bitter to a fever-stricken patient, however sweet and acceptable to one who is well again, for those in sound health enjoy it. *More to be desired than gold and precious stone, much though it be, and sweeter than honey and the honeycomb.*

12. [V. 12] *For thy servant keepeth them.* Their sweetness thy servant experiences by keeping them, not by talking about them. Thy servant keeps them because they are both sweet at the present time and advantageous for the future, since *in keeping them there is a great reward.* But the heretic, in love with his own foolhardiness, neither sees their glory nor tastes their sweetness.

13. [V. 13] *Who* indeed *can understand sins?* Father, forgive them, for they know not what they do.[27] Therefore, says the Psalmist, that man is thy servant who preserves this sweetness, this tenderness of charity, this love of unity. But I who do preserve it, the Psalmist continues, I

supplicate thee, for *who*, indeed, *can understand sins?* May human weaknesses never steal upon me, and man as I am entangle me unawares: *From my secret ones cleanse me, O Lord.* These are the words we first chanted, and now you see we have come to them in our discourse. Let us utter them, and sing them with understanding; let us pray as we sing and obtain our petition as we pray. Let us repeat: *From my secret ones cleanse me, O Lord.* Who indeed can understand sins? If darkness could be seen, then sins could be understood. Now it is only when we repent of our sins that we finally enjoy the light. For when a man is all wrapped up in his sin, his eyes are so to speak darkened and blindfolded and he cannot see the sin, just as when your bodily eye is bandaged you can see nothing, not even the bandage.

Therefore let us cry to God, who can see what He is to cleanse and can look into what He is to heal; let us say to Him: *From my secret ones cleanse me, O Lord;* [V. 14] *and from those of others spare thy servant.* My own sins, the Psalmist says, defile me, other men's sins afflict me; cleanse me from the one, spare me from the other. Take away from my heart the dangerous train of thought, drive away from me the evil adviser; this is the force of the words: *From my secret ones cleanse me, O Lord, and from those of others spare thy servant.* For these two classes of sins, our own and those of others, became evident from the first, even from the beginning. The devil fell by his own sin, Adam he overthrew by the sin of another. This same servant of God, who keeps God's judgments and finds therein a great reward, prays thus in another Psalm: *Let not the foot of pride come to me, and let not the hands of sinners move me.*[28] Let not the foot of pride come near me, he begs; in other words: *From my secret ones cleanse me, O Lord.* And let not the hands of sinners move me: *From those of others spare thy servant.*

14. *If* my own secret sins and those of others *shall have no dominion over me, then I shall be without spot.* This is no bold reliance on his own strength, but the Psalmist entreats the Lord to accomplish it, praying in the words of another Psalm: *Direct my ways according to thy word, and let no iniquity have dominion over me.*[29] Fear not, if you are a Christian, any man's lordship from without; but the Lord your God you must fear always. Fear the evil within you, your own base desires, not what God made in you but what you have made for yourself. The Lord made you a good servant; you have created for yourself an evil master in your own heart. Well do you deserve to be subject to iniquity, well do you deserve to be subject to the master you have created for yourself, since you refused to be subject to Him who made you.

15. The Psalmist continues, however: *If they shall have no dominion over me, then I shall be without spot, and I shall be cleansed from the great sin.* From what sin, are we to suppose? What is this great sin? Possibly it is not what I am going to say, yet I will not hide my opinion. This great sin, I consider, is pride. This is perhaps what he expresses in other terms by saying: *And I shall be cleansed from the great sin.* Do you ask how great that sin is which overthrew an angel, which changed an angel into a devil and closed the kingdom of heaven against him forever? A great sin it surely is, and the head and origin of all sins. For the Scripture tells us: *Pride is the beginning of all sin;* and for fear you should disregard this as a light matter, it adds: *The beginning of the pride of man is to fall off from God.*[30] No, my brethren, this vice is no slight fault. Those high and mighty personages whom you see

addicted to this vice find Christian humility distasteful.
It is this vice which makes them scorn to bend their necks
beneath the yoke of Christ, constrained though they are
yet more tightly by the yoke of sin. Serve they must, yet
serve they will not, even when it would be to their advantage. By refusing to serve they merely withdraw their
service from a good Master without finding any escape
from servitude, since any one who will not serve love
must needs become the slave of sin. That vice, the source
of all vices, since all the rest spring from it, has caused a
falling off from God, when a soul, by a deplorable misuse
of its free will, plunges into darkness and all other sins
follow on. Thus the soul squanders its substance in living
riotously with prostitutes, and the former companion of
angels becomes through want a feeder of swine.³¹ It was
because of this vice, because of this enormous sin of pride,
that God came in humility. This enormous sin, this mon-
strous disease of souls, was the very thing which brought
the almighty Physician down from heaven, humbled Him
even to taking the form of a slave, exposed Him to igno-
miny, hung Him upon the tree, that by the saving strength
of so potent a remedy this tumor might be healed. And
now finally let man blush to be proud, for whose sake
God has become humble. So, says the Psalmist, *I shall be
cleansed from the great sin*, because God resists the proud
and gives grace to the humble.³²

16. [V. 15] *And thereby may the words of my mouth
be pleasing, and the meditation of my heart always in thy
sight.* For unless I am cleansed from the great sin, my
words will be pleasing in men's sight but not in thine. The
proud soul desires to shine in the sight of men, the humble
soul in secret, where God beholds it. If any one pleases
men by a good deed, let him rejoice for their sakes who

are pleased by it, and not for his own; the fact of having done the good deed ought to suffice. For *our glory*, says the Apostle, *is this, the testimony of our conscience.*[33] And therefore let us add what follows: *O Lord, my helper and my Redeemer:* my helper in good, my Redeemer from evil. My helper, that I may abide in thy love; my Redeemer, to set me free from my iniquity.

DISCOURSE ON PSALM 19

1. [Verse 1] *Unto the end, a Psalm for David.* The title is a familiar one. It is not Christ who is speaking, however, but the prophet who speaks to Christ, and in the form of a prayer sings of things to come.

2. [V. 2] *May the Lord hear thee in the day of tribulation.* May the Lord listen to thee when thou hast cried: *Father, glorify thy Son.*[1] *May the name of the God of Jacob protect thee.* For the nation born of the younger brother is thine, since the elder is to serve the younger.[2]

3. [V. 3] *May He send thee help from the sanctuary and defend thee out of Sion,* by fashioning for thee a hallowed Body, the Church, secure in her contemplation[3] and awaiting thy return from the marriage feast.[4]

4. [V. 4] *May He be mindful of all thy sacrifices.* May He never let us forget all the outrages and insults thou didst endure for us. *And may thy whole-burnt offering be made fat.* May the cross, on which thou didst offer thyself as a complete holocaust to God, be transformed into the gladness of the resurrection. (*Diapsalma.*[5])

5. [V. 5] *May He give thee according to thy own heart.* May the Lord answer thee, not indeed according to the desires of those who persecuted thee in the hope of destroying thee utterly, but according to thine own heart's

desire, since thou hast known the fruit thy passion would reap. *And fulfil all thy counsel.* May He crown all thy plans with fulfilment, not only thy purpose to lay down thy life for thy friends[6] in order that the dead grain may spring up again with a richer yield,[7] but also that whereby blindness has fallen upon a part of Israel, until the fulness of the Gentiles has come in, when the whole of Israel will find salvation.[8]

6. [V. 6] *We will rejoice in thy salvation.* We shall rejoice that death can in no wise hurt thee, for thus thou wouldst prove that neither shall it hurt us. *And in the name of our God we shall be exalted.* By extolling thy name we shall be led, not indeed to our destruction, but rather to our own glorification.

7. [V. 7] *The Lord fulfil all thy petitions.* May the Lord grant not only the requests thou didst proffer on earth, but also those by which thou dost plead for us in heaven. *Now have I known that the Lord hath saved His anointed.* The spirit of prophecy has now taught me that the Lord is to raise up His Christ from the dead. *He will hear him from His holy heaven.* God will answer not only when from earth our Lord prays to be glorified,[9] but when in heaven He intercedes for us at the right hand of His Father[10] and pours forth from thence the Holy Ghost on all who believe in Himself.[11] *The salvation of His right hand is in mighty acts.* Our mighty acts proceed from His beneficent favor, seeing that He so sustains us in affliction that it is when we are weak that we become most powerful.[12] For vain is the salvation of men[13] which comes from the left, not from the right hand of God. It elates with excessive pride all who, sinners that they are, have rested secure in the things of this world.

8. [V. 8] *Some trust in chariots, and some in horses.*[14]

Some are carried away on the whirling wheel of fortune, others attain to honors which foster pride, and revel in them. *But we will exult in the name of the Lord our God.* Our hope, on the contrary, is fixed in eternal joys, and without any thought of self-glory we will exult in the name of the Lord our God.

9. [V. 9] *They are bound and have fallen.* The men aforesaid, bound hand and foot by their love of temporal benefits, were afraid to spare our Lord's life lest the Romans should make an end of their country;[15] and thus, tripping on the stumbling stone and rock of scandal, they forfeited their heavenly hope.[16] They fell into the blindness which struck part of Israel;[17] and having failed to recognize God's way of justification they tried to institute a way of their own.[18] *But we are risen and are set upright.* And we, the Gentile nations who were to enter in, from being once stones have been raised up to be children of Abraham,[19] and whereas we never aimed at justifying ourselves, yet we have embraced justice[20] and have risen up. Not however by our own strength, but in virtue of the justification which comes of faith do we stand erect.

10. [V. 10] *O Lord, save the king,* in order that after having taught us in His passion how to wage war, He may now offer our sacrifices also,[21] who is the High Priest raised from the dead and set on His throne in the heavens. *And hear us in the day that we shall call upon thee.* Since He now makes offering for us, answer us in the day when we call upon thee.

DISCOURSE ON PSALM 20

1. [Verse 1] *Unto the end, a Psalm for David himself.* The title is familiar: Christ is the theme of the song.

2. [V. 2] *In thy strength, O Lord, the king shall joy.* Christ Jesus in His human nature will exult, O Lord, in that strength of thine which has clothed with flesh the eternal Word. *And in thy salvation He shall rejoice exceedingly.* In that power which imparts life to every creature He will rejoice exceedingly.

3. [V. 3] *Thou hast granted him his soul's desire.* He longed to eat the Passover,[1] to lay down His life when He so willed and freely to take it up again afterwards:[2] thou hast granted His wish. *Thou hast not deprived him of the request of his lips.* He said: *My peace I leave with you,*[3] and so it was accorded.

4. [V. 4] *For thou hast prevented him with blessings of sweetness.* As He had already drunk deep of the blessing of thy sweetness, the gall of our sins did Him no harm. (*Diapsalma.*[4]) *Thou hast set on his head a crown of precious stones.* From the outset of His ministry thou didst surround Him with clusters of precious stones, His disciples, who were the first to proclaim His message to the world.

5. [V. 5] *He asked life, and thou gavest it him.* The resurrection He besought in the words, *Father, glorify thy Son,*[5] thou hast granted. *Length of days forever and ever:* the ages of this world which measure out the duration of the Church, and after that the unfailing ages of the world without end.

6. [V. 6] *His glory is great in thy salvation.* In raising Him from the dead thou hast indeed crowned Him with glory in thy saving help. *Glory and great beauty shalt thou lay upon him.* Yet more wilt thou add to His splendor and great majesty when thou dost enthrone Him at thy right hand in heaven.

7. [V. 7] *For thou shalt give him a blessing forever and*

ever. The everlasting blessing thou art to bestow is this: *Thou shalt make him joyful in gladness with thy countenance.* The sight of thy face will give unspeakable joy to that human nature which our Lord has raised to thy side.[6]

8. [V. 8] *For the king hopeth in the Lord.* This king without pride and lowly of heart trusts in the Lord. *And through the mercy of the Most High he shall not be moved.* And in the mercy of the Most High, the obedience which is to bring Him even to the death of the cross will not shake His humility.

9. [V. 9] *Let thy hand be found by all thy enemies.* When thou dost sit in judgment, O King, let all thy enemies feel that power which they failed to discern beneath thy lowly estate. *Let thy right hand find out all them that hate thee.* May the light of glory in which thou reignest at the Father's right hand search out on the day of judgment and punish all who bore thee malice, since here below they took no cognizance of that glory.

10. [V. 10] *Thou shalt make them as an oven of fire.* At thy bidding the consciousness of their evil-doing will become a fiery furnace within them. *In the time of thy anger,* when thou dost openly come as Judge. *The Lord shall trouble them in His wrath, and fire shall devour them.* Thereupon, whirled away by the Lord's vengeance, a prey to remorse of conscience, they will be consigned to devouring flames for all eternity.

11. [V. 11] *Their fruit shalt thou destroy from the earth.* Because it is merely earthly, thou wilt rid the earth of their fruit. *And their seed from among the children of men.* Thou shalt wipe out their works; in other words, thou wilt not reckon those they have led astray among the sons of men whom thou hast called to an everlasting inheritance.

12. [V. 12] *For they have intended evils against thee.* Such is the chastisement they have provoked in supposing that by putting thee to death they would avert the evils they dreaded hadst thou become their king. *They devised counsel, which they have not been able to establish.* They formed this plan when they said: *It is expedient that one should die for all.*[1] They could not fulfil it, since they did not know what they were saying.

13. [V. 13] *For thou shalt make them turn their back:* thou wilt rank them among those from whom thou dost turn away with disregard and disdain. *In thy remnants thou shalt prepare their face.* What thou dost set aside, namely ambitions for an earthly kingdom, will incite their insolence in the Passion for which thou dost prepare thyself.

14. [V. 14]) *Be thou exalted, O Lord, in thy own strength.* O Lord, whom they did not recognize in thy lowliness, be thou exalted in that strength of thine which they thought to be weakness. *We will sing and praise thy power.* Our hearts and deeds shall celebrate and make known thy wonders.

First Discourse on Psalm 21

1. [Verse 1] *Unto the end, for the morning protection, a Psalm of David.* Unto the end, or for our Lord Jesus Christ, who Himself proclaims His own resurrection. For it was in the morning of the first day of the week that He rose from the dead[1] and was thereby admitted into eternal life, where death shall no more have dominion over Him.[2] The whole Psalm is spoken in the Person of our crucified Lord. It opens, notice, with the words He used when, hanging on the cross, He uttered a great cry, thus signify-

ing the old self whose mortality He had assumed. Together with Him, then, our former nature has been nailed
to the cross.[3]

2. [V. 2] *O God, my God, look upon me, why hast
thou forsaken me far from my salvation?*[4] Thou art far
from coming to my aid, since salvation is far from sinners.[5]
The words of my sins: for the prayer I utter is not that of
a righteous man but of one laden with sins. He who thus
prays nailed to the cross is indeed our old self who does
not even know why God has forsaken him.[6] Or the text
may run: *Far from my salvation* are *the words of my sins.*

3. [V. 3] *O my God, I shall cry to thee by day, and
thou wilt not hear.*[7] My God, when things go well in this
life, I shall beg thee not to alter them, and thou wilt pay
no heed, because this cry of mine will be that of my sins.
And by night, and it shall not be reputed as folly in me.
And when things go badly here below, then undoubtedly
shall I beg thee to prosper my ways, and again thou wilt
return no answer. Thou dost act thus not to drive me to
foolishness, but rather to teach me what thou wouldst
have me implore of thee; no longer in these words of sin
which desire a fleeting life, but in the supplications of one
turned wholly towards thyself, to possess life everlasting.

4. [V. 4] *But thou dwellest in the holy place, the praise
of Israel.* Thou dwellest in the holy of holies, and therefore
thou dost ignore the impure prayers of sin. Thou art the
glory of him who keeps his eyes upon thee, not of him
who sought his own glory by eating of the forbidden
fruit, so that when his bodily eyes were opened,[8] he tried
to escape from thy sight.

5. [V. 5] *In thee have our fathers hoped.* All the just
who have sought not their own glory but thine *have hoped,
and thou hast delivered them.*

6. [V. 6] *They cried to thee, and they were saved.* Their prayer came unto thee; because it was not in sinful words far removed from salvation, thou didst therefore deliver them. *They trusted in thee and were not confounded.* They placed their trust in thee, and thou didst not betray the trust, for their hope did not play them false.

7. [V. 7] *But I am a worm and no man.* Now I no longer speak as Adam, but I, Jesus Christ, speak in my own name: without begetting[9] was I born in human flesh, that as man I might be above men, yet in such a manner that human pride should perhaps stoop to imitate my abasement. *The reproach of men and the outcast of the people.* My lowliness has made me the butt of men's ridicule, so that they could say by way of outrage and abuse: *Be thou His disciple,*[10] and so lead the rabble to despise me.

8. [V. 8] *All that caught sight of me fell to mocking.* I was the laughingstock of all who looked on me. *They spoke with the lips and wagged the head.* Their hearts were silent: they merely spoke with their lips.

9. For tossing their heads in derision, they cried: [V. 9] *He hoped in the Lord, let Him deliver him; let Him save him, seeing He delighteth in him.* Such were their words, but they flowed merely from their lips.

10. [V. 10] *For thou art He that hast drawn me out of the womb.* Thy hand drew me forth, not only from a virginal womb, for to be drawn out of his mother's womb is the law of every human being; but thou hast also drawn me out of the womb of the Jewish race, that womb which still envelops in darkness all those unborn as yet to the light of Christ, who place their salvation in the exterior observance of the Sabbath, in circumcision, and suchlike ceremonies. *My hope from the breasts of my mother.* My hope, O God, not only from the moment I fed at the

Virgin's breast, for thou wast my hope long before; but from the time thou didst draw me not only from the womb but from the breasts of the synagogue, in order to preserve me from being fed on formal observances.

11. [V. 11] *I was strengthened in thee from the womb:* the womb of the synagogue which rejected me instead of bearing me; and if I did not fall, it was because thou didst uphold me. *From my mother's womb thou art my God.* Yes, *from my mother's womb,* for notwithstanding my human birth I never became unmindful of thee like a mere infant.

12. *Thou art my God,* [V. 12] *depart not from me, for tribulation is very near.* Since thou art my God, do not depart from me, because tribulation is at hand; it has already beset my body. *For there is none to help me:* who will help me, if not thou?

13. [V. 13] *Many calves have surrounded me:* A horde of dissolute ruffians has encircled me. *Fat bulls have besieged me.* And their ringleaders in their turn have hemmed me in, triumphant at my overthrow.

14. [V. 14] *They have opened their mouths against me.* Their lips have given vent, not to the words of thy Holy Scriptures, but to the cries of their own passions against me. *As a lion ravening and roaring:* This lion's prey was myself, when I was seized and led forth to die; and its roaring: *Crucify Him, crucify Him!*[11]

15. [V. 15] *I was poured out like water, and all my bones were scattered.* I was poured out like water when my persecutors fell to the ground, and my disciples, who formed the framework of my Body, the Church, left me, scattered by fear.[12] *My heart is become like molten wax in the midst of my belly.* The words which Wisdom has recorded concerning me in the sacred books were un-

comprehended as if hard and obscure; but when the fire of my sufferings was applied, it melted them, so to say, showed them up clearly and enshrined them in the memory of my Church.

16. [V. 16] *My strength is dried up like a potsherd.* My sufferings have shriveled up my strength, not like grass, but like clay which fire bakes all the harder. *And my tongue hath cleaved to my jaws.* Those who were to be my mouthpiece have observed my precepts in their own lives. *And thou hast brought me down into the dust of death.* Thou hast thrown me into the hands of evildoers marked out for death, whom the wind will sweep like dust from the face of the earth.[13]

17. [V. 17] *For many dogs have encompassed me.* I have been hemmed in by a pack of hounds, barking not in the name of truth, but in the name of their tradition. *The council of the malignant hath besieged me. They have dug my hands and feet.*[14] They have pierced my hands and feet with nails.

18. [V. 18] *They have numbered all my bones.* They have marked every bone in my body stretched on the wood of the cross. *And they have looked and stared upon me.* The same men, with no change of heart, stood watching and gloating over me.

19. [V. 19] *They parted my garments amongst them, and upon my vesture they cast lots.*

20. [V. 20] *But thou, O Lord, remove not thy help to a distance from me.* But do thou, O Lord, raise me to life again without delay, not at the end of the world like the rest of mankind. *Look towards my defense.* Watch over me, that they do me no harm.

21. [V. 21] *Deliver my soul from the sword:* Preserve my soul from tongues which cause dissension, *and my only*

one from the hand of the dog. Rescue my Church from
the clutches of this nation so clamorous on behalf of its
traditions.

22. [V. 22] *Save me from the lion's mouth.* Save me
from the maw of this world's empire. *And my lowliness
from the horns of the unicorns.* Preserve my humble state
from the arrogance of the proud who would eclipse all
men and brook no rival.

23. [V. 23] *I will declare thy name to my brethren.*
I will proclaim thy renown to the humble who are my
brethren, and who love one another as I have loved them.[15]
In the midst of the church will I extol thee. With joy I
shall make known thy glory throughout my Church.

24. [V. 24] *Ye that fear the Lord, praise Him.* All you
that worship the Lord, seek His honor, not your own.
All ye seed of Jacob, magnify Him. Glorify God, you
who are all sons of him who is to be served by his elder
brother.

25. [V. 25] *Let all the seed of Israel fear Him.* Let all
who have been regenerated to a new life and restored to
the vision of God pay Him reverence. *Because He hath
not slighted nor despised the supplication of the poor man.*
He has heeded the supplication, the appeal, that is, of the
poor man devoid of ostentation, a stranger to frivolous
pomp; not the appeal of the man who cried to God in
sinful words and refused to abandon his foolish life.
Neither hath He turned away His face from me, as He did
to the man who complained: Thou dost not answer when
I cry out to thee.[16] *And when I cried to Him, He heard
me.*

26. [V. 26] *With thee is my praise.* For I do not seek
glory for myself, since I find my glory in thee who dwellest in the holy place. And thou who art the praise of

Israel dost give ear to the Holy One who now beseeches thee. *In a great church I will confess to thee:* I will bless thee in the Church throughout the whole world. *I will pay my vows in the sight of them that fear Him.* I will offer the sacraments of my body and blood in the sight of His worshipers.

27. [V. 27] *The poor shall eat and be filled.*[17] Those who are humble, who despise the world, shall eat their fill and become like me, so as neither to desire this world's abundance nor to fear its want. *And they shall praise the Lord that seek Him.* Praise of the Lord is the outpouring of the soul filled with His fulness. *Their hearts shall live forever and ever,* for He Himself is the food of the heart.

28. [V. 28] *All the ends of the earth shall remember and shall be converted to the Lord.* They shall recall to mind; for God had been forgotten by the nations born in death and bent on outward things; but henceforth the furthest dwellers on earth will come back to the Lord. *And all the kindreds of the Gentiles shall adore in His sight:* All the races of the universe will offer Him worship within their own hearts.

29. [V. 29] *For the kingdom is the Lord's, and He shall have dominion over the nations.* It is to the Lord, not to men of pride, that empire belongs; and He shall hold sway over the nations.

30. [V. 30] *All the rich ones of the earth have eaten and have adored.* Even the great ones of the earth have received the body of their Lord in His lowliness, and although they have not partaken to the extent of doing as He did like the poor man, nevertheless they have adored Him. *In His sight all they that go down to the earth shall fall.* God alone witnesses the fall of all who abandon a

heavenly mode of life, and who prefer to flaunt a false happiness before men who do not perceive their ruin.

31. [V. 31] *And to Him my soul shall live:* And my soul, which in despising this world seems dead in men's sight, will forget itself in order to live in Him. *And my seed shall serve Him:* My deeds, those whom I lead to believe in Him, will serve Him.

32. [V. 32] *There shall be declared to the Lord a generation to come.* The children of the New Testament will be extolled to the glory of the Lord. *And they shall show forth*[18] *His justice:* the heralds of the Gospel will proclaim His justice. *To a people that shall be born, which the Lord hath made:* a people begotten by faith in our Lord.

SECOND DISCOURSE ON PSALM 21[1]

1. What God would not permit His Scriptures to pass over in silence, we too may not pass over in silence. And you shall listen to it. Our Lord's passion, as we know, happened but once; Christ died once, the just for the unjust.[2] And we know, we possess it as certain and hold with unshakable faith, *that Christ rising again from the dead, dieth now no more, and death shall no more have dominion over Him.*[3] These are the Apostle's words. Yet, for fear we should forget what occurred but once, it is re-enacted every year for us to remember. Does Christ die as often as the celebration of Easter comes round? No; the yearly remembrance brings before our eyes, in a way, what once happened long ago and stirs in us the same emotions as if we beheld our Lord hanging upon the cross; not in mockery, of course, but as believers. For as He hung on the tree He was mocked; seated in heaven He is worshiped.

Or rather, is He not still being mocked, though now our
anger is not directed against the Jews, who at any rate
derided Him as He was dying, not when He was reigning?
And who is there that even today derides Christ? Would
there were but one, would there were but two, would
they could be numbered! All the chaff of His own threshing floor mocks Him, and the wheat groans to witness its
Lord insulted. I would groan over it with you; indeed,
it is the season for mourning. We are celebrating our
Lord's passion; it is the season for sighing and weeping,
the season for making confession and supplication. Yet
who among us is capable of shedding tears in proportion
to such immense sorrow? But what does the prophet say
about it? *Who will give water to my head and a fountain
of tears to my eyes?*[4] If there really were a fountain of
tears in our eyes, even that would not be enough. Christ
is being mocked when the truth is quite clear, when nobody can say: "I did not understand." He who possesses
the whole round world is offered a part of it. He who sits
at the right hand of the Father is told: "See what thou
hast here"; and instead of the whole world He is shown
Africa only.[5]

2. What, brethren, are we to make of the words we
have just heard? If only they could be written with our
tears! Who was the woman who came in with the ointment?[6] Of what was she a type? Surely, of the Church?
What did this ointment typify? Was it not that sweet odor
of which the Apostle declares: *We are the good odor of
Christ in every place?*[7] The Apostle was referring to the
Church herself, and in saying *We are* he was speaking to
the faithful. Now what did he say? We are the fragrant
perfume of Christ in every place. Paul has told us that
all the faithful are the sweet odor of Christ in every place,

and now these people contradict him, saying that Africa alone has a pleasant perfume, the world at large reeks of corruption. Who is it that says we are the good odor of Christ in every place? The Church. This fragrance was typified by that box of ointment with which our Lord was anointed. Let us see if our Lord Himself does not bear witness to it. Some who thought of their own gain, being covetous and dishonest, in particular Judas himself, complained about that ointment, saying: *To what purpose is this waste?* The precious substance might have been sold and benefited the poor. He wished to make merchandise of the sweet odor of Christ. And what did our Lord reply? *Why do you trouble the woman? For she hath wrought a good work upon me.* And what need I add, since He Himself said: *Wheresoever this gospel shall be preached in the whole world, that also which this woman hath done shall be told.*[8] Is there anything to add to this, or anything to take away? Is there any reason why we should lend our ears to calumniators? Was our Lord lying, or was He deceived? Let them take their choice which to say: either the Truth has spoken falsely or the Truth has been deceived. *Wheresoever this gospel shall be preached.* And as though you were asking Him: "But where shall it be preached?" He goes on, *In the whole world.* Let us listen to the Psalm and see whether it says the same thing. Let us listen to its song of lament, and truly there is reason for mourning when it falls upon deaf ears. I wonder, brethren, whether this Psalm is being read today among the Donatists? I ask you, my brethren, I confess to you, Christ's mercy is my witness: are they made of stone so that they cannot hear? What could be said more clearly even to the deaf? Christ's passion is set forth as clearly here as in the Gospel, and the Psalm was composed I know not how many years before our Lord was born of the Virgin Mary: the Psalmist was a herald announcing the Judge to come. Let us study it as fully as our limited space of time permits, not as fully as the promptings of our sorrow would move us, but, as I said, as fully as the short space of time permits.

3. [V. 2] *O God, my God, look upon me; why hast thou forsaken me?* This first verse we heard from the cross, when our Lord cried: *Eli, Eli: My God, my God, Lama sabachthani: why hast thou forsaken me?*[9] The Evangelist has translated the words, telling us that He said in Hebrew: *My God, my God, why hast thou forsaken me?* What did our Lord mean? God had not forsaken Him, since He Himself was God. Beyond all doubt the Son of God was God, beyond all doubt the Word of God was God. Listen to the first words of that Evangelist who poured forth what he had drunk in from our Lord's breast.[10] Let us see whether Christ is God: *In the beginning was the Word, and the Word was with God, and the Word was God.* That very Word which was God *was made flesh and dwelt among us.*[11] And when the Word of God was made flesh, He hung upon the cross and cried: *My God, my God, look upon me; why hast thou forsaken me?* Why were these words used, if not because we were present there, because the Church is Christ's Body?[12] To what end did He exclaim: *My God, my God, look upon me; why hast thou forsaken me?* except as it were to draw our attention and tell us: "This Psalm is written about me"? *Far from my salvation are the words of my sins.* What sin could be imputed to Him *who did no sin,* as it is written, *neither was guile found in His mouth?*[13] How then can He say *my sins,* unless He Himself is pray-

ing on behalf of our sins, and making our sins His own, so
as to make His justice ours also?

4. [V. 3] *O my God, I shall cry to thee by day, and
thou wilt not hear; and by night, and it shall not be reputed
as folly in me.* He was speaking of me, of you, of the other
man; for He was bearing with Him His Body, the Church.
Surely, brethren, you do not suppose that when our Lord
cried: *My father, if it be possible, let this chalice pass from
me*,[14] He was afraid to die? The soldier is not braver than
his commander. It is enough for the servant to be like his
master.[15] Paul, the soldier of Christ the King, declares:
*I am straitened between two, having a desire to be dissolved
and to be with Christ.*[16] He desires death so as to be with
Christ, and is Christ Himself afraid of death? No, but
since He bore our weakness, He spoke thus for the sake
of those who are members of His Body and yet are afraid
of death. Hence this prayer was the prayer not of the
Head but of His own members, as likewise the words
which follow: *By day and by night I have cried, and thou
wilt not hear.* Many cry out in trouble and are not heard:
but this is for their well-being and not to show their folly.
Paul cried out to be rid of the sting of the flesh, yet he was
not set free from it by way of reply; rather he was told:
*My grace is sufficient for thee, for power is made perfect
in infirmity.*[17] So he went unheard, not to manifest his
folly but to increase his wisdom, that man may understand
that God is a physician, and trouble a saving remedy, not
a doom and a penalty. Under medical treatment you are
cauterized, you are cut, you cry out; the physician does
not trouble about your wishes but about restoring your
health.

5. [V. 4] *But thou dwellest in the holy place, the praise
of Israel.* Thou dwellest among those whom thou hast

sanctified, enabling them to understand that some thou dost refuse to hear for their own interest, while others thou hearest for their condemnation. Paul went unheard, and this for his good; the devil was heard, but for his condemnation. He asked that he might tempt Job, and the request was granted him.[18] The demons asked that they might enter into the swine, and were given permission.[19] The demons obtained a hearing, the Apostle did not; but they were heard for their condemnation, the Apostle went unheeded for his salvation; for *it shall not be reputed as folly in me. But thou dwellest in the holy place, the praise of Israel.*

Why dost thou not hear even thine own? Why am I repeating all this? Remember how we always say, "Thanks be to God."[20] Besides, there is a great concourse here, and some have come who are not in the habit of coming. I tell you all, that a Christian enduring trials is being tested, unless he has forsaken his God. For when all goes well with a man, the Christian is left to himself. Fire is put into a furnace, and indeed the goldsmith's furnace has a deep and mysterious meaning. There we find both gold and chaff, and there too fire working in a confined space. The fire is the same, yet its effects are different; it reduces the chaff to ashes, it frees the gold from its impurities. Now those in whom God dwells are undoubtedly improved under tribulation, they are refined like gold. And if perchance our enemy the devil should ask leave to try some one, and be allowed to do so, either by some bodily ill or by some loss or bereavement, the sufferer must keep his heart firmly fixed on the One who does not withdraw Himself. Even if God seems to turn His ear away from his laments, yet He heaps mercy upon his entreaties. He who made us knows what to do; He knows how to remake us. He who built the house is a good builder; and if anything in it has fallen into decay, He knows how to repair it.

6. [V. 5] And notice how the speaker continues: *In thee have our fathers hoped; they have hoped, and thou hast delivered them.* We know from having read it how many of our fathers God delivered because they hoped in Him. He brought forth the whole people of Israel from the land of Egypt;[21] He rescued the three youths from the fiery furnace;[22] He delivered Daniel from the den of lions; He saved Susanna from the false accusation.[23] They all called upon Him and were delivered. Did He fail His own Son, so as not to listen to Him as He hung upon the cross? How comes it that He was not delivered on the spot, when He cried: *In thee have our fathers hoped, and thou hast delivered them?*

7. [V. 7] *But I am a worm and no man. A worm and no man.* Truly, man is a worm as well; but He is *a worm and no man.* Why no man? Because He is God. Why then did He so abase Himself as to say *a worm?* Is it because a worm is born of flesh without coition, as Christ was of the Virgin Mary? Both a worm then, and yet no man. Why a worm? Because He was mortal, because He was born of the flesh, because He was born without human generation. Why is He no man? Because *in the beginning was the Word, and the Word was with God and the Word was God.*[24]

8. *The reproach of men and the outcast of the people.* See how much He suffered. But now, before the recital of His passion, in order that we may approach it with greater sorrow, consider first how much He suffers, and then consider why He suffers. What was the fruit of it all? Observe, our fathers hoped, and they were brought out

from the land of Egypt. And, as I have said, so many have
called upon God and been delivered at once, without waiting for the life to come. Job, for instance, at the devil's
request was handed over to him, rotting and full of worms;
yet in this life he regained his health and recovered twice
as much as he had lost.[25] But our Lord was scourged and
there was none to help; He was defiled with spittle and
there was none to help; He was struck with blows and
there was none to help; He was crowned with thorns,
there was none to help; He was raised on the tree, there
was none to rescue Him. He cries out: *My God, my God,
why hast thou forsaken me?*[26] and is given no help. Why,
my brethren, why? What did He gain by suffering so
much? All these sufferings of His are the price of something. Let us recount what cost Him so much and let us
see what He says. First we must inquire what He suffered,
and then why He suffered, and let us realize how greatly
those men are Christ's enemies, who acknowledge that He
has endured such sufferings and yet conceal the reason.
So we must listen to the whole matter in this Psalm, both
what and why He suffered. Bear in mind these two points,
what and why. First let me explain what. We need not
dwell at length on this, and thus the actual words of the
Psalm will reach you the more forcibly. See what our
Lord suffers, take heed, Christians: *The reproach of men
and the outcast of the people.*

9. [V. 8, 9] *All they that saw me fell to mocking, they
spoke with the lips and wagged the head. He hoped in
the Lord, let Him deliver him; let Him save him, seeing
He delighteth in him.* But why did they speak thus? Because He had become man, they treated Him as a man and
nothing more.

10. [V. 10] *For thou art He that hast drawn me out of*

the womb. Would they have spoken as they did against the Word which was in the beginning, that Word which was with God? That Word by whom all things were made was not drawn forth from the womb except when the Word was made flesh and dwelt among us. *For thou hast drawn me out of the womb: my God*[27] *from the breasts of my mother.* Before the ages thou wast my Father, from my infancy thou art my God.

11. [V. 11] *I was cast upon thee from the womb:* that thou alone shouldst be my hope, in my state as man, as weak, as the Word made flesh. *From my mother's womb thou art my God.* It is not as coming from thyself that thou art my God, for in that relation thou art my Father: but from my human birth thou art my God.

12. [V. 12] *Depart not from me, for tribulation is very near, for there is none to help me.* Consider Him in His abandonment; and woe to ourselves if He should abandon us, *for there is none to help.*

13. [V. 13] *Many calves have surrounded me; fat bulls have besieged me.* These are the people and their leaders: the people, or the calves without number; their leaders, the bulls in their strength.

14. [V. 14] *They have opened their mouths against me, as a lion ravening and roaring.* Listen to their roaring in the Gospel: *Crucify Him, crucify Him!*[28]

15. [V. 15] *I am poured out like water, and all my bones are scattered.* He calls His staunch ones His bones; for bones stand firm in the body. When did He scatter His bones? When He said to them: *Behold I send you as lambs in the midst of wolves.*[29] He scattered His staunch ones, and He was poured forth like water. Now when water is poured out it either cleanses or irrigates. Christ has been poured forth like water, the filthy have been

cleansed, men's minds have been bedewed. *My heart is become like wax melting in the midst of my bowels.* His bowels symbolize the weak ones in His Church. How has His heart become like wax? His heart is His Scripture, or rather His wisdom enclosed in the Scriptures. The Scriptures were a closed book which no one understood; our Lord was crucified and then the Scriptures melted like wax, so that even the weakest might penetrate their meaning. That is why the veil of the temple was rent,[30] because what had been veiled has been unveiled.

16. [V. 16] *My strength is dried up like a potsherd.* A superb expression: my name has been established all the more firmly by my suffering. For just as a potsherd is soft before it is baked but firm after baking, so before the Passion our Lord's name was despised, but after the Passion it was honored. *And my tongue hath cleaved to my jaws.* As that member of our body is of use only for speaking, so He declared that His preachers, His tongue, had cleaved to His jaws, because it was from His inner life they were to draw wisdom. *And thou hast brought me down into the dust of death.*

17. [V. 17] *For many dogs have encompassed me, the council of the malignant hath besieged me.* Here, too, look at the Gospel. *They have dug my hands and my feet.* Then were those wounds made, the scars of which were handled by that doubting disciple who said: *Unless I put my fingers into the scars of His wounds I will not believe.* When He said to him: *Come, put in thy hand, faithless one,* he put in his hand and cried out: *My Lord and my God!* And our Lord replied: *Because thou hast seen me, thou hast believed; blessed are they that see not and believe.*[31] *They have dug my hands and my feet.*

18. [V. 18] *They have numbered all my bones:* when

He was stretched out hanging on the tree. No words can better describe the stretching of His body upon the tree than these: *They have numbered all my bones.*

19. [V. 19] *And they have looked and stared upon me:* They looked and did not understand; they stared and did not see. They had eyes for His body but not a heart that could penetrate to the Word. *They parted my garments amongst them.* His garments are His sacraments. Notice, brethren; His garments, His sacraments could be parted through heresies, but there was a vesture there that nobody divided. *And upon my vesture they cast lots.* Now the *coat,* the Evangelist tells us, *was woven from the top,*[32] woven in heaven, woven by the Father, woven by the Holy Spirit. What is this coat but charity, which nobody can divide? What is this coat but unity? They draw lots for it, but nobody divides it. Heretics have been able to divide the sacraments among themselves, but charity they have not divided. And being unable to divide it, they withdrew; but it remains entire. To some it has fallen by lot; he who possesses it is safe. Nobody can dislodge him from the Catholic Church, and if any one outside the Church begins to possess it, he is brought inside, as the olive branch was brought into the ark by the dove.[33]

20. [V. 20] *But thou, O Lord,* remove not thy help to *a distance.* And so it was: after three days He rose again. *Look towards my defense.*

21. [V. 21] *Deliver my soul from the sword:* in other words, from death. For the sword is a blade, and by a blade the Psalmist would have us understand death. *And my only one from the hand of the dog. My soul, my only one,* Head and Body; His Church He calls His *only one; from the hand,* that is, from the power of the dog. Who are the dogs? Those who bark like dogs, without knowing

why. Nobody is hurting them, yet they bark. What harm does a passer-by do to a dog? Yet it will bark. They who rage blindly, not perceiving against whom or in what cause, these are the dogs.

22. [V. 22] *Save me from the lion's mouth.* You know who the roaring lion is, prowling round and seeking some one to devour.[34] *And my lowliness from the horns of the unicorns.* The unicorns must represent the proud; and therefore he added *my lowliness.*

23. You have heard what He suffered and how He prayed to be delivered from these sufferings. Now let us consider why He suffered. Just reflect, brethren; how can he be a Christian who does not belong to those for whom Christ suffered? We already know what He suffered. His bones were counted, He was mocked, His garments were divided and they cast lots for His coat, men surrounded Him raging with fury and all His bones were scattered. We listen to the story and read it in the Gospels. Now let us look into the reason. O Christ, Son of God, hadst thou not willed it, thou wouldst not have suffered; show us the fruit of thy passion. Listen, He replies, to the fruit: it is not that I am silent, but that men are deaf. Listen, He replies, to the fruit of all these sufferings of mine. [V. 23] *I will declare thy name to my brethren.* Let us see whether He declares God's name to His brethren in any separate part. *I will declare thy name to my brethren; in the midst of the church will I extol thee.* That is how it is done. But let us see what this church is. For He has said: *In the midst of the church I will sing thy praise.* Let us look at the church for which He suffered.

24. [V. 24] *Ye that fear the Lord, praise Him.* Wherever God is feared and praised, there you find the Church of Christ. See, my brethren, whether the singing of Amen

and Alleluia all over the world is for no reason. Is not God feared there? Is not God praised there? Donatus has left us, saying: "God is not feared at all; the whole world has come to grief." You have no reason to declare that the whole world has come to grief. So a small part of it in Africa has remained faithful? Does Christ say nothing, then, to stop these men's mouths? Does He say nothing to silence the tongues that utter such things? Let us look and perhaps we shall find something. Now it is we who are told: *In the midst of the church.* The Church He speaks of is ours. *Ye who fear the Lord, praise Him.* Let us see whether these folk praise the Lord, and find out whether He is speaking of them and whether it is in the midst of their church that He is praised. How can they praise Christ when they say: "He has lost the whole world, the devil has robbed Him of all of it, and He remains only in one portion"? However, let us look a little further, let Him declare Himself more openly, let Him speak more plainly; let there be no room for inter-pretation or conjecture. *All ye seed of Jacob, magnify Him.* Perhaps they will go further and say: "We are the seed of Jacob." Let us see whether they are.

25. [V. 25] *Let all the seed of Israel fear Him.* Again they may say: "We are the seed of Israel"; let us grant them that, let them say it. *Because He hath not slighted nor despised the supplication of the poor.* What poor? Not those that rely upon themselves. Let us judge whether they are poor who say: "We are the righteous." Christ cries out: *Far from my salvation are the words of my sins.* But let them go on saying what they will. *Neither hath He turned away His face from me; and when I cried to Him, He heard me.* Why did He hear him? To what purpose?

26. [V. 26] *With thee is my praise.* To God he has

entrusted His praise, teaching us not to rely upon man. Let them continue saying what they will. Already they are beginning to feel the fire; it is coming nearer; there is no one that can hide himself from its heat.[35] But supposing they say further: "We too have entrusted our praise to Him, we too do not rely upon ourselves"; well, let them say it. *In a great church I will confess to thee.* Here, I think, He touches them to the quick. Now what is a great church, brethren? Surely a tiny portion of the world is not a great church? A great church is one which embraces the whole world. However, should any one wish to contradict Christ, saying: "Thou hast said, *In a great church I will confess to thee:* tell us, which great church? Thou art reduced to a morsel of Africa, the rest of the world thou hast lost; thou didst shed thy blood for the whole world, but thou hast been defeated by an usurper." We have spoken thus to our Lord as if by way of inquiry, though we know what we intend to answer. Let us suppose, then, that we do not know what He is going to say; would not His answer be: "Peace; I am going to say what nobody can call in question"? Let us await His reply, then. I wanted simply to state the matter and not let men interpret these words of Christ in any other way. *In a great church.* And you tell us that He is confined to a remote corner. And still they dare to say: "Ours is the great Church; what about Bagai and Tamugade?"[36] And unless Christ gives an answer which will stop their mouths, they will go on to say that Numidia alone is the great Church.

27. Let us see, let us listen to our Lord again: *I will pay my vows in the sight of them that fear Him.* What are these vows of His? The sacrifice He offered to God. Do you know what kind of sacrifice? The faithful know what vows He offered in the sight of them that fear Him;

for there follows: [V. 27] *The poor shall eat and be filled.* Blessed are the poor, who eat that they may be filled. It is the poor who eat. As for the rich, they are not filled because they are not hungry. The poor shall eat; among them was Peter the fisherman, among them was the other fisherman John and James his brother, among them too was Matthew the publican. These were among the poor who ate and were filled, because they suffered like the victim they consumed. In giving His supper, He has given His passion; the man who suffers as He did is filled. The poor have done as He did; for they have suffered in order to follow in Christ's footsteps. *The poor shall eat.* But why the poor? *And they shall praise the Lord that seek Him.* The rich praise themselves, the poor praise the Lord. Why are they poor? Because they praise the Lord and seek the Lord. The Lord is the wealth of the poor; therefore their home is empty, while their hearts are full of wealth. Let the rich aim at filling their coffers; the poor aim at filling their heart; and when they have filled it, they that seek Him praise the Lord. And see, brethren, in what treasure they are rich that are truly poor; their wealth is not in the money chest, nor in the granary, nor in the storehouse: *Their hearts shall live forever and ever.*

28. Now pay attention. Our Lord has suffered; He has endured all you have heard. We inquire why He has suffered, and He began to tell us: *I will declare thy name to my brethren; in the midst of the church will I extol thee.* But these men still say: "This is the Church." *Let all the seed of Israel fear Him.* They repeat: "We are the seed of Israel." *Because He hath not slighted nor despised the supplication of the poor man.* Again they say: "We are they." *Neither hath He turned away His face from me.* Christ

our Lord has not turned away from Himself, in other words from the Church which is His Body. *With thee is my praise.* You wish to praise yourselves. But they reply: "Indeed, we also praise Him." *I will pay my vows in the sight of them that fear Him.* The sacrifice of peace, the sacrifice of love, the sacrifice of His Body, all this the faithful know already; I cannot now discuss it. *I will pay my vows in the sight of them that fear Him.* Let the publicans eat, let the fishermen eat, let them be fed, let them imitate the Lord, let them suffer, let them be satisfied. Our Lord Himself has died, the poor die too; the death of the disciples is united to the death of the Master. Why? Show me the results.

[V. 28] *All the ends of the earth shall remember and shall be converted to the Lord.* There you are, brethren. Why do you ask us what answer to give to the Donatists? Look at the Psalm; among us it is read today, and among them too it is read today. Let us write it on our foreheads, let us go forward with it. Our tongue must take no rest, it must repeat the words: See, Christ has suffered; see, the Merchant displays His gains, see the price He gave in shedding His blood. He carried the price of us in a sackcloth bag: He was pierced with a lance, the bag was rent, and the price of the whole world poured out. What are you going to answer me, you heretic? That it is not the price of the whole world? That only Africa has been redeemed? You dare not say: "The whole world was redeemed, but has been lost." From what usurper has Christ suffered so severely as to forfeit His own possession? Look, *all the ends of the earth shall remember and shall be converted to the Lord.* Let this satisfy you, and let Him speak. Had He said "the ends of the earth," and not *all the ends of the earth,* they might have been able to say:

"Why, we have the ends of the earth in Mauretania."
Actually He said *all the ends of the earth*. You heretic, He
said *all*. What way out have you to escape the difficulty?
You have no way out, but there is a way in.

29. I do not wish to discuss this further, for fear any
one should attribute value to words of mine; I beg you to
go to the Psalm, to read the Psalm. There you find how
Christ has suffered, how His blood has been outpoured:
there you will find our Redeemer and the price we have
cost Him. Tell me, what did He buy? Why do we ask?
Supposing some one should say to me: "Why do you ask,
you simpleton? You have the book in your hands, there
you have what He paid; look and see what He bought.
Look, there you have it: *All the ends of the earth shall remember, and shall be converted to the Lord*. The ends of
the earth shall remember." But the heretics have forgotten,
even though they hear it every year. Do you suppose they
listen when their reader recites: *All the ends of the earth
shall remember, and shall be converted to the Lord?* Well,
perhaps that is but one verse: your thoughts were elsewhere, you were chatting with your neighbor while it
was being read. Wake up and listen, for he repeats it and
knocks on deaf men's ears: *And all the kindreds of the
Gentiles shall adore in His sight*. He is still deaf, he does
not hear, we must knock again. [V. 29] *For the kingdom
is the Lord's, and He shall have dominion over the nations.*
Keep these three verses in mind, brethren. Today they
have been chanted even in their assembly; or perhaps they
have erased them. Believe me, my brethren, I am so agi-
tated, so shocked, that I marvel at this astounding deafness
and hardness of their hearts; indeed I sometimes doubt
whether they have this text in their copies. Today all are
hastening to the church, today all are attentively listening

to this Psalm, every one is listening with heart uplifted. But supposing they are not attentive, is there only the one verse: *All the ends of the earth shall remember, and shall be converted to the Lord?* You are waking up, but you are still rubbing your eyes: *And all the kindreds of the Gentiles shall adore in His sight.* Shake off your sleep, you are still drowsy. Listen: *For the kingdom is the Lord's, and He shall have dominion over the nations.*

30. Whether they have anything else to say, I cannot tell; let them dispute with the Scriptures, not with us. Now here is the book itself, let them contend against that. Where is that saying of theirs: "We preserved the Scriptures from being burnt"?[37] They have been preserved to burn you. What did you preserve? Open the book and read; you have preserved it and you attack it. Why did you preserve from the flames what you would destroy with the tongue? I do not believe it, I do not believe you preserved them. I do not believe it at all; you did not preserve them. Our people are right in saying that you treacherously handed them over. He is proved the traitor who reads the will and declines to implement it. Here you are; it is read, and I follow it up; it is read, and you refuse to do so. Whose hand threw it into the flames? His who believes and follows it up, or his who is sorry there is anything to read? I do not want to know who saved it: wherever the book has been found and our Father's will has reappeared from some hiding place or other, no matter what thieves wanted to steal it or what persecutors to burn it, wherever it comes to light, it must be read. Why dispute? We are brothers, why dispute? Our Father has not died intestate. He made a will and then died: He died and He rose again. Disputes arise over the inheritance left by the dead, until the will is publicly produced. And when

the will is produced in public, all are silent for the opening
and reading of the document. The judge listens attentively,
the legal men hold their peace, the heralds procure silence,
everybody is in suspense while the words of the deceased,
unconscious in the tomb, are read. The testator lies un-
heeding in his grave, yet his words have force; Christ is
enthroned in heaven, and is His will to be gainsaid? Open
it and let us read it. We are brothers, why must we dispute? Let us calm our minds; our Father has not left us
without a will. He who made the will lives forever; He
hears our words, He recognizes His own. Let us read;
what are we quarelling about? When the whole inheritance has been found, let us hold to it. Open the will and
read in the very beginning of the Psalter: *Ask of me.*[38]
But who is speaking? Perhaps it is not Christ. Well, there
you find, *The Lord said to me: Thou art my Son, this day
have I begotten thee.*[39] So the Son of God is speaking, or
rather the Father is speaking to His Son. What, then, does
He say to the Son? *Ask of me and I will give thee the
Gentiles for thy inheritance, and the utmost parts of the
earth for thy possession.* When an estate is contested, in-
quiries are usually made among the owners of the adjoin-
ing lands, and between this or that neighbor, to find the
heir to whom it pertains by gift or purchase. Which
neighbors can supply information? Those who possess
land on the right hand and the left. But He who has no
limits to His inheritance has no neighbor. On whatever
side you turn, Christ is the owner. You have the uttermost
parts of the earth for your inheritance; come, possess it all
with me. Why do you dispute and offer only a portion?
Come here; it is for your own advantage to lose your
action, since you will have the whole. Are you still quibbling? I have read the will, yet you are still quibbling. Are

you still quibbling because He spoke of the utmost parts of the earth and not of all the utmost parts of the earth? Let us read it, then. What was read out? *All the ends of the earth shall remember and shall be converted to the Lord. And all the nations of the Gentiles shall adore in His sight. For the kingdom is the Lord's, and He shall have dominion over the nations.* His it is, not yours. Acknowledge the Lord; acknowledge the Lord's possession.

31. But you now, because you wish to hold your own goods in private and not in the general unity with Christ—for you wish to rule on earth, not to reign with Him in heaven—you possess your own establishments. And sometimes we have gone to these people to say to them: "Let us seek the truth and let us find it." And they answer: "Keep what you have: you have your sheep, I have mine; leave my sheep in peace as I leave yours." Good heavens! My sheep, his sheep—what did Christ purchase then? No; these sheep are neither mine nor thine; let them belong to Him who purchased them, Him who branded them. Neither he who planted counts for anything nor he who waters, but God who gives fruitfulness.[40] Why must I have mine and you yours? If Christ is with you, let mine go in that direction, for they are none of mine; if Christ is with us, let yours come this way, for they are none of yours. As far as possessions are concerned, let us kiss brow and hands and let there be an end of aliens.

But he says: "The possession is not mine." What means this? Let us see whether the possession is not yours; let us see whether you do not claim it for yourself. I labor for the name of Christ, you for the name of Donatus. For if you are looking for Christ, Christ is to be found everywhere. You say: "Look, here is Christ";[41] I say: "He is all over the world." Praise the Lord, ye children, praise the

name of the Lord.[42] Where does His praise begin and
where does it end? From the rising of the sun even to its
going down, praise the name of the Lord. See what
Church I am pointing out to you, see what Christ has
bought, see what He has redeemed, see for what He has
given His blood. But what is it you say? "I too gather for
Him." *He that gathereth not with me*, Christ says, *scatter-
eth*.[43] You split up unity, you seek for possessions of your
own.

And why have they the name of Christ attached to
them? Because to guarantee your own property you have
affixed to it the title of Christ. Do not some men do the
same in their own homes? To safeguard his house against
a powerful aggressor, a man will fasten to it the title of
some influential magnate. The title is a lie. The man himself wants to be the owner but wishes to have the front
of his house protected by another person's title, hoping
that when the assailant reads it he will be overawed by
the influence of the name and abstain from attacking the
house. Now this they did when they condemned the
Maximianists. They pleaded before the magistrates and
read out the decrees of their council,[44] by way of demon-
strating their claim to be regarded as bishops. Then the
magistrate asked: "Who is this other bishop of the party
of Donatus?" Their representative answered: "We
acknowledge no one but Aurelius the Catholic." For fear
of the law they mentioned only one bishop. To gain the
ear of the magistrate, they placarded the name of Christ:
they placarded their own property with His title. The
Lord is good, may He spare them, and where He finds
His own title, may He claim the possession for His own.
Mighty is His mercy to do so much for them; may He
gather together whomsoever He finds bearing the name

of Christ. And consider, brethren, when a person of power comes across his own title, is he not justified in claiming the property as his own, saying: "This man would not placard my name unless the property were mine. He has affixed my title, the property is mine; whatever I find marked with my name is mine." Would he change the title? No, the title remains as before; the ownership is changed, the title is not. Similarly with those who possess the baptism of Christ; if they return to unity, we do not change or destroy their title, but we acknowledge the title of our King, the title of our Commander. What are we to say? O wretched patrimony, let Him whose title you bear own you; you bear the title of Christ, do not be the property of Donatus.

32. We have spoken at great length, brethren; but bear in mind what has been read today. There now, I repeat it, and it must often be repeated: by this day, or rather by the mysteries celebrated on this day, I adjure you not to let these words go out of your minds. *All the ends of the earth shall remember and shall be converted to the Lord. And all the nations of the Gentiles shall adore in His sight. For the kingdom is the Lord's, and He shall have dominion over the nations.* Against Christ's ownership, so evident and so clearly proved, do not listen to the words of a deceiver. Whatever they say to contradict it, they are but men that speak; but these are the words of God.

DISCOURSE ON PSALM 22

1. [Verse 1] *A Psalm for David himself.* It is the Church who addresses Christ: *The Lord feedeth me, and*

I shall want nothing. Our Lord Jesus Christ is my shepherd; I shall lack nothing.

2. [V. 2] *He hath set me in a place of pasture.* He has led me to the faith, setting me for my sustenance in a place of springing herbage. *He hath brought me up on the water of refreshment.* He has brought me up on the water of baptism, which restores health and strength to those who have lost them.

3. [V. 3] *He hath converted my soul. He hath led me on the paths of justice for His own name's sake.* He has led me along the narrow and seldom trodden paths[1] of His justice, not for any merits of mine, but for the glory of His own name.

4. [V. 4] *For though I should walk in the midst of the shadow of death.* Should I walk in the midst of this life, which is the shadow of death, *I will fear no evils, for thou art with me.* I will fear no evils, because thou dwellest by faith in my heart; and thou art with me here, that when the shadow of death is left behind, I too may be with thee hereafter.

Thy rod and thy staff, they have comforted me. Thy chastisement resembles the shepherd's crook guiding his flock, or the staff felt by children now growing up and passing from a life of mere sensation to a life of the spirit. Far from discouraging, they have consoled me, as being but a proof of thy watchful care.

5. [V. 5] *Thou hast prepared a table before me against them that afflict me.* The rod which controlled my infancy and unreasoning youth whilst at pasture with the flock, that rod, I say, gave place to thy staff. Thereupon thou didst spread a banquet before my eyes, in which the milk of infancy was no longer to sustain me; but as one grown up I was to take solid food[2] to strengthen me in the face of

my persecutors. *Thou hast anointed my head with oil: Thou hast* gladdened my soul with spiritual joy. *And thy inebriating cup, how goodly is it!*[3] How sweet is that cup of thine which drives away all remembrance of the foolish pleasures of the past!

6. [V. 6]   *And thy mercy will follow me all the days of my life,* as long as I live in this mortal life, which is not thine but mine. *And that I may dwell in the house of the Lord unto length of days.* It will follow me not only here below, but it will also bestow upon me the freedom of the Lord's house forever and ever.

DISCOURSE ON PSALM 23

1. [Verse 1] *A Psalm for David himself, on the first day of the week.* A Psalm for David himself, touching the glorification and resurrection of our Lord, which took place early on the first day of the week, ever since known as the Lord's day.

2. *The earth is the Lord's and the fulness thereof, the world and all they that dwell therein,* since the Lord in His glory is offered to the faith of all nations, and His Church embraces the whole world. [V. 2] *For He hath founded it upon the seas.* He has built that Church on solid foundations above the floods of this world; she is to dominate and suffer no harm therefrom. *And hath prepared it upon the rivers.* As rivers flow into the sea, so do covetous men overspread the earth, yet the Church rules even such as these; mastering by God's grace the unholy desires of the worldly, she prepares herself by means of charity to receive the prize of immortality.

3. [V. 3] *Who shall ascend into the mountain of the Lord?* Who will climb to the summit of God's righteous-

ness? *Or who shall stand in His holy place?* And having reached this sanctuary founded upon the seas and prepared upon the rivers, who shall be able to stand his ground?

4. [V. 4] *The innocent in hands and clean of heart.* Who, then, can rise to such heights and remain there, but the man who is blameless in act, pure of heart? *Who hath not taken his soul in vain:* who never accounted his soul among perishable things, but realizing its immortality, set his heart upon an enduring, immutable eternity. *Nor sworn in deceit to his neighbor:* who acted towards his brethren without treachery, but with the simplicity and truth of all that is eternal.

5. [V. 5] *He shall receive a blessing from the Lord, and mercy from God his Saviour.*

6. [V. 6] *This is the generation of them that seek Him.* Such is the nature of all who seek Him, *of them that seek the face of the God of Jacob (diapsalma).*[1] They seek the face of that God who gave the birthright to the younger son.[2]

7. [V. 7] *Take away your gates, ye princes.* You who crave for domination over your fellow men, take away these gates of cupidity and fear which you have erected; otherwise they may prove a hindrance. *And be ye lifted up, O eternal gates,* gates of life everlasting, gates of renunciation of the world, and of return to God. *And the King of glory shall enter in.* Then shall enter that King in whom we may glory without pride; He has shattered the gates of death, thrown open to Himself the heavens, fulfilled His own injunction: *Rejoice, for I have overcome the world.*[3]

8. [V. 8] *Who is this King of glory?* Awe-struck with wonder, human nature asks: *Who is this King of glory?*

He is *the Lord who is strong and mighty*, whom you
thought weak and vanquished. *The Lord mighty in battle.*
Handle His scars: you will find them healed, and human
frailty restored to immortality. The glory due to the dust
of the earth was paid back in full when the Lord wrestled
with death in triumphant victory.

9. [V. 9] *Take away your gates, ye princes.* From this
point let us go straight into heaven. Let the prophet's
trumpet re-echo anew: Take away, ye heavenly princes,
those gates by which you enter with the souls of those
who adore the celestial host.[4] *And be ye lifted up, O
eternal gates.* Be ye lifted up, gates of eternal justice, love
and chastity, whereby the soul is united to the only true
God and refuses to offer many other so-called gods an
adulterous worship. *And the King of glory shall enter in.*
Yes, He will enter, this King of glory who is to sit at the
right hand of the Father to make intercession for us.[5]

10. [V. 10] *Who is this King of glory?* Whence comes
your amazement, prince of the domain of this air,[6] and
why your question: *Who is this King of glory?* Who but
the Lord of hosts, He is *the King of glory*. In a body now
risen from the dead, He who was once subjected to your
temptation now mounts above you on high; He whom
the crafty spirit tempted ascends above all the angels. Let
none of you therefore thrust himself forward to bar our
way and to make us worship him as if he were God; for
no principality, angel or power henceforth separates us
from the love of Christ.[7] Better trust the Lord than rely
on a prince;[8] if anyone glories, therefore, let him glory in
the Lord.[9] Those angel hosts do indeed play a part in the
providential ruling of the world, but *The Lord of hosts,
He is the King of glory.*

DISCOURSE ON PSALM 24

1. [Verse 1] *Unto the end, a Psalm for David himself.* Christ is here speaking in the name of His Church, for the content of the Psalm applies rather to the Christian people already converted to God.

2. *To thee, O Lord, have I lifted up my soul,* by spiritual longing, for in its unholy desires my soul lay groveling on the earth. [V. 2] *In thee, O my God, I put my trust: let me not be ashamed.* My God, my self-reliance has driven me into this human frailty. I abandoned God, wished to put myself in God's place,[1] yet was so terrified of being killed by the tiniest insect that I was forced to blush at my ridiculous pride. But now that my trust is in thee, no longer may I be put to shame.

3. [V. 3] *Neither let my enemies laugh at me.* Let not them mock me whose venomous and insidious suggestions have proved so many snares, and who with their rallying cry "Bravo, bravo" have thus degraded me. *For none of them that wait on thee shall be confounded.*

4. [V. 4] *Let them be confounded who wantonly do vain things.* Shame to those who do evil deeds for the sake of obtaining transitory benefits. *Show, O Lord, thy ways to me, and teach me thy paths.* They are neither broad nor do they lead the many to perdition; teach me the narrow paths which are thine and known to few.[2]

5. [V. 5] *Direct me in thy truth,* in my avoidance of error. *And teach me,* for by myself I have learnt nothing but falsehood. *For thou art the God of my salvation, and on thee have I waited all the day long.* Since thou hast cast me out of Paradise,[3] and I have traveled into a far country,[4] I cannot return to thee unless thou meet the

wanderer. Throughout the course of my life on earth, my return to thee has depended upon thy mercy.

6. [V. 6] *Remember, O Lord, thy bowels of compassion.* Remember, Lord, thy gracious works, for men accuse thee of seeming forgetfulness. *And that thy mercies are from the beginning of the world.* Above all, forget not that thy mercies are from eternity. Indeed they are inseparable from thee, since thou hast subjected sinful man to vanity, yet not without hope;[5] and thou hast lavished on thy creature so many and such great consolations.

7. [V. 7] *The sins of my youth and of my ignorance do not remember.* Do not store up for retribution the follies I have committed through impudent presumption or ignorance; efface them, so to speak, from thy memory. *According to thy mercy, be mindful of me*, O God. Think of me, indeed, not in terms of the chastisement which is my due, but in terms of the mercy which is thine. *For thy goodness' sake, O Lord:* not according to my desert, O Lord, but according to thy loving-kindness.

8. [V. 8] *The Lord is sweet and righteous.* The Lord is sweet in that He has so far pitied sinners and evildoers as to wipe out all their past sins. But the Lord is also righteous, for after bestowing the unmerited grace of vocation and pardon, He will look on the last day for merits proportionate to such grace. *Therefore He will give a law to sinners in the way*, for it is in order to guide them along the right path that He has first shown mercy.

9. [V. 9] *He will guide the meek in judgment.* He will train the peaceful man, and at the judgment He will not throw into consternation those who follow His will and do not resist that will by preferring their own. *He will teach the gentle His ways.* He will teach His ways, not to those who want to rush ahead as if they were more

capable of directing their own course, but to those who do not stiffen their necks or stubbornly kick when the mild yoke and the light burden are laid upon them.[6]

10. [V. 10] *All the ways of the Lord are mercy and truth.*[7] What ways, then, will He teach them, if not that mercy which is easily moved to pity, and that truth which is proof against corruption? The first He has exercised in forgiving sins, the second in apportioning our merits. Hence all the ways of the Lord are reduced to the two comings of the Son of God, the one to exercise mercy, the other judgment. That man attains to God by the path ordained, therefore, who acknowledging that he has been set at liberty through no merits of his own, lays aside his pride and from that time onwards dreads the severe scrutiny of the Judge whose gracious succor he has already experienced. *To them that seek after His covenant and His testimonies.* For it is those who in meekness and gentleness search into the covenant by which our Lord has redeemed us unto newness of life in His own blood, and study His witnesses in the Prophets and Evangelists, who recognize His mercy in His first coming, His judgment in His second.

11. [V. 11] *For thy name's sake, O Lord, thou wilt pardon my sin; for it is great.* Not only hast thou pardoned the faults I committed before I reached the faith, but the sacrifice of a contrite heart[8] will make thee deal mercifully when considering my present sin which is grievous indeed, for even the true path is by no means free from stumbling block.

12. [V. 12] *Who is the man that feareth the Lord,* and who thus advances towards wisdom? *He will appoint him a law in the way he hath chosen.* The Lord will dictate to him the ordinances governing the way he has freely

chosen to tread, so that he may no longer sin with impunity.

13. [V. 13] *His soul shall dwell in good things, and his seed shall possess the land by inheritance.* His deeds will obtain for him the secure possession of a body restored to life.

14. [V. 14] *The Lord is a firmament to them that fear Him.* Fear seems proper only to the weak, but the Lord is the strength of those who fear Him. And the name of the Lord, glorified throughout the world, supports those who look on Him with reverence. *And His covenant shall be made manifest to them.* He will make His covenant a revelation to them, for the nations and the farthest ends of the earth are Christ's heritage.

15. [V. 15] *My eyes are ever towards the Lord, for He shall pluck my feet out of the snare.*[9] I have nothing to fear from earth's perils so long as I do not gaze earthwards, for He upon whom I fix my eyes will save my feet from the snare.

16. [V. 16] *Look thou upon me and have mercy on me, for I am alone and poor,* representing as I do thy one and only people who preserve the lowly estate of thy one and only Church, which suffers neither schism nor heresy.

17. [V. 17] *The troubles of my heart are multiplied.* My heart has been sorely afflicted as I see wickedness abound and charity grow cold.[10] *Bring me out of my necessities.* Since I must needs suffer thus, so that by enduring to the end I may be saved,[11] spare me from needs such as these.

18. [V. 18] *See my abjection and my labor.* See my self-abasement; never do I take such pride in my right-

eousness as to cast myself forth from unity; see, too, my distress in enduring the unruly folk who surround me. *And forgive me all my sins.* Be appeased by these sacrifices and pardon my sins, not only the follies of my youth and ignorance before I believed in thee, but also those into which I have fallen through frailty and the darkness of this life even now that I walk by faith.

19. [V. 19] *Consider my enemies, for they are multiplied.* Not only have I encountered them outside, but even within the very communion of the Church. *They have hated me with an unjust hatred,* returning for my love a bitter grudge.

20. [V. 20] *Keep thou my soul and deliver me.* Take my soul into thy keeping for fear I should stoop so low as to imitate them, and set me free from the distress I feel at being in association with them. *I shall not be ashamed, for I have hoped in thee.* Should they make a stand against me, I shall not be put to shame, for it is in thee and not in myself that I have placed my trust.

21. [V. 21] *The innocent and the upright have adhered to me, because I have waited on thee, O Lord.* The pure and upright of heart, unlike the wicked, are united to me not by bodily presence alone, but by our common love of purity and justice. I have never abandoned thee to model myself on evildoers, but I have patiently waited upon thee and do yet wait for the final winnowing of thy harvest.

22. [V. 22] *Deliver Israel, O God, from all his tribulations.* Deliver thy people, not only from the troubles which beset them without, but also from those they endure within, for thou, O God, hast prepared thy people to enjoy the vision of thyself.

FIRST DISCOURSE ON PSALM 25

1. [Verse 1] *For David himself.* David himself may here signify, not the Mediator Christ Jesus in His humanity, but the whole Church now perfectly established in Christ.

2. *Judge me, O Lord, for I have walked in my innocence.* Be thou my judge, O Lord, for after having first received thy mercy, have I not acquired a certain merit from keeping to the path of my innocence? *And trusting in the Lord I shall not waver.* Nevertheless I place my confidence not in myself but in the Lord, and I shall abide in Him.

3. [V. 2] *Prove me, O Lord, and try me.* For fear, however, that some secret faults escape me, do thou, O Lord, try me and prove me; lay them open, not to thyself who seest all, but to myself and my fellow men. *Burn my reins and my heart.* Apply to my inmost desires and thoughts a remedy which will purify them like fire. [V. 3] *For thy mercy is before my eyes.* To save me from being entirely consumed by this fire, I fix my eyes not on any merits of my own, but on thy loving-kindness which has led me to embrace such a life. *And I am well pleased with thy truth.* I have loathed all my own falseness, whereas thy truth has delighted me; in and with that truth I have been enabled to please thee.

4. [V. 4] *I have not sat with the council of vanity.* I have not chosen for boon companions men who strive to find in the enjoyment of the transitory things of life a happiness which is impossible. *Neither will I go in with the doers of unjust things.* And because this is the root of all evil, I will not reach any secret understanding with evildoers.

5. [V. 5] *I have hated the assembly of the malignant.* In order to form this aforesaid *council of vanity,* evildoers assemble in groups, which I have held in abhorrence. *And with the wicked I will not sit.* Therefore I will not sit down among guilty men in such a company; I will never, in other words, give my approval. *And with the wicked I will not sit.*

6. [V. 6] *I will wash my hands among the innocent.* I shall work spotless deeds among thy pure ones, and with the clean of heart I shall wash these hands which are to lay hold of thy sublime mysteries.[1] *And I will compass thy altar, O Lord.*

7. [V. 7] *That I may hear the voice of thy praise,* to teach me how to praise thee. *And tell of all thy wondrous works.* When I have learned my lesson, I shall set forth all thy wonderful deeds.

8. [V. 8] *I have loved, O Lord, the beauty of thy house,* the Church; *and the place where thy glory dwelleth,* the abode in which thou art glorified.

9. [V. 9] *Take not away my soul with the wicked.* Destroy not, then, together with those who hate thee, this soul of mine which has loved thy house in all its beauty. *Nor my life with bloodthirsty men,* with the man who detests his neighbor, since both commandments beautify thy house.

10. [V. 10] *In whose hands are iniquities.* Destroy me not, I say, with the guilty and bloodthirsty committed to works of evil. *Their right hand is filled with gifts.* What was given to them to obtain eternal salvation, they have diverted to procure themselves this world's goods, thinking to make gain from religion.[2]

11. [V. 11] *But as for me, I have walked in my innocence; redeem me and have mercy on me.* May the

inestimable price of my Lord's blood avail for my perfect liberation, and amid the perils of life may thy mercy never forsake me.

12. [V. 12] *My foot hath stood in uprightness.* My love has never deviated from thy justice.[3] *In the churches I will bless thee, O Lord.* Lord, since I unite love of my neighbor to my love for thine own self, I will never leave thine elect in ignorance of the blessing thou dost bestow.

Second Discourse on Psalm 25[1]

1. During the reading from Paul the Apostle, you and I, holy brethren, heard him say: *As the truth is in Jesus to put off, according to former conversation, the old man, him who is corrupted according to deceitful lusts; and be renewed in the spirit of your mind, and put on the new man who according to God is created in justice and holiness of truth.*[2] No one must imagine that there is question here of laying aside some material object, like shedding a coat; or of putting something on externally, like wearing a garment, casting off one coat to don another. For fear so literal an interpretation should hinder men from carrying out his injunctions in a spiritual manner within their own souls, the Apostle immediately explains the signification of ridding oneself of the old man to be clothed with the new. The rest of the passage, in fact, is devoted to an explanation of this theme. He seems to be answering this question: How am I to strip off the old man and clothe myself with the new? Or am I myself to be a third person who must discard the old self which was mine, and take over a new self which was not? In that event would there not be three men, so that he who is to leave the old and attach himself to the new stands in the middle? For fear

therefore that we should be perplexed by a conception so crude, and failing to carry out the precept should find an excuse in the obscurity of the passage, the Apostle adds: *Wherefore, putting away lying, speak ye the truth.* That is the essence of putting off the old man and putting on the new. *Wherefore, putting away lying, speak ye the truth, every man with his neighbor, for we are members one of another.*

2. Let none of you imagine, brethren, that while you must tell the truth to a Christian, you may tell a lie to a pagan.[3] Speak with your neighbor. Your neighbor, like yourself, is a child of Adam and Eve. We are all kinsmen by reason of our human birth; but we are brethren in a fuller sense through the hope of a heavenly inheritance. You must treat every man as your neighbor even before he becomes a Christian. For you do not know what he is before God, you are ignorant of God's designs in his regard. So-and-so worships stones and you laugh at him; lo, one day he is converted, he adores God, and your erstwhile laughingstock possibly becomes much more religious-minded than you are. We therefore possess brethren concealed among men who are not as yet children of the Church, just as there are those concealed in the Church who are far from being one with us. Accordingly, since we are unaware of the future, let us look upon every man as our neighbor, not merely by reason of our common human nature which makes us share the same lot here below, but also by reason of our heavenly inheritance, since we do not know what he, who as yet is of no account, is destined to become.

3. Now listen to St. Paul's further instructions regarding the putting on of the new self and the putting off of the old. *Putting away lying, speak ye the truth, every*

man with his neighbor. For we are members one of another. Be angry and sin not.[4] If you fall into a rage with your servant for committing some fault, turn your anger against yourself for fear you also fall into sin. *Let not the sun go down upon your anger.*[5] That, brethren, marks the limits of its duration. For if through human frailty, if through the weakness of this mortal flesh which is our lot, anger seizes upon a Christian unawares, it must not be nursed and carried over to the morrow. Cast it out of your heart before this visible light go down, for fear the light invisible should abandon you.

Nevertheless this passage may well bear another interpretation. It may signify Christ who is the Truth, our Sun of Justice; not that sun which pagans and Manicheans worship, and even sinners behold, but that other Sun whose truth is the light of human nature and the joy of the angels. As for man, although the eyes of his heart are so weak as to shrink from His rays, they may nevertheless be strengthened by the practice of the commandments and thus enabled to contemplate Him. When this Sun has begun to dwell in man by faith, you must take care not to let the wrath which arises in you so far gain the upper hand that the sun goes down upon your anger, or rather that Christ abandons your mind. Christ will not dwell with your anger. One would suppose that He had gone down from you, whereas in reality it is you who have gone down from Him; for resentment harbored turns to hatred, and once it has become hatred you are already a murderer. *Whosoever hateth his brother*, St. John tells us, *is a murderer.*[6] And again, *Everyone that hateth his brother*, he declares, *abideth in darkness.*[7] No wonder such a man is living in darkness, since his sunlight has been quenched.

4. Possibly this is also the meaning of what you have heard in the Gospel: *The ship was in peril on the lake, and Jesus was asleep.*[8] Now we too are sailing across a kind of lake where there is no lack of wind and storm; every day the trials of this life are on the point of swamping our vessel. Why? Surely it is because Jesus is asleep? Were Jesus not asleep within you, you would never encounter these squalls, but you would enjoy inward tranquility because Jesus was keeping watch with you. What do we mean by saying Jesus is asleep? Your faith which comes from Jesus has fallen asleep. Storms come down upon this lake, you see evildoers flourishing, good men in affliction; there you see the temptation, there the threatening wave. And your soul cries: O God, is this thy justice, that evil men should joyfully prosper and the good toil in woe? You argue with God: Is this thy justice? And God replies: Is this your faith? Was this what I promised you? Was it in order to have a prosperous time in this world that you became a Christian? Are you in torments at seeing the wicked flourish here and now, when hereafter they will suffer torments with the devil for company? Why such complaint? Why are you fainthearted because of the waves and storms on the lake? Why? Because Jesus is asleep, or rather your faith which comes from Jesus has fallen asleep in your heart. What are you to do to get out of danger? Rouse Jesus with the cry: *Master, we perish.*[9] The hazards of the deep terrify us: we are sinking. Our Lord will awake; in other words, your faith will return to you, and with His help you will see in your soul that the gift given today to the wicked will not be theirs forever. It will either part from them while they are yet alive, or they will have to part from it when they come to die. As for the gift held in pledge for you, it will be yours for all eternity.

The happiness granted them for a time soon vanishes. It blossoms indeed like grass in flower.[10] All flesh is grass; the grass is withered and the flower is faded; but the word of the Lord endureth for ever. Turn your back, then, on all that falls away, and your face towards all that is eternal. When Christ rises up, your heart will no longer be buffeted by the storm, nor your boat submerged beneath the waves; because your faith will command the winds and the sea, and the danger will pass over. That, brethren, is what the Apostle's counsel to put off the old self amounts to. *Be angry and sin not; let not the sun go down upon your anger; and give not place to the devil.* The old self fell an easy prey to the devil, the new one must not do likewise. *He that stole, let him now steal no more.*[11] As the old self was a thief, so the new must be a thief no longer. The new self is a man also, he is one and the same man; but whereas he was Adam, he must become Christ; he was the old man, he must be the new; and so forth throughout the passage.

5. But let us examine the Psalm a little more carefully and see how every one who makes any headway in virtue in the Church has to put up with evil men in the Church. Such a man will not mind them; often the many who complain of the wicked are wicked in their turn. In the same way, a man in health bears with two sick men far more easily than two sick men bear with each other. Therefore, brethren, take this warning: the Church on earth is a threshing floor; I have frequently said it. I shall go on saying it. It contains both chaff and grain. No one can hope to get rid of the chaff entirely until the time of winnowing. Let no man depart from the threshing floor before the winnowing, on the plea that he finds sinners insupportable; otherwise on being found outside the floor,

he is more likely to be picked up by the birds than to find himself inside the barn. Pay attention, brethren, to what all this signifies. In the early stages of threshing, the grains of corn do not touch one another amid the chaff; they are so to say strangers, by reason of the chaff which separates them. Someone looking at the threshing floor from a distance may perceive nothing but chaff. Unless he looks more carefully, unless he puts out his hand and separates the mixture by blowing it apart with breath from his mouth, he will hardly succeed in distinguishing the grain. Indeed it may happen that the grains themselves are apparently so separated from one another, so unconnected, that the Christian who advances in virtue may consider himself isolated. This thought, brethren, proved a temptation to Elias, mighty though he was, and as the Apostle reminds us, he complained to God: *They have slain thy prophets, they have dug down thy altars, and I am left alone, and they seek my life. But what saith the divine answer to him? "I have left me seven thousand men that have not bowed their knees before Baal."*[12] God did not reply: You have two or three others like yourself; but rather: Do not imagine you are the only one. There are seven thousand others, He told him, and yet you think yourself unique!

Briefly, then, this is the recommendation with which I began. Listen, venerable brethren, with attention, and I pray God to touch your hearts in His mercy in order that you may understand it, so that it will work in you and bear fruit. Here it is in a few words: If anyone is still wicked, he must not imagine that no one is good; if anyone is good, he must not suppose that he is the only good one. Have you fully grasped it? Listen, I am going to repeat it. Notice what I say: If any man who is still a wrongdoer questions his conscience and finds in it only self-condemnation, he must not suppose that no one else is good; if any man is good, he must not suppose he is the only good one, nor must he be afraid, for all his upright-ness, of associating with the wicked, for the time of separation will come. Thus we have been singing today: *Take not away my soul with the wicked, nor my life with bloodthirsty men.*[13] What is the meaning of *Take not away my soul with the wicked?* Do not destroy my soul at the same time. Why does he dread the same ruin? I think he is saying to God: At present thou dost allow us to be intermingled, but do not involve in the same destruc-tion those whom thou dost suffer to dwell together. This is the main idea throughout the Psalm, which I should like to examine quickly with you, venerable brethren, for it is short.

6. [Verse 1] *Judge me, O Lord.* A desire to be judged is a serious wish and dangerous, one would think, to him-self. What is this judgment he craves? His separation from the wicked. He defines this judgment of separation in clear terms in another place: *Judge me, O God, and dis-tinguish my cause from the nation that is not holy.*[14] That shows the implication of the verb *judge:* Let not the good and wicked go forth together into everlasting fire as the good and wicked at present enter into the Church to-gether, without any apparent discrimination. *Judge me, O Lord.* Why? *For I have walked in my innocence, and trusting in the Lord I shall not waver.* What does the phrase *trusting in the Lord* mean? He who falters among the wicked is the man who places no trust in the Lord; men such as these instigate schisms.[15] They have shivered at finding themselves among sinners, they who were so much worse themselves, righteous men forced so to speak

to keep company with rogues. Ah, if only they had been real corn, they would have put up with the chaff on the threshing floor until the winnowing of the harvest. But because they were merely chaff, a wind has arisen to forestall the final winnowing, and catching up the chaff from the barn has flung it out among thorns. It is true that chaff has been blown away from the floor, but does nothing but corn remain? Nothing but chaff is carried away before the winnowing, yet there remains chaff along with the corn, nor will this chaff be separated until the time of winnowing comes. This the Psalmist has expressed in the words: *I have walked in my innocence, and trusting in the Lord I shall not waver.* If I had simply trusted in man, I might possibly see that very man leading a disorderly life at some time, failing to follow the paths of justice which he has learned or even himself taught in the Church, and wandering along paths mapped out by the devil. Had I placed my trust in man, it would have wavered when man wavered, fallen when man fell; but as my confidence is in the Lord, it will remain unshakable.

7. [V. 2] *Prove me, O Lord, and try me,* the Psalmist continues; *burn my reins and my heart.* What is the force of *burn my reins and my heart?* Try by fire my inmost desires, try my thoughts (the heart symbolizes thoughts, the reins desires), and prove that my thoughts do not dwell on evil, no evil arouses my passions. What fire is to try my desires? The fire of thy word. What fire is to try my heart? The flame of thy spirit. This is the fire described elsewhere in the words: *And there is no one that can hide himself from his heat;*[16] and of this fire our Lord said in His turn: *I have come to cast fire on the earth.*[17]

8. Therefore the Psalmist goes on to say: [V. 3] *For thy mercy is before my eyes, and I am well pleased with*

thy truth. That is to say, I have never sought to please men; my desire has been to please thee inwardly where thy eyes penetrate, and I have cared little about giving displeasure in the sight of men, according to the Apostle's injunction: *Let everyone prove his own work, and so shall he have glory in himself only and not in another.*[18]

9. [V. 4] *I have not sat,* declares the Psalmist, *with the council of vanity.* Now the exact meaning of *I have not sat* demands your close attention, venerable brethren. In saying *I have not sat* he appeals to God who sees all. You may be absent perhaps from an assembly, yet sitting there all the same. For instance, you are not at the theater, but the show is absorbing your thoughts, in direct opposition to the petition: *Burn my reins;* you are seated there in heart, notwithstanding your absence of body. On the other hand it may happen that someone presses you to enter and detains you there, or some charitable duty forces you to take a seat in the theater. How is that possible? It can happen that a servant of God has some good work to perform which necessitates his being present in the amphitheater. He may wish to rescue some gladiator or other, and it may so fall out that he has to sit and wait for the appearance of the man he wants to save. You see, then, that in spite of his bodily presence for all to see, this man has not sat with the council of vanity. What is symbolized by sitting? It means to be of one heart with those who are consorting together. If your heart is not there, notwithstanding your presence you have not sat down; if your heart is there, you have sat down in spite of being absent. *Neither will I go in with the doers of unjust things.*[19] [V. 5] *I have hated the assembly of the malignant.* You see it is a question of an inward attitude. *And with the wicked I will not sit.*

10. [V. 6] *I will wash my hands among the innocent,* not with visible water. You wash your hands when you perform your works with holy and pure thoughts in the sight of God, for an altar stands before God's eyes, to which that Priest has entrance who first offered Himself for our sakes. That altar is on high, and no one can lay hold of it without having washed his hands among the innocent. Many, it is true, approach the altar you see here unworthily, and God permits His sacraments to be profaned for a time. Nevertheless, my brethren, will the heavenly Jerusalem resemble these visible walls? By no means; you may enter with the wicked within the walls of this church, you will not enter with the wicked into Abraham's bosom. Have no fear, therefore; wash your hands clean. *And I will compass the altar of the Lord,* where you offer your gifts to the Lord, where you pour out your petitions, where your conscience is clear, where you tell God who you are; and if there is anything in you that perhaps displeases God, He to whom you acknowledge it will put it right. Wash your hands, then, among the innocent and take your place among them at the altar of the Lord, in order to listen to the sound of His praise.

11. These words in fact follow: [V. 7] *That I may hear the voice of thy praise and tell of all thy wondrous works.* What is the meaning of: *That I may hear the voice of thy praise?* The Psalmist means: So that I may understand it. Now to hear before God does not mean to catch audible sounds to which many listen and many others do not. How many there are who are listening to me, yet are deaf to God! How many have ears, but not the ears of which Jesus spoke when He cried: *He that hath ears to hear, let him hear!*[20] What, then, does the voice of praise denote? I shall tell you if I can, with the help of God's

mercy and your prayers. To hear the voice of praise is to
realize inwardly that whatever in you is corrupted by sin
comes from yourself; whatever is good, whatever makes
for righteousness, comes from God. Thus you must so hear
the voice of praise as never to praise yourself, however
virtuous you may be; for in lauding your own goodness
you become blameworthy. Humility had made you good,
pride makes you wicked. You had sought enlightenment
by your conversion, and that conversion of yours filled
you with light, it made you radiant. But to whom were
you converted? To yourself? If you could receive enlightenment by returning to yourself, you should never
know darkness, because you are never absent from yourself. Whence comes your light? It comes from your having turned to something outside yourself. What is the
something outside yourself? God is light. You indeed were
not light because of your sins. In his desire to make this
voice of praise audible to his converts, the Apostle tells
them: *For you were heretofore darkness, but now light.*[21]
What does *you were heretofore darkness* stand for, if not
the old self? *But now light;* it is not without reason that
you are now light who once were darkness, since you have
received illumination.[22] Beware of thinking yourself the
light; the light is that which enlightens every man that
comes into this world.[23] As for you, your nature, your
perversity, your estrangement from God had made you
darkness, whereas now you have become light. For fear,
however, of making proud those whom he has compli-
mented by saying: You are *now light,* the Apostle immediately adds: *in the Lord.* His words are these: *You
were heretofore darkness, but now light in the Lord.* If
there is no light apart from the Lord, and if you are light
precisely because you are in our Lord, then *what hast thou*

that thou hast not received? And if thou hast received,
why dost thou glory as if thou hadst not received it?[24] It is
thus the Apostle speaks elsewhere to men who were vainglorious, anxious to arrogate to themselves what belonged
to God alone, and to boast of their gifts as if they originated with themselves. *What hast thou,* he asks them, *that*
thou hast not received? And if thou hast received, why
dost thou glory as if thou hadst not received it? He who
has given to the humble, takes away from the proud; He
who has given is able also to take back the gift. This then,
brethren, is the sense of the words, if indeed I have succeeded in explaining them to you; and if I have not
succeeded as I would, at least I have done what I could;
this is the sense of the words: *I will wash my hands among*
the innocent, and I will compass thy altar, O Lord, that I
may hear the voice of thy praise; that is to say, the good
which is in me gives me not presumptuous trust in myself,
but trust in thee who hast given me it, and I do not seek
my own glory in myself, but rather thine in thee. Therefore the Psalmist adds: *That I may hear the voice of thy*
praise and tell of all thy wondrous works. Yes, thy works,
not mine.

Well now, brethren, turn your attention to this man
who truly loves God, who has placed his trust in God.
There he is in the midst of evildoers asking God not to
let him be destroyed with the wicked, because when God
judges He makes no mistake. As for you, when you see
men gathering in the same place, you assume that they are
of equal merit; but have no fear, God cannot be deceived
like that. You need a current of air to distinguish chaff
from grain; you require a draught to stir it for you, and
since you are not the wind yourself, you have to create a
stream of air to help you. With the winnowing fan you

then stir both chaff and grain, whereupon the air drives
away all that is light and what is solid remains. You have
recourse to air, then, to sift the threshing floor. But does
God stand in need of anyone to help Him to judge, for
fear of destroying good and bad together? Well, therefore, do not be afraid; remain upright in all security, surrounded though you are with the wicked, and repeat the
words you now hear: [V. 8] *I have loved, O Lord, the
beauty of thy house.* This house of God is the Church; as
yet it contains wrongdoers, but the beauty of God's house
consists in the just, in the saints: this is the beauty I have
loved in thy house. *And the place where thy glory
dwelleth.* What do these words signify? They have the
same meaning, somewhat obscure I admit, as the explanation I have already given you. May our Lord come to my
aid, and the same Lord dispose your hearts to pay close attention. What is the force of *the place where thy glory
dwelleth?* The Psalmist has just said, *the beauty of thy
house,* and in order to explain this beauty of God's house
he adds, *the place where thy glory dwelleth.* He is not
satisfied with saying, "the place where God dwells"; he
has to say, "the place where God's glory dwells." What is
this glory of God? It is what I was explaining to you a
short while ago: he who advances in virtue must glory, not
in himself but in the Lord.[25] For all have sinned and do
need the glory of God.[26] Those therefore in whom the
Lord dwells in such wise that He is Himself glorified in
His gifts, those who have no desire to attribute to themselves or claim as their own what they have received from
Him, these are the men who form the beauty of God's
house. The Scriptures would not have drawn the distinction so deliberately had there not been others who possess
God's gift indeed, but who far from glorying in God,

glory rather in themselves; doubtless they possess the gift of God but they contribute nothing to the beauty of His dwelling. They who participate in the beauty of God's house, in whom God's glory dwells, they form the abiding place of God's glory. In whom does God's glory abide, I ask, if not in those who so glory as to make the Lord their glory, not themselves? Therefore, since I have loved the beauty of thy house, that is to say all who dwell therein and seek thy glory, since I have placed no trust in man or given my assent to the ungodly, since I refuse to enter or sit down in their company; since all this has been my conduct in God's Church, what is to be my reward? The next verse provides us with the answer: [V. 9] *Take not away my soul with the wicked, nor my life with bloodthirsty men.*

13. [V. 10] *In whose hands are iniquities, their right hand is filled with gifts.* Gifts do not consist solely in riches, in gold, silver or precious objects, nor do all who accept them necessarily accept bribes. Why, the Church sometimes accepts them. I go further: Peter accepted gifts, our Lord accepted them; He possessed a purse, and what others put into it Judas stole.[27] What does the Psalmist mean by "accepting gifts"? To praise a man for reward, to flatter him, to cajole and curry favor, to deliver an unjust verdict for the sake of bribes. For what bribes? He who delivers a false judgment not from mere love of gold or silver or suchlike, but rather from love of praise, accepts a gift, and a gift than which nothing is more worthless. He has opened his hand to receive the witness of another's tongue and has forfeited the witness of his own conscience. *In whose hands,* therefore, *are iniquities, their right hand is filled with gifts.* You see, my brethren, they are under the eye of God, these men whose hands are un-

ST. AUGUSTINE

stained by guilt, whose right hand is free from bribes; they
are obviously under the eye of God and can say to God
alone: "Thou knowest"; to Him alone can they say:
*Take not away my soul with the wicked, nor my life with
bloodthirsty men,* for He alone can see that they take no
bribes.

Let me take an example. It so happens that two men
have to settle a dispute before a servant of God. Each
thinks his own case the just one; if he thought it unjust,
he would not have recourse to an arbitrator. The one
considers himself in the right, so does the other. They
present themselves before the judge. Before the verdict is
pronounced, each assures him: "We accept your decision;
God forbid that we should reject your award! What are
you to say? Simply pass judgment as seems best to you,
only give a verdict. May I be anathema if I contradict in
any way." Before the sentence both are well-disposed towards the judge. Nevertheless, the verdict to be given will
go against one of the two, though neither knows which
will be condemned. Now if the judge wants to please
either, he will accept by way of bribe the praise of men.
But having accepted a gift of one kind, notice what kind
of gift he forfeits. He accepts a word which sounds on
the air and dies away, he rejects that which is reiterated
and never dies away. The Word of God is ever being
uttered without ever passing away; man's word vanishes
in its very utterance. Such a man, therefore, lets go the
substance to cling to the shadow. If on the contrary he
keeps his eyes on God alone, he will pronounce sentence
against one of the two, bearing God in mind whose deputy
he is in thus passing judgment. Now let us consider the
man who loses the case: supposing the sentence cannot be
quashed because it is maintained not merely by ecclesi-

astical law but by that of the civil rulers, who have conceded to the Church that the decisions of an ecclesiastical
court shall not be annulled;[28] if, I say, the sentence cannot
be quashed, the loser, far from wishing to examine his own
conscience, turns blinded eyes upon the judge and maligns
him with all his might. "He wanted," so he says, "to please
my adversary, he has favored the man with money, he has
accepted bribes, he has been afraid of offending him."
The accuser takes it for granted that the judge has accepted bribes.

Supposing, however, a poor man is prosecuting a rich
one, and judgment is delivered in the poor man's favor,
the rich man uses precisely the same language: "The judge
has accepted bribes." What bribes can a beggar offer?
"The judge observed his poverty," he replies, "and for
fear of incurring blame if he brought in a verdict to a poor
man's disadvantage, he violated justice and pronounced
sentence against the truth." Since, then, these recrimina-
tions are inevitable, realize that God alone sees those who
accept or reject bribes, and it is only in His presence that
those who refuse them can say: [V. 11] *But as for me, I
have walked in my innocence; redeem me and have mercy
on me; my foot hath stood in uprightness.* I have been
much perturbed undoubtedly by the accusations and exer-
tions of those who with human rashness have protested in
every quarter against my verdict, but *my foot hath stood
in uprightness.* How *in uprightness?* Because, as he said to
begin with, *And trusting in the Lord, I shall not waver.*

14. Now how does the Psalmist conclude? *In the
churches I will bless thee, O Lord.* In other words it is not
myself I shall bless in the churches as if human beings
were the ground of my hope, but it is thyself whom I
shall bless by my works. To bless God in the churches,

brethren, means so to live that each one's life may give
glory to God. To bless God in word and curse Him in
deed is by no means to bless Him in the churches. Almost
all bless Him with their tongues, but not all by their
works. Some bless by words, others by their lives. But
those whose conduct is inconsistent with their profession
cause God to be blasphemed. Those who are not as yet
members of the Church, for instance, even though the
true motive of their refusal to be Christians may be attachment to their disorderly lives, make bad Christians their
excuse. They flatter and delude themselves: "Why urge
me to become a Christian?" they ask. "A Christian has
cheated me. Would I cheat? Never. A Christian has
broken his solemn word to me. But I? Never." By arguing
thus, they block the way of salvation, and the fact that
they could be much worse—not that they are as yet really
good—profits them nothing. Just as a man in the midst of
darkness will open his eyes in vain, so it will be equally
useless to face the light if he keeps his eyes closed. There
you have the image of a pagan (I prefer to speak of them
as if they lead good lives), standing with eyes wide-open
in the midst of darkness, because he does not acknowledge
our Lord as his light. The Christian, on the other hand,
who leads a bad life is, I admit, standing in God's light and
none other, but his eyes are closed. Refusing in his de-
pravity to look upon Christ to whose ranks he nominally
belongs, he resembles a blind man in broad daylight, dead
to every life-giving ray of Him who is Very Light.

First Discourse on Psalm 26

1. [Verse 1] *For David himself, before he was
anointed.* Christ's young recruit speaks as he comes newly

to the faith. *The Lord is my light and my salvation: whom shall I fear?* The Lord will give me both knowledge of Himself and salvation; who shall wrest me from Him? *The Lord is the protector of my life: of whom shall I be afraid?* The Lord will repulse all the attacks of my enemy, both open and concealed; of no man will I be afraid.

2. [V. 2] *Whilst the wicked draw near against me, to eat my flesh:* whilst evildoers approach to recognize and insult me and to vaunt themselves over me in my change for the better, so that with their reviling tooth they may gnaw away not myself but rather my unregenerate desires. *My enemies that trouble me.* Not only those who harass me with reproaches in the name of friendship to turn me away from my purpose, but my enemies too. They *have themselves been weakened and have fallen.* In acting thus to defend their own opinion, they have weakened their power of believing higher things, and yielded to hatred for the word of salvation which prompts me to do what displeases them.

3. [V. 3] *If armies in camp should stand against me, my heart shall not fear.* Yea, even if a multitude of opponents conspires to stand together against me, my heart will not be impelled by fear to join them. *If a battle should rise up against me, in this will I be confident.* If persecution from the world should burst upon me, I will set my hope in this prayer that I am pondering.

4. [V. 4] *One thing I have asked of the Lord, this will I seek after.* One petition have I begged of the Lord, and for this I will go on asking. *That I may dwell in the house of the Lord all the days of my life:* that as long as I live, no adversities may shut me out from the number of those who guard the Lord's faith in truth and unity throughout the world. *That I may contemplate the delight of the*

Lord: with this end, that perseverance in faith may reveal to me the vision of bliss and I may contemplate it face to face. *And I may be protected, His temple:* and when death is swallowed up in victory,[1] I, His temple, may be clad in immortality.

5. [V. 5] *For He hath hidden me in His tabernacle in the day of my evils.* For He has hidden me in the economy of His Incarnate Word during the time of temptation to which my mortal life is exposed. *He hath protected me in the secret places of His tabernacle:* He has protected me, since the faith that justifies has reigned in my heart.[2]

6. [V. 6] *He hath exalted me upon a rock.* And to lead me to salvation by the open acknowledgment of my faith, He has made my confession stand forth fortress-like upon the foundation of His own strength. *And now He hath lifted up my head above my enemies.* What is He reserving for me at the last, when even now, while the body is dead because of sin,[3] I feel in truth that my mind is serving the law of God, and not being led captive under the rebellious law of sin?[4] *I have gone round and have offered in His tabernacle a sacrifice of jubilation.* I have considered the whole round world believing in Christ, and because in this temporal order God was humbled for our sakes, I have praised Him with rejoicing; for with such sacrifice He is well pleased. *I will sing and give praise to the Lord.* Heart and deed shall witness to my joy in the Lord.

7. [V. 7] *Hear, O Lord, my voice, with which I have cried to thee.* Listen, O Lord, to my inner voice, which my intense desire sends up to thy ears. *Have mercy on me and hear me.* Show mercy to me and listen to my supplication.

8. [V. 8] *My heart hath said to thee: I have sought thy face.* I have not made a display of myself before men, but

in secret, where thou alone hearest, my heart has said to thee: I have sought from thee no reward apart from thyself, but only thy countenance. *Thy face, O Lord, will I seek.* Upon this search I will persistently persevere. Not anything of small value will I seek, O Lord, but thy countenance, that I may love thee freely, since I can find nothing more precious.

9. [V. 9] *Turn not away thy face from me,* that so I may find what I seek. *Decline not in thy wrath from thy servant,* or whilst seeking thee I may become involved in something else. What indeed could be a more grievous punishment to one who loves and longs for the truth of thy countenance? *Be thou my helper:* how shall I find thee unless thou help me? *Forsake me not; do not thou despise me, O God my Saviour.* Scorn not the boldness of a mortal who seeks the Eternal, for thou, O God, dost heal the wound left by my sin.

10. [V. 10] *For my father and my mother have left me:* for the kingdom of this world and the city of this world, which gave me my temporal and mortal birth, have failed me because I searched for thee and disdained what they offered; they could not give what I seek. *But the Lord hath taken me up.* But the Lord, who can bestow Himself upon me, has taken me into His care.

11. [V. 11] *Set me, O Lord, a law in thy way.* As I start out towards thee, and embark upon the lofty undertaking of attaining by fear to wisdom, do thou, O Lord, teach me the way thou hast ordained, lest I should go astray and thy guidance abandon me. *And guide me in the right path because of my enemies.* And direct me aright in its narrow course; for it is not enough merely to begin, since enemies will not cease to harass me until I reach my goal.

12. [V. 12] *Deliver me not over to the will of them that trouble me.* Do not allow those who beset me to feast on my misfortunes. *For unjust witnesses have risen up against me.* Men have stood up to accuse me falsely, to steal me away and alienate me from thee, as if I were seeking praise from men. *And iniquity hath lied to itself.* Iniquity can congratulate itself on nothing but its own falsehood, for it has failed to disturb me; rather has a greater reward on this account been promised me in heaven.

13. [V. 13] *I believe to see the good things of the Lord in the land of the living.* And since my Lord has suffered all this before me, if I too despise the tongues of the dying (for the mouth that lies kills the soul[5]), I believe that I shall see the good things of the Lord in the land of the living, where there is no place for untruthfulness.

14. [V. 14] *Wait for the Lord, do manfully; and let thy heart take courage, and wait thou for the Lord.* But when will that be? It is hard for a mortal, it is slow for a lover: but listen to the trustworthy voice of him who counsels you: *Wait thou for the Lord.* Endure manfully the fire which purges your passions, and stoutly that which purges your heart. Do not suppose that what you do not as yet receive is denied you. You will not faint from despair, if you mark the words: *Wait thou for the Lord.*

SECOND DISCOURSE ON PSALM 26[1]

1. The Lord our God, who beholds us eating our bread according to His just decree in the sweat of our face,[2] wishing to speak words of consolation to us, deigns to borrow our language to show that He is not only our Creator but also our Indweller. If we claim that the words

of this Psalm, which we have heard and partially sung, are ours, we must be reverently careful how we state the truth; they are rather the words of God's Spirit than our own. If, on the other hand, we declare that they are not ours, this is manifestly untrue. The Psalm is one long complaint of souls in trouble; could these doleful and tearfilled cries which here resound possibly be assigned to One who can never know distress? Our Lord, then, is full of mercy, we are in need of mercy; in His compassion He bends down to speak to the miserable, nay even to use in their midst the language of the miserable. Thus each statement is true, both that the words are ours and that they are not ours, that they are and are not the words of God's Spirit. They are the words of God's Spirit because they fall from our lips solely by His inspiration. They are not His in that He feels neither misery nor fatigue, whereas these are cries of sorrow and toil. Again they are ours because they reveal our misery; and yet not ours, since it is through His grace that we are enabled even to lament.

2. [Verse 1] *The Psalm of David before he was anointed.* Thus runs the title of the Psalm: *The Psalm of David before he was anointed,* before, that is, he received the unction. He was in fact anointed as king.[3] At that time the anointing was reserved for the king and the priest; in those days only these two persons received the holy oil. In these two persons was prefigured one to come who should be both King and Priest, the one Christ holding both offices, and called the Christ by reason of His anointing. Not only has our Head, however, been anointed, but we ourselves also who are His Body. Now He is King because He rules and leads us, Priest because He makes intercession for us.[4]

He is moreover the only Priest to be at the same time

the sacrificial Victim; for the sacrifice He offered to God was none other than Himself. Apart from Himself He could not find a rational victim of perfect purity. Like a spotless lamb, He redeemed us by the shedding of His blood, incorporating us with Himself, making us His members, that with Him we may make one and the same Christ. That is why all Christians share in the anointing which formerly under the Old Testament was the exclusive prerogative of two men. From this it is evident that we are Christ's Body, because we all share in the anointing and in Him we are all both Christ's and Christ, since in a certain way the whole Christ consists in both Head and Body. This anointing will perfect us spiritually in that life which is promised to us. This Psalm, then, is the prayer of one who longs for that life and begs insistently for the grace of God which is to be perfected in us at the last. Hence the title: *before he was anointed*. Here below we receive the anointing sacramentally, and the sacrament is the figure of what we are yet to be. And this ineffable something that lies ahead is what we ought to long for, groaning while we receive the sacrament, so that one day we may rejoice in the reality of which the sacrament is but a symbol.

3. Notice the speaker's words: *The Lord is my light and my salvation: whom shall I fear?* He enlightens me; begone darkness! He saves me; away with all weakness! Walking resolutely in the light, whom shall I fear? The salvation God bestows is not such as man can snatch from me, nor is His light such as man can extinguish. Our Lord enlightens, we are the enlightened; our Lord saves, we are the saved. If He is the enlightener and we the enlightened, He the Saviour, we the saved, then apart from Him we are simply darkness and weakness. But since in Him we

possess a hope that is sure, fixed and true, whom shall we fear? The Lord is your light, the Lord is your Saviour. Find another more powerful and fear him. I belong to the most mighty of all, to Him who is almighty; it is He who enlightens, He who saves; I fear Him and none other. *The Lord is the protector of my life: of whom shall I be afraid?*

4. [V. 2] *Whilst the wicked draw near against me, to eat my flesh, my enemies that trouble me have themselves been weakened and have fallen.* Then what have I to fear? Of whom shall I be afraid? Who or what shall make me tremble? See, it is my persecutors who reel and fall. Now why do they pursue me? *To eat my flesh.* What is meant by *my flesh?* The impulses of my lower nature. Let them rage in their pursuit; nothing in me can die but what is mortal. Something will remain in me which my pursuer cannot reach, the sanctuary in which my God dwells. Let them feast upon my flesh; when my flesh is consumed, I shall be spirit and spiritualized. And indeed my Lord promises me so complete a salvation that even this mortal flesh of mine, which seems to have fallen a prey to persecutors, shall not perish forever, but what has been manifested in the resurrection of my Head may be hoped for by all His members. Whom shall my soul fear, so long as God dwells in it? Whom shall my flesh fear, when this corruptible body has been clad in incorruption?[5]

Do you wish to know why we need have no fear even for this flesh of ours, although it be consumed by those that pursue us? *It is sown a natural body, it shall rise a spiritual body.*[6] What confidence he should have who has learnt to say: *The Lord is my light and my salvation: whom shall I fear? The Lord is the protector of my life: of whom shall I be afraid?* The emperor is protected by guards and fears nothing; a mortal is protected by mortals and is free from anxiety: a mortal is protected by the Immortal, and shall he be alarmed and afraid?

5. Now hear what confidence he ought to possess who speaks thus: [V. 3] *If armies in camp should stand together against me, my heart shall not fear.* Camps are strongly defended, but what stronger defense is there than God? *If war should rise up against me.* What can a warlike attack do to me? Can it take away my hope from me? Can it take away from me the gift of the Almighty? As He who gives is invincible, so what He gives cannot be taken away. To carry off the gift is to defeat the giver. Therefore, my brethren, nobody can deprive us even of those temporal things we receive, except He who gave them. As for the spiritual gifts He bestows, He will only take them back if you waste them. Natural and temporal things He does take away, since whoever else removes them does so in virtue of power received from Him. All this we know; and we read in the Book of Job how not even the devil, who appears so to speak all-powerful for the time being, can do anything without permission.[7] He received power over the lowest things and forfeited all that was greatest and noblest. And this power of his is not the mastery of one inflicting punishment, but the penalty of one who is himself condemned. Hence not even he can exercise any power without permission. You can see this both in the book I have quoted and in the Gospel where our Lord says: *This night Satan hath desired to have you, that he may sift you as wheat; and I have prayed for thee, Peter, that thy faith fail not.*[8] God grants this power either to punish or to try us. Therefore, since nobody can take away what God bestows, let us fear none but God. What-

ever the threat, whatever the insolent attack launched against us, let not our heart be afraid.

6. *If war should rise up against me, in this will I be confident.* In what? [V. 4] *One thing I have asked of the Lord.*[9] The speaker has named some boon in the feminine gender as though to say *Unam petitionem,* "one petition." In ordinary conversation, for instance, we Latins often put the word "two" in the feminine plural accusative, thus saying *Duas habes,* not *duo;* Holy Scripture here uses the same manner of speech: *Unam,* it says, *One thing I have asked of the Lord, this will I seek after.* Let us see what this man who fears nothing is asking for. What carefree confidence of soul! Would you also fear nothing? Make this sole request of the man who fears nothing—or has he made the request in order to fear nothing? *One thing,* he declares, *I have asked of the Lord, this will I seek after.* This is the practice of those who walk uprightly. Well, what is it? What is this one thing? *That I may dwell in the house of the Lord all the days of my life.* This is the one thing; *house* is the name for the place where we shall abide eternally. In this state of pilgrimage the word "house" is used, but properly speaking we should call it a tent. A tent belongs to travelers, to those in some way at war and fighting against an enemy. When we speak of a tent in this life, obviously there is an enemy concerned; those who share tents in common are called tent fellows, which as you know is another name for soldiers. So it is a tent for us here and a house hereafter. Sometimes, because of their resemblance, the tent is inaccurately called a house, and similarly a house is sometimes called a tent; but properly speaking heaven is the house, here below we are in tents.

7. In another Psalm the Psalmist tells us precisely what

we are to do in that house: *Blessed are they that dwell in thy house: they shall praise thee forever and ever.*[10] On fire, so to speak, with this desire, and burning with this love, he longs to dwell all the days of his life in the house of the Lord; to abide in the Lord's house all his days, not days that come to an end but days that last forever. For the word "days" is used in the same way as the word "years" in the text: *And thy years shall not fail.*[11] The day of life everlasting is a single day which never closes. Thus, then, the speaker addresses the Lord: I have longed for this, it is my one prayer, I shall go on asking for it. Well, suppose we say to him: "And what will you do there? What will constitute your enjoyment there? What will be the recreation of your soul? What pleasures will be the source of your delight? You will not stay there unless you are happy; but whence will that happiness come?" For in this life the human race finds many kinds of happiness, and a man is considered unhappy when he is deprived of what he loves. Men in fact have different tastes, and when anyone appears to possess what he loves, he is termed happy. But he is truly happy, not when he has what he loves, but when he loves what is worthy of his love. Indeed, many men are more miserable in having what they love than in being without it; they are miserable in loving harmful things and more so in possessing them. And when we love amiss, God in His mercy denies us what we crave for, whereas it is in His anger that He gives another man the object of his guilty desire. You find the Apostle declaring roundly: *God gave them up to the desires of their heart.*[12] He gave them what they delighted in, but for their condemnation. Again you find God refusing a request: *For which thing*, says St. Paul, *thrice I besought the Lord that He would take it*—the sting of the flesh—*from me, and He said to me: My grace is sufficient for thee; for power is made perfect in infirmity.*[13] As you see, He gave over the philosophers to the desires of their hearts, while He rejected the Apostle Paul's petition. He heard the former for their condemnation, refused the latter for his sound welfare. But when we love what God would have us love, beyond any doubt He will grant us it. And the one thing we should love above all else is to dwell in the house of the Lord all the days of our life.

8. Now in their dwelling places here on earth, men find satisfaction in various kinds of comfort and pleasure; every one would like to live in a house where there is nothing to annoy and plenty to please him; but let the pleasurable delights vanish and the man will want to move elsewhere. So let us question the Psalmist more insistently, so to speak, and let him tell us what he, and we too with him, will do in that house where he wishes, chooses and longs to be, and where, as his one gift from the Lord, he begs that he may dwell all the days of his life. What will you do there, I ask you; what is it you are longing for? Listen to the answer: *That I may contemplate the delight of the Lord.* There you see what it is I love, there you see why I wish to dwell in the house of the Lord all the days of my life. Marvelous sight, to gaze upon the beauty of the Lord Himself! When his night is ended, he longs to repose forever in God's light. Then our night will be no more; morning will have dawned for us. That is why the Psalmist says elsewhere: *In the morning I will stand before thee and will behold.*[14] Now that I am prostrate, I cannot contemplate thee; but then I shall stand upright and I shall behold. The voice of mankind speaks thus, for it is man who has fallen, and unless we had fallen, the One who was sent to raise us up would not have come.

We have fallen, He has come down. He has ascended, we are lifted up; for no man has ascended but He who descended.[15] He who fell headlong is raised up; He who came down ascends. If He has ascended alone, we must not therefore despair. For He came simply to raise us up from our fall; one day we shall be set on our feet, we shall behold, and we shall enjoy ineffable delight.

There now, I have spoken thus and you have cried out with longing for some vision of beauty not yet granted. Let your soul transcend all ordinary things, let your thought reach out beyond all the habitual reflections of your lower nature, derived from your corporal senses and creating all kinds of illusions. Cast all this out of your mind, reject whatever presents itself: recognize the weakness of your heart, and in so far as anything you are able to imagine does occur to you, say: "It is not that; had it been that, it would not have presented itself to me." Thus you will long for some kind of good. What kind of good? The goodness of all good, whence all good proceeds, the good to which no further good can be added. For we speak of a good man, a good field, a good house, a good animal, a good tree, a good body, a good soul; you have added something whenever you said "good." But here it is the absolute Good, the essential Good, which makes all things good, the Good from which all good things flow. This is the delight of the Lord; this is what we shall contemplate. Mark, brethren: if all that we call good here below possesses a charm for us, if we are enamored of good things which are not good in their essence—since nothing changeable is goodness in its essence—what will be the contemplation of the unchangeable Good, eternal and ever-abiding, ever the selfsame? For those things which are called good would give us no pleasure were they not good; nor could they be good by any other means unless they originated from Him who is the absolute Good.

9. Now you see, says the Psalmist, why I wish to dwell in the house of the Lord all the days of my life. I have told you the reason: *That I may contemplate the delight of the Lord*. But to enable me to contemplate it unceasingly so that no annoyance may befall me in my contemplation, no temptation turn me aside, no alien power sweep me away, that I may be the butt of no enemy in my contemplation but have thorough and undisturbed enjoyment of my delight which is the Lord my God Himself, what must He do for me? He must protect me. Hence, the speaker continues, I long not only to contemplate the delight of the Lord but also to be protected as His temple. So that He may protect me as His temple, I shall become His temple and shall be in His keeping. Does God's temple resemble the temples of idols? The idols of the Gentiles are guarded by their temples; the Lord our God protects His own temple and I shall be safe. To contemplate Him will be my happiness, His protection will be my safety. As my contemplation is perfect, so also will be His protection; and the more perfect the bliss of contemplation, the more perfectly imperishable shall be my well-being. These two expressions, *That I may contemplate the delight of the Lord and be protected, His temple*, are implied in the two with which the Psalm begins: *The Lord is my light and my salvation: whom shall I fear?* The Lord is my light, since I shall behold His beauty. He is my salvation, since He will guard me as His temple.

10. By what means, then, does He finally accord us this favor? [V. 5] *For He hath hidden me in His tabernacle in the day of my evils*. So I shall dwell in His house all the days of my life, in order to gaze upon the delight

of the Lord and be protected as His temple. But whence my assurance of arriving thither? *For He hath hidden me in His tabernacle in the day of my evils.* Then indeed my days of misfortune will be no longer; but now in these difficult days of mine He has kept His eyes upon me. And since He has looked upon me with eyes of mercy when I was afar off, what blessings will He bestow upon me when I enjoy His presence? My request for that one thing, then, was not unseemly; nor did my heart say to me: "What are you asking?" or "From whom are you asking it? Miserable sinner that you are, do you dare to address yourself to God? Do you dare to hope that you will enjoy any contemplation of God, you who are so weak and unclean of heart?" Yes, I dare to hope, not from myself but from God's ineffable love; this hope is not presumption on my part, it is a pledge of His love. Will He who has given so great a pledge to the exile desert him when he reaches home? *For He hath hidden me in His tabernacle in the day of my evils.* See now: our evil days are the days of our life. Days of evil come to the ungodly in one way and to the faithful in another. Even believers are as yet absent from the Lord, *for*, as the Apostle tells us, *as long as we are in this body we are absent from the Lord.*[16] If they do not undergo evil days, if we are not living in days of evil, why have we that petition in the Lord's prayer, *Deliver us from evil?*[17] Far differently, however, do those who as yet have not the faith spend the days of evil; yet even these He has not despised. For Christ died for sinners.[18] Let the soul of man, then, dare to feel confidence and to ask that one boon; it will obtain it and hold it in all security. Since in its loathsomeness it has been so loved, how will it shine forth in the splendor of its beauty?

For He hath hidden me in His tabernacle in the day of

my evils; He hath protected me in the secret place of His tabernacle. What is the secret place of His tabernacle? What is it? There are many parts of the tabernacle, so to speak, to be seen from without. There is also, as it were, the shrine, which is called the secret sanctuary, the innermost recess of the temple.[19] And what is this? The place which the priest alone entered. And perhaps this High Priest is Himself the secret of God's tabernacle. For He formed a body from this tabernacle and became for us a hidden sanctuary, so that the rest of His members, believing in Him, might constitute His tabernacle, but He Himself be its secret sanctuary. *For you are dead,* says the Apostle, *and your life is hid with Christ in God.*[20]

11. Would you know that it is of this the Psalmist is speaking? Remember that the rock is Christ.[21] Hear what follows: *For He hath hidden me in His tabernacle in the day of my evils; He hath protected me in the secret place of His tabernacle.* You were asking what is the secret place of the tabernacle. Listen to what comes next: [V. 6] *He hath exalted me upon a rock.* That is to say, He has raised me up in Christ. Because you have humbled yourself in the dust, He has raised you upon a rock. But Christ is above, and you are still below. Listen to the words that follow: *And now He hath lifted up my head above my enemies. And now,* even before I come to that house where I wish to dwell all the days of my life, even before I come to that contemplation of the Lord, *And now He hath lifted up my head above my enemies.* I still suffer from the enemies of Christ's Body, I have not as yet been exalted above these enemies; yet *He hath lifted up my head above my enemies.* Christ our Head is already in heaven. Our enemies are still able to rage against us, we are not yet exalted beyond their reach; but our Head is there

already. From thence He used the words: *Saul, Saul, why persecutest thou me?*[22] He thus showed that He was in us here below; therefore we too are in Him there on high, since *now He hath lifted up my head above my enemies.* See what a pledge we possess, through which by faith and hope and charity we are in heaven in union with our Head forever, because He Himself by His divinity, His goodness, and His unity with us, is on earth even until the consummation of the world.[23]

12. *I have gone round and have offered in His tabernacle a sacrifice of jubilation.* We offer up a sacrifice of jubilation, we offer up a sacrifice of gladness, a sacrifice of rejoicing, a sacrifice of thanksgiving, which no words can express. But where do we offer it? In His own tabernacle, in Holy Church. And what is the sacrifice we offer? An overflowing and ineffable joy, beyond words, not to be expressed in speech. This is the sacrifice of jubilation. Where seek for it, how find it? By looking everywhere. *I have gone round,* says the Psalmist, *and have offered in His tabernacle a sacrifice of jubilation.* Let your mind roam through the whole creation; everywhere the created world will cry out to you: "God made me." Whatever pleases you in a work of art brings to your mind the artist who wrought it; much more, when you survey the universe, does the consideration of it evoke praise for its Maker. You look on the heavens; they are God's great work. You behold the earth; God made its numbers of seeds, its varieties of plants, its multitude of animals. Go round the heavens again and back to the earth, leave out nothing; on all sides everything cries out to you of its Author; nay the very forms of created things are as it were the voices with which they praise their Creator. But who can fathom the whole creation? Who shall set forth

its praises? Who shall worthily praise heaven and earth, the sea, and all things that are in them? And these indeed are visible things. Who shall worthily praise the angels, thrones, dominations, principalities and powers? Who shall worthily praise that power which works actively within ourselves, quickening the body, giving movement to the members, bringing the senses into play, embracing so many things in the memory, distinguishing so many things by the intelligence; who can worthily praise it? Now if in considering these creatures of God human language is so at a loss, what is it to do in regard to the Creator? When words fail, can aught but triumphant music remain? *I have gone round and have offered in His tabernacle a sacrifice of jubilation.*

13. There is also another interpretation, which seems to me in closer harmony with the rest of the Psalm. Since the speaker has told us that he has been set up on the rock which is Christ, and that Christ his Head has been exalted above His enemies, he would thus have us understand that he himself, set up on the rock, has been raised up, in the person of his Head, beyond the reach of his enemies. Hereby he alludes to the glory of the Church, before which its persecutors have had to yield the victory; and because this victory has been achieved throughout the world by faith, *I have gone round,* the Psalmist declares, *and have offered in His tabernacle a sacrifice of jubilation.* In other words, I have pondered on the faith of the whole world, this faith which exalts my Head above my persecutors, and in that tabernacle of His, or rather in the Church which embraces the whole world, I have praised the Lord in a way no words can tell.

14. *I will sing and will give praise to the Lord.* Free from care at last, we shall sing to the Lord without fear;

without fear we shall bless Him as we gaze upon His beauty, while He guards us as His temple, and we enjoy incorruptible perfection, since death will be swallowed up in victory.[24] But what of the present? I have spoken of those joys which will be ours when we have gained that one petition. But what of the present? [V. 7] *Hear, O Lord, my voice.* For the present we must groan, we must pray. Groaning is the lot of the wretched, praying the lot of the needy. Prayer shall pass away and give place to praise; weeping shall pass away and give place to joy. In the meantime, however, whilst we live in the time of our misfortunes, our prayer to God must not cease. We must ask of Him that one petition and never interrupt our prayer until by His gift and guidance we attain to it. *Hear, O Lord, my prayer, with which I have cried to thee; have mercy on me and hear me.* The Psalmist makes that one petition; beseeching, weeping, groaning, persistently he begs but one thing. He has done with all his lower desires; only one thing remains to be granted.

15. Now listen to his reason for this petition: [V. 8] *My heart hath said to thee: I have sought thy face.* This was the speaker's meaning when he said a little earlier: *That I may contemplate the delight of the Lord. My heart hath said to thee: I have sought thy face.* Were our joy in this visible sun of ours, it would not be our heart but our bodily eyes that exclaimed, *I have sought thy face.* But to whom else does our heart cry, *I have sought thy face,* if not to Him who is visible only to the heart's eye? The eyes of the flesh seek this world's light, those of the heart that other light. Well, do you wish to behold that light which is seen by the eyes of the heart? That light is God Himself. For *God is light,* says John, *and in Him there is no darkness.*[25] Would you look upon that light? Cleanse

the eye with which it is to be seen: *Blessed are the clean of heart, for they shall see God.*[26]

16. *My heart hath said to thee: I have sought thy face; thy face, O Lord, will I seek.* One thing I have asked from the Lord, this I will seek: thy face. [V. 9] *Turn not away thy face from me.* See how the speaker has persisted in that one petition! Do you really want to obtain your request? Then seek nothing else. Be satisfied with one thing, for it will be sufficient for you. *My heart hath said to thee: I have sought thy face; thy face, O Lord, will I seek. Turn not away thy face from me; decline not in thy wrath from thy servant.* Superb! Nothing could be more sublimely spoken. They who truly love will understand. Another man might wish to live happily forever among the earthly desires and pleasures he loves: and on that account he might possibly offer God adoration and prayer in the hope of obtaining a long life surrounded by everything he enjoys. He should never lose anything that earthly ambition could possess, neither gold nor silver nor any domain that charms his eyes; neither his friends, nor his children, nor his wife nor his dependents should die; amid the enjoyment of all such pleasant things he would wish to live forever. But since he knows he is mortal and cannot live forever, it may be that he worships God, prays and sighs to God, for the one object, that all these things may accompany him even to old age. And were God to say to him: "Look, I make you immortal amidst these things," he would accept this as a great boon, and in the excitement of his self-congratulation would hardly be able to contain himself. Such is not the desire of this man who has asked but one thing of the Lord. But what does he want? To gaze upon the Lord's loveliness all the days of his life.

On the other hand, the man who would worship God

in the way and for the end mentioned, so long as he could procure these temporal advantages, would fear God's anger only because of the risk that He might take them away. The Psalmist does not fear His anger on this account, since he had said of his enemies: Let them eat my flesh. Then why is he afraid of God's anger? For fear that He should deprive him of the object of his love. What has he loved? Thy face. Hence he considers it a sign of God's anger if He turns away His face from him. O Lord, *decline not in thy wrath from thy servant*. One might reply: "Why fear that He may turn away from you in anger? Rather, if He turns away from you in anger, you will have less to fear from His vengeance, whereas if you fall into His hands in His anger He certainly will punish you. It would be better to choose that He should turn away from you in His anger." "No," replies the man, for he knows what he wants. "His anger is nothing else but the turning away of His face." Supposing He let you live forever amid the delights and pleasures of earthly enjoyments? A lover such as this answers: "I do not want them; whatever I have besides Himself has no charms for me. Far from me be every gift whatsoever that my Lord might bestow; let Him give me Himself." *Decline not in thy wrath from thy servant*. Sometimes He turns from us but not in anger, as for instance from those who beg Him: *Turn away thy face from my sins.*[27] To turn away His face from your sins is not to depart from you in anger. May He indeed turn away His face from your sins, but not turn His face away from yourself.

17. *Be thou my helper, forsake me not*. For see, I am on my journey; I have asked of thee one thing, to dwell in thy house all the days of my life, to contemplate thy beauty and be protected as thy temple. This one boon I

have asked; and I am on my journey to reach it. Perhaps thou wilt tell me: Make an effort, put your best foot forward; I have given you free will, you are your own master; go forward on your journey, seek after peace and pursue it.[28] Do not turn aside from the road, do not loiter there, do not look back; persevere in your journey, for he who perseveres to the end shall be saved.[29] But now you with your free will are relying so to speak upon your own power to walk.[30] Do not rely on yourself; if God leaves you, you will faint by the wayside, you will fall, you will go astray, you will come to a standstill. Say to Him, then: "Thou hast indeed given me a free will, but without thee all my efforts come to nothing: *Be thou my helper, forsake me not, do not thou despise me, O God my Saviour*. Thou who didst fashion me helpest me; thou who didst create me dost not desert me."

18. [V. 10] *For my father and my mother have left me*. The speaker has made himself a little child before God; he has chosen Him as his father, he has made Him his mother. He is a father because He has created him, because He calls him to His service, He directs him, He governs him: a mother, in that He cherishes him, feeds him, suckles him, nurses him. *My father and my mother have left me, but the Lord hath taken me up*, both to guide me and to nourish me. Mortal parents procreate, the children take their place, mortals give place to mortals, children are born to succeed to those who begot them, and those who begot them depart. He who created me will never depart; nor shall I ever be separated from Him. *My father and my mother have left me, but the Lord hath taken me up*. Besides these two parents, of whose flesh we were born, the father a man, the mother a woman, like Adam and Eve; besides these two parents, we also

have here, or rather we had, another father and another mother. The father of things worldly is the devil, and when we were unbelievers he was our father; for our Lord tells unbelievers: *You are of your father the devil.*[31] If he who works on the children of unbelief[32] is the father of all the ungodly, who is their mother? There is a certain city which is called Babylon; this city is the home of all the lost, from east to west; it holds sway over the empire of earth. It is the capital of what you call the Republic,[33] which you now see growing old and waning: this was our first mother, from her we were born. But we have acknowledged another father, God; we have done with the devil. How dare he approach us, who have been adopted by the Conqueror of all? We have acknowledged another mother, the heavenly Jerusalem which is Holy Church, a portion of which is in exile on earth. We have done with Babylon. *My father and my mother have left me:* they have nothing further to bestow upon me. Even when they seemed to give to me, it was thou who gavest, and I attributed the gift to them.

19. Who but God alone is able to confer any good on man even in this world below? Or what can be taken away from a man without the command or permission of the Giver? But men in their delusion imagine that these things are given by the demons they worship; and sometimes they say to themselves: "We need God for life eternal, for a wholly spiritual life, but we have to worship those other powers for the sake of these temporal things." Oh the folly of mankind! You really prefer those things for the sake of which you want to worship such beings; in fact you are more inclined to worship them than God Himself, or if not actually more, at least as much. But God will not share His altar with them, no, not even though He be

given much greater honor and they much less. What then, you will say, are not they too needed for obtaining such things? No. But is there not reason to fear they may do us harm when angered? They will do no harm unless He permits it. These beings are always ready to do us harm, and neither peace offerings nor entreaties will weaken their implacable desire to injure us. This is characteristic of their malevolence. Therefore what will you gain by worshiping them? You will only offend God, who in anger will deliver you into their power; powerless to hurt so long as He is favorable to you, they will be able to do whatever they like when He is displeased. See, you who hold such opinions, how useless it is to worship these beings in the hope of temporal gains: of all who worship Neptune have none ever suffered shipwreck, and of all who blaspheme Neptune have none ever come safe to port? Have all the women who worship Juno had a happy delivery, or all who blaspheme Juno an unfortunate one? From this, beloved brethren, you may understand the foolishness of those men who would honor those demons merely for temporal benefits. For if they must be worshiped to obtain these temporal benefits, their worshipers alone would make immense fortunes. Yet even if it were so, we at any rate ought to shun such gifts and ask but one petition of the Lord. It should be added that He is the giver of all these things—and to worship such spirits is to offend Him. Away then with father and mother, away with the devil, away with the city of Babylon; our Lord shall receive us as His children, to comfort us with perishable things and bless us with imperishable ones. *For my father and my mother have left me, but the Lord hath taken me up.*

20. The Psalmist, then, has now been taken under the

Lord's protection; he has abandoned that city and its ruler the devil, for the devil is the ruler of the ungodly, the ruler of the world of this darkness. What darkness? The darkness of sinners, of unbelievers. Hence the Apostle tells those who now believe: *You were heretofore darkness, but now light in the Lord.*[34] Now that we are adopted by Him, what are we to say? [V. 11] *Set me, O Lord, a law in thy way.* Have you dared to ask for a law? What if He should say to you: "Will you fulfill the law? If I give you a law, will you fulfil it?" The speaker would not dare to ask, unless he had previously declared: *But the Lord hath taken me up.* He would not dare to ask, unless he had previously prayed: *Be thou my helper.* If thou dost receive me, if thou dost help me, give me a law: *Set me, O Lord, a law in thy way.* Give me a law, accordingly, in thy Christ. For the Way Himself has spoken to us, saying: *I am the way, and the truth, and the life.*[35] A law in Christ is a law with mercy. This is the wisdom of which we are told: *And she bears the law and clemency on her tongue.*[36] If you are guilty of an infraction of the law, confess it, and you will obtain pardon of Him who has shed His blood for you. Only do not forsake the way; say to Him: Be thou my upholder. *And guide me in the right path because of my enemies.* Give me a law, but do not deprive me of thy mercy. In another Psalm the prophet has said: *For He will show mercy who gaveth the law.*[37] Thus the words: *Set me, O Lord, a law in thy way,* refer to precept. Is there a reference also to mercy? Yes. *And guide me,* says the Psalmist, *in the right path because of my enemies.*

21. [V. 12] *Deliver me not over to the will of them that trouble me:* in other words, do not allow me to assent to my oppressors. For if you acquiesce in the designs of

him who oppresses you, he will not, so to speak, devour
your flesh, but by his perverse determination he will eat
up your soul. *Deliver me not over to the will of them that
trouble me.* Deliver me, if it please thee, into the hands of
my persecutors. Such was the prayer the martyrs made,
and He has delivered His own into the hands of their
persecutors. But what was it He delivered? Simply their
flesh. This is indicated in the Book of Job: *The earth is
given into the hands of the wicked;*[38] the flesh is delivered
into the hands of the persecutor. *Deliver me not; me,* not
my flesh but my very self. As a soul I address thee, as a
human spirit I appeal to thee; I do not ask: "Deliver not
my flesh into the hands of them that trouble me," but:
Deliver me not over to the will of them that trouble me.
And in what way are men betrayed to the will of their
oppressors? *For unjust witnesses have risen up against me.*
Now since there are false witnesses, who heap up accusations against me and defame me with a mass of calumnies,
were I given over to their will I too should be a liar and
one of their company, not a partaker in thy truth but a
confederate in lying against thee. *Unjust witnesses have
risen up against me, and iniquity hath lied to itself.* To
itself, not to me; let it always lie to itself, but let it not lie
to me. If I am delivered to the will of my enemies, if, that
is to say, I associate myself with their plans, then iniquity
will have lied not only to itself but also to me. But let
them unleash all their fury, let them exert their utmost
endeavor to block my course; yet, provided that thou dost
not abandon me to their will, so long as I refuse to acquiesce in their designs I shall stand firm, constant in thy
truth, and the lies of iniquity will turn not against me but
against itself.

22. After all these dangers, after toil and tribulation,

gasping, panting, struggling in the hands of those who harass and persecute him, but ever steadfast and full of confidence in Him who upholds him, sustains him, leads him, governs him, the Psalmist returns to his one and only petition. He has rejoiced in surveying the universe, he has exulted in bliss, he has groaned beneath the weight of toil, yet he concludes with a sigh: [V. 13] *I believe to see the good things of the Lord in the land of the living.* Oh these good things of the Lord, sweet, immortal, beyond comparison, eternal, unchangeable as they are! And when shall I gaze upon you, ye good things of the Lord? I look forward to beholding you, but not in the land of the dying. *I believe to see the good things of the Lord in the land of the living.* Our Lord, who for my sake did not disdain to take upon Himself mortal clay and to suffer death at the hands of the dying, will rescue me from the land of the dying. *I believe to see the good things of the Lord in the land of the living.* The Psalmist has spoken with a sigh, he has spoken in distress, he has spoken in peril from trials without number, yet he hopes all from the mercy of Him to whom he has said: *Set me, O Lord, a law.*

23. Now what does He say who has set him a law? Let us also listen to this voice of our Lord, a voice of encouragement and consolation reaching us from above, the voice of Him who holds the place of the father and mother who have forsaken us. Let us listen to His voice, for He has heard our groans, He has observed our sighs, He has understood our longings; and that sole petition of ours, that one request we make through Christ our Advocate, He has graciously received. And so long as we are on this journey of ours, during which He will defer but not take away what He has promised, He has told us: [V. 14]

Wait for the Lord. You will not be waiting for one who can deceive or be deceived, nor for one who will be unable to find the wherewithal to give. He who has promised is the Almighty, He who has promised is faithful, He who has promised is true. *Wait for the Lord, do manfully.* Do not yield to exhaustion; do not be among those of whom we are told: *Woe to them that have lost patience!*[39] *Wait for the Lord* is said to all of us, although it is said only to one man. We are one in Christ; we who desire that one petition, who ask for that one boon, we who groan in these days of our misfortune, we who trust to see the good things of the Lord in the land of the living— we are the Body of Christ. To all of us, who are one in one Man, are addressed the words: *Wait for the Lord, do manfully; and let thy heart take courage, and wait thou for the Lord.* What else should He say to you, except to repeat what you have already heard? *Wait for the Lord, do manfully.* He who has lost endurance has become weak and womanish. Let both men and women take heed of this, for man and woman are one in the one Man. He is no longer man or woman who lives in Christ.[40] *Wait for the Lord, do manfully; and let thy heart take courage, and wait thou for the Lord.* By patient waiting for the Lord you will possess Him, you will possess Him for whom you wait. If you can find anything grander, better or sweeter, set your heart on that.

DISCOURSE ON PSALM 27

1. [Verse 1] *Of David himself.* The voice is that of the Mediator whose arm was mighty[1] in the combat of His passion. The evils He seems to invoke upon His enemies are not curses; rather are they prophecies of the chastise-

ment in store for them. So also in the Gospel, when our Lord speaks of the cities which witnessed the miracles He wrought without believing in Him,[2] He does not strike them with anathemas, He simply predicts their impending punishment.

2. *Unto thee have I cried, O Lord; O my God, be not thou silent to me.* Unto thee, O Lord, I have cried; break not, O my God, the union of thy Word with my human nature. Keep not silence from me, *or I shall be like them that go down into the pit.* The unbroken union of thine eternal Word with my own self makes me unlike the rest of men who are born into the deep misery of this world, where thy Word goes unrecognized, as if thou wert keeping silence. [V. 2] *Hear the voice of my supplication, when I pray to thee, when I lift up my hands to thy holy temple:* when I am nailed to the cross, for the salvation of those who by faith will become thy holy temple.

3. [V. 3] *Draw not away my soul with the wicked, and with the workers of iniquity destroy me not: with those who speak peace with their neighbour*, such as the men who assure me: *We know that thou art come a teacher from God.*[3] *But evils are in their hearts:* their hearts are cogitating nothing but evil.

4. [V. 4] *Give them according to their works.* Repay them in their own coin: this is plain justice. *And according to the malice of their intentions*, for in making evil their aim, they can no longer find goodness. *According to the works of their hands give thou to them.* Their deeds may have contributed to the salvation of others; yet in spite of that, do thou repay them as the intention of their deeds deserves. *Render to them their reward.* Since in exchange for the truth they were taught, they intended to return falsehood, let them be the dupes of their own deceit.

5. [V. 5] *Because they have no discernment in the works of the Lord.* And why, obviously, has this punishment befallen them? The answer is, *because they have no discernment in the works of the Lord.* Small wonder if that was their immediate recompense. With malicious intent they tempted the Man whom they failed to recognize as God, even as they failed to see the Father's plan in sending Him clothed in our flesh. *And the operations of His hands.* They took no heed of the notable works which were wrought before their very eyes. *Thou shalt destroy them and shalt not build them up.* Let them do me no harm; rather, let their repeated attempts to stir up intrigues against my Church be brought to naught.

6. [V. 6] *Blessed be the Lord, for He hath heard the voice of my supplication.*

7. [V. 7] *The Lord is my helper and my protector.* The Lord is my strength in my bitter suffering, and my shield in granting me resurrection and immortality. *In Him hath my heart confided, and I have been helped. And my flesh hath flourished again,* in other words, it has risen from the dead. *And with my will I will give praise to Him.* Hence, the fear of death being now no more, they who believe in me will praise the Lord, no longer constrained by fear under the law, but by their free choice in conformity with the law; and as I am in them, it is I who will give praise.

8. [V. 8] *The Lord is the strength of His people.* Not of that people who do not recognize God's way of justification and strive to institute their own,[4] but of the people who place no reliance on their own strength, because it is the Lord who supports His chosen ones amid the difficulties of this life, in their warfare with the devil. *And the protector of the salvation of His anointed.* Having saved

His people by Christ His anointed and sustained their courage in the fight, He will finally uphold them in peace forevermore.

9. [V. 9] *Save thy people and bless thy inheritance.* My flesh has risen from the dead, and since thou hast said to me: *Ask of me, and I will give thee the Gentiles for thy inheritance,* therefore I now make the request: *Save thy people and bless thy inheritance,*[5] because all I have is thine.[6] *And rule them and exalt them forever.* Guide them during their life on earth, and thereafter raise them up unto life everlasting.

DISCOURSE ON PSALM 28

1. [Verse 1] *A Psalm of the completion of the tabernacle, for David himself.* A Psalm in honor of the Mediator mighty of hand,[1] concerning the completion of His Church in this world, where she daily wages war against the devil.

2. The prophet is speaking: *Bring to the Lord, O ye children of God, bring to the Lord the offspring of rams.* Offer yourselves to the Lord, you whom the apostles, the leaders of the flocks, have begotten through the Gospel.[2] [V. 2] *Bring to the Lord glory and honor.* May your deeds give praise and glory to the Lord. *Bring to the Lord glory to His name.* Proclaim His glory throughout the world. *Adore ye the Lord in His holy court.* Adore the Lord in hearts which are hallowed and all-embracing, for you yourselves are His royal and holy dwelling place.

3. [V. 3] *The voice of the Lord is upon the waters:* Christ's voice over the nations. *The God of majesty hath thundered.* From the midst of the cloud of His human flesh, the God of majesty with fearful voice has uttered a

call to penance.[3] *The Lord is upon many waters.* When our Lord Jesus had made His voice heard throughout the awe-stricken nations, He converted them to His law and took up His abode in them.

4. [V. 4] *The voice of the Lord is in power.* Already they speak with the voice of the Lord which communicates to them their power. *The voice of the Lord in magnificence.* The voice of the Lord works in them mighty wonders.

5. [V. 5] *The voice of the Lord breaking the cedars:* the voice of the Lord humbling the proud through heartfelt sorrow. *Yea, the Lord shall break the cedars of Libanus.* The Lord shall break by repentance those who glory in the distinction of their earthly nobility; they will stand abashed when He makes choice of the base things of this world[4] to show forth in them His divine power.

6. [V. 6] *And shall reduce them to pieces as a calf of Libanus.* He will throw down their haughty pride and will reduce them to imitate the lowliness of Him who, like a calf,[5] was led to slaughter by the great ones of this world: *The kings of the earth stood up, and the princes met together against the Lord and against His Christ.*[6]

And as the beloved son of unicorns. For He, the well-beloved and only Son of the Father, dispossessed Himself of His rank;[7] He was made man, as a child of those Jews who did not recognize God's way of justification[8] but congratulated themselves with pride on their own as if it were the only true justice.

7. [V. 7] *The voice of the Lord cleaving the flame of fire.* The voice of the Lord who opens up a way and passes unharmed through those that dog His steps with the most implacable hatred, or who splits the ranks of His bitterly-raging persecutors, so that some ask: Is not this indeed the

Christ? while others retort: No, but He seduces the people.[9] He thus divides the insensate crowd: some He draws to Himself by love, others He abandons to their own malice.

8. [V. 8] *The voice of the Lord rocking the wilderness.* In order to lead them to the faith, the voice of the Lord rouses those nations who were once without hope and without God in the midst of this world,[10] where so to speak man had never dwelt, since it contained no prophet, no preacher of the word of God. *And the Lord shall shake the desert of Cades.* Then will the Lord sound forth the sacred word of His Scriptures, which the Jews neglected and failed to appreciate.

9. [V. 9] *The voice of the Lord perfecting the stags.* For the voice of the Lord has above all led to perfection those who know how to control and discountenance venomous tongues.[11] *And He will reveal the woods.* He will then lay bare to them the obscurities of the divine books, the mysteries hidden in shadow, so that they may browse at large in their pastures. *And in His temple every man speaks His glory.* And in His Church all who have been regenerated to the hope of eternal life bless God, each man according to the gift he has received from the Holy Spirit.

10. [V. 10] *The Lord inhabiteth the flood.* The Lord first of all inhabits the flood of this world by His presence in the saints, whom He keeps safe within the Church as in an ark.[12] *And the Lord shall sit King forever.* And thereafter He will sit enthroned as King in His elect for all eternity.

11. [V. 11] *The Lord will give strength to His people.* Because the Lord must give His people courage as they battle against the storms and hurricanes of this life: He

has never promised them tranquility here below. *The Lord will bless His people with peace.* That same Lord who is to bless His people will give them peace in Himself; for *My peace I give unto you,* He said, *my peace I leave with you.*[13]

FIRST DISCOURSE ON PSALM 29

1. [Verse 1] *Unto the end, a Psalm of a canticle at the dedication of the house, for David himself.* Unto the end. A joyful song of the resurrection which has renewed the body, not only of our Lord but also of the whole Church, and has altered its condition to one of immortality. In the last Psalm, the tabernacle in which we have to dwell as long as our warfare lasts reached completion;[1] this Psalm is concerned with the dedication of the house which is to endure everlastingly in unbroken peace.

2. It is Christ, therefore, who speaks in His totality:[2] [V. 2] *I will extol thee, O Lord, for thou hast upheld me.* I will praise thy majesty, O Lord, for having taken me under thy protection. *Thou hast not made my enemies to rejoice over me.* Thou hast not allowed those to triumph over me, who have so often sought everywhere and by every means to crush me beneath persecution.

3. [V. 3] *O Lord my God, I have cried to thee and thou hast healed me.* I have called upon thee, O Lord my God, and I am no longer burdened with a feeble body subject to disease and death.

4. [V. 4] *Thou hast brought back, O Lord, my soul from hell, thou hast saved me from them that go down into the pit.* Thou hast rescued me from a state of utter blindness[3] and from a corruptible body of common clay.

5. [V. 5] *Sing to the Lord, O ye His saints.* The

prophet gazing into the future he now foretells, cries out in a transport of joy: *Sing to the Lord, O ye His saints. And give praise to the memory of His holiness.* Praise Him, for He has not forgotten the holiness He has bestowed on you, although this time of waiting may seem long to your desire.

6. [V. 6] *For wrath is in His indignation.* He has exacted a penalty from you for original sin, which you have expiated by death. *And life in His good will.* He has bestowed on you life everlasting, to which you could attain by no efforts of your own, because it was His good pleasure. *In the evening weeping shall have place.*[4] This evening fell when the light of wisdom was extinguished in sinful man and he was condemned to death: from that fateful evening, tears must flow as long as God's people, amid toil and temptation, await the day of the Lord. *And in the morning gladness.* Man is to wait until the morning that is to witness the joy of his resurrection, which burst forth into its first blossom when our Lord rose at daybreak.

7. [V. 7] *And in my abundance I said: I shall never be moved.* As for me, who from the very first have been speaking in the name of God's people, in the days of prosperity when I no longer suffered want, I declared: *I shall never be moved.*

8. [V. 8] *O Lord, in thy favor thou gavest strength to my beauty.* But, Lord, such prosperity came to me not from myself but from that bounty of thine which bestowed upon me strength and beauty, as I learned when *Thou didst turn away thy face from me, and I became troubled;* for my sins indeed made thee sometimes turn away thy face and I lost all peace, when the light born of knowing thee faded from my soul.

9. [V. 9] *To thee, O Lord, will I cry, and I will make supplication to my God.* When I recall my days of trouble and misery, as if still plunged therein, I hear the voice of thy first-born, my Leader who is about to die for me, crying aloud: *To thee, O Lord, will I cry, and I will make supplication to my God.*

10. [V. 10] *What profit is there in my blood, whilst I go down to corruption?* How will it profit thee to shed my blood, if I am made the prey of corruption? *Shall dust confess to thee?* If I am not restored at once to life, if my body is left to decay, *shall dust confess to thee?* In other words, can the multitude of the ungodly whom my resurrection was to make righteous, give praise to thee? *Or declare thy truth?* Can they convince others of the truth of thy salvation?

11. [V. 11] *The Lord hath heard and hath had mercy on me; the Lord became my helper.* He has not allowed His holy one to see corruption.[5]

12. [V. 12] *Thou hast turned for me my mourning into joy.* I, thy Church, imitating this first-born from the dead, now sing at the dedication of thy house: *Thou hast turned for me my mourning into joy. Thou hast cut my sackcloth and hast girded me with gladness.* Thou hast ripped away the covering of my sins, the sadness of my mortal existence, in order to clothe me in the best robe,[6] and in never-ending joy.

13. [V. 13] *To the end that my glory may sing to thee, and I may not be pierced:* No longer to mourn in lowliness but in glory to sing thy praise, because thou hast now raised me out of humiliation so that neither consciousness of sin, fear of death nor dread of judgment can pierce my heart. *O Lord my God, I will confess to thee forever.* My glory, O Lord my God, consists in this: to

proclaim to thine everlasting praise that there is nothing in me of my own, but that all good whatsoever is from thee, who art God all in all.[7]

Second Discourse on Psalm 29

1. As you all know, we have been singing:[1] [Verse 2] *I will extol thee, O Lord, for thou hast upheld me and hast not made my enemies to rejoice over me.* If the Holy Scriptures have taught us to recognize our enemies, we can grasp the real meaning of this hymn; if, however, the wisdom of the flesh has so deluded us that we no longer recognize the adversary with whom we wrestle,[2] the very opening lines of this Psalm pose an insoluble problem. For whose are we to suppose is the voice that praises and thanks God, and cries out in excess of joy: *I will extol thee, O Lord, for thou hast upheld me and hast not made my enemies to rejoice over me?* Let us consider in the first place that it is our Lord Himself, who in the human nature which He has deigned to assume has every right to make these prophetic words of the Psalmist His own. As man, He was weak; as weak man, He prayed. We have just heard, when the Gospel was read, that He withdrew from His disciples to go into the desert, where they searched for Him and found Him. Being in a lonely spot, *there He prayed*, and when His disciples discovered Him they told Him: *All seek for thee.* To which He made answer: *Let us go into other places and towns to preach, for to this purpose am I come.*[3] If you regard only our Lord Jesus Christ's Godhead, who is He that is praying? To whom? With what object? Can a God pray? Can He pray to His equal? What motive for praying could He have who is ever blessed, ever almighty, ever immutable,

eternal, and coeternal with the Father? If we listen to His voice thundering through John as through some cloud: *In the beginning was the Word, and the Word was with God, and the Word was God; the same was in the beginning with God; all things were made by Him, and without Him was made nothing; what hath been made in Him is life, and the life was the light of men, and the light shineth in darkness, and the darkness did not comprehend it,*[4] we find in these words neither prayer, nor matter for prayer, nor occasion for prayer, nor desire for prayer. But when a little further on we are told: *And the Word was made flesh and dwelt among us,*[5] we are given both the Divine Majesty to whom we pray, and a human being who will make supplication on our behalf. The Apostle uses these very words, in fact, even after the resurrection of our Lord Jesus Christ, *who sitteth,* he says, *at the right hand of God, who also maketh intercession for us.*[6] Why does He intercede for us? Because He has deigned to become our Mediator. What do we mean by a Mediator between God and men? I do not say between the Father and men, but between God and men. What is God? Father, Son and Holy Ghost. What are men? Sinners, evildoers, mortals. Between that Trinity and mankind with its frailty and guilt, one Man has been made Mediator, a Man free from guilt but nevertheless weak, so that in His innocence He could give you access to God, and in His infirmity could have access to you. Thus it is that *the Word was made flesh,* or the Word was made man, in order to become the Mediator between man and God. The term "flesh" of course typifies mankind, as we know from the text: *All flesh shall see the salvation of God.*[7] All flesh, in other words, all men. The Apostle has also told us: *For our wrestling is not against flesh and blood,*

that is to say, against human beings, *but against principalities and powers and the rulers of the world of this
darkness,*[8] of whom, by the help of God, we shall speak
later. It was necessary, however, to draw this distinction in
order to understand this Psalm which I have undertaken in
the name of our Lord to explain to you, holy brethren. I
have quoted these few examples to show you that "flesh"
designates men, and when we say, *And the Word was
made flesh,* we mean: And the Word was made man.

2. It is not without reason that I have emphasized this
point. You are aware, dear brethren, that there were once
certain heretics called Apollinarians,[9] perhaps indeed there
are some left even to this day. Now many of them erred
in speaking of the human nature which the Wisdom of
God assumed (and in which He manifested His Person,
not as He does in mankind at large, but according to the
words of the Psalm: *God, thy God, hath anointed thee
with the oil of gladness above thy fellows,*[10] with an
unction, in other words, superior to that of thy fellow
men; for fear anyone should imagine that Christ's anointing resembled that of ordinary mortals, of other just men,
such as the patriarchs, prophets, apostles, martyrs or any
other outstanding figure of the human race. Now among
all mankind there is none greater than John the Baptist;[11]
there has risen no greater son of woman. If you are in
search of the highest human nobility, you will find it in
John the Baptist. But there was One, the latchet of whose
shoes John declared he was unworthy to loose[12]—what was
He, I ask, if not something beyond the rest of men? Even
in His very human nature He was something more than
any other man. As God, in His divine nature, as the Word
who was from the beginning, the Word who was with
God, the Word who was God, He is equal to the Father

and above every creature. But we are speaking at present of His manhood. It is possible, brethren, that someone among you may believe that the human nature which was assumed by the Wisdom of God was exactly like the rest of men. Now in your human bodies there is a great difference between the head and the other members. Although all without doubt make up one and the same body, nevertheless the head is far superior to the remaining members. In all the others you simply have the sense of touch; it is by actually touching that they receive impressions, whereas by the head you see, you hear, you smell, you taste, you touch. If the head is so much superior to the other members of the body, how much more noble is He who is Head of the whole Church, this Man,[13] in other words, whom God has willed to become Mediator between God and man?).

Well then, as I was saying, those heretics maintained that the human nature which the Word assumed when the Word was made flesh, had no human mind, but only a soul without any human understanding. You know of what man consists: of soul and body. But the human soul possesses something more than the souls of beasts. For animals also have *anima*, a soul: hence their name of animals. We should not call them animals unless they had *anima*, a soul; and we know they have because they too are alive. What has man, however, over and above, which stamps upon him the image of God? He understands, he reasons, he distinguishes between good and evil: it is in this way that he is made to the image and likeness of God.[14] He has something in him, you see, which the beasts have not. And when he despises that quality of his which raises him above the beasts, he destroys in himself, he defaces and in a way degrades God's image, so that such men are given the warning: *Do not become like the horse and the mule who have no understanding.*[15] These heretics, then, argued that our Lord Jesus Christ had neither human mind nor that which the Greeks call λογικόν and we term rational, the power by which man reasons, a power unknown to other animals. What precisely is their doctrine? That the very Word of God, in Christ's human nature, stood in place of the mind which is in us.[16] The Church cast them out, the Catholic faith held them in horror, whereupon they went into heresy. Catholic faith has ordained that this man whom the Wisdom of God took to Himself was exactly like other men: He lacked nothing whatever which contributes to the integrity of human nature; but the pre-eminence of His Person made Him so much greater than other men. For one may say of others that they are partakers of the Word of God since the Word of God dwells in them, but none of them can be given the actual title Word of God, as He was of whom we are told: *The Word was made flesh.*[17]

3. Other heretics also have arisen, sprung from the last-named, who have denied to the Man who is Christ, the Mediator between God and men, not merely a human mind but even a human soul. He was simply the Word and flesh, they have argued, but in that union there was no human mind, no human soul. This was their teaching. What precisely was there then?[18] Merely the Word and flesh. The Catholic Church has disowned these likewise, and expelled them from her flock and from the one, true faith; she has confirmed her dogma, as I have already said, that the Man who was our Mediator was man in every sense of the word, sin excepted. Actually we witness Him performing many physical acts which make clear to us that His body was not fictitious but real: how, for in-

stance, do we learn that He had a body? Why, He walked, He sat, He fell asleep, He was seized, scourged, buffeted, nailed to a cross, and He died. Take away the body and all those things become impossible. Therefore from the indications given in the Gospel we can satisfy ourselves that our Lord had a real body, to which more-over He testified after the resurrection: *Handle and see,* He said, *for a spirit hath not flesh and bones, as you see me to have;*[19] and as from these signs and these actions we be-lieve, understand and acknowledge that our Lord Jesus had a body, in the same way other natural functions teach us that He had a soul. To feel hunger and thirst is char-acteristic of the soul: take away the soul and the dead body will not feel such things. If the heretics maintain these feelings are fictitious, all that has been deduced from the body will be a fable also; but if the reality of the physical acts proves that the body is real, the truth of the soul's actions proves that the soul was likewise real.

4. What is the lesson? O whoever you are here listening to me, our Lord has made Himself weak for your sake, but do not therefore imagine that God is like yourself. You are a mere creature, He is your Creator. That the Word, the Son of God, that your God has become man on your account, is no reason to compare Him in His manhood with yourself, but rather to exalt Him, both above your-self in that He is your Mediator, and above every creature in that He is God. And realize furthermore that He who has become man for your sake, can without loss of dignity intercede for you; and if such prayer does not impair His dignity, He can likewise without loss of dignity utter in your name the words: *I will extol thee, O Lord, for thou hast upheld me and hast not made my enemies to rejoice over me.* But unless we really understand who the enemies

are, we shall falsify these words if we think of them as issuing from our Lord Jesus Christ Himself. For how can Christ our Lord say with truth: *I will extol thee, O Lord, for thou hast upheld me?* How can it be true of Christ in His human nature, in His weakness, in His mortal flesh? For His enemies did in fact triumph over Him when they crucified Him, held Him fast, scourged Him and buffeted Him, saying as they did so: *Prophesy unto us, O Christ.*[20] This triumph of theirs almost forces us to think that the words *Thou hast not made my enemies to rejoice over me* are untrue. To add to that, while He was hanging on the cross they passed up and down, or stood by watching, and tossed their heads with the taunt: *Behold the Son of God, He saved others, Himself He cannot save; let Him now come down from the cross, and we will believe in Him.*[21] Were they not gloating over Him when they hurled such insults? What then becomes of the voice which cries: *I will extol thee, O Lord, for thou hast upheld me and hast not made my enemies to rejoice over me?*

5. Possibly the voice which speaks is not that of our Lord Jesus Christ, but that of mankind itself, of the whole Church, of the entire Christian people, because in Christ all men form but a single man, and all Christians unite to form but one man. Possibly it is this man, this unity of Christendom that says: *I will extol thee, O Lord, for thou hast upheld me and hast not made my enemies to rejoice over me.* But is that true in their regard? Were the apostles not seized, beaten, scourged, put to death, nailed to a cross, burnt alive, condemned to the beasts? Do we not celebrate their memory to this day? When men were wreaking their worst on them, was not the victory apparently theirs? How is it possible, therefore, for even the Christian people to say: *I will extol thee, O Lord, for thou*

hast upheld me and hast not made my enemies to rejoice over me?

6. We shall understand it if we first study the title of the Psalm. Now the title runs: [V. 1] *Unto the end, a Psalm of a canticle at the dedication of the house, for David himself.* The entire hidden meaning and all hope of elucidating the difficulty are to be found in the title. The house in process of building will one day be dedicated. This house which is the Church is at present merely under construction, later on it will be dedicated. At that dedication the splendor of the Christian people, as yet invisible, will burst forth in glory. Let our enemies rage against us, humiliate us, do, not what they would, but whatever they are divinely permitted to do here below. We must not however attribute to our enemies all that we suffer at their hands; it sometimes comes from the Lord our God. For our Mediator has shown us by His own example that when He divinely allows men to do us harm, the ill will is not given from above, but merely the power to perform it. Every evildoer cherishes in his heart a desire to injure, but to carry it into effect is beyond his power. The intention renders him already guilty, but the power to act comes by a mysterious dispensation of God's providence which allows the evildoer to punish one, to test another, and to send a third to his crown. To punish, as He allowed the ἀλλόφυλοι, the foreigners, to capture the people of Israel for their sin against God.[22] To put to the test, as He allowed the devil to try Job:[23] to Job's triumph, to the devil's shame. To crown, as He allowed their persecutors to crown the martyrs. The martyrs were slaughtered and their executioners fancied themselves victors; these achieved a hollow triumph before the eyes of all, the others in secret won an invisible but real crown. The power thus

given, therefore, is part of the mysterious working of God's providence; but whereas the desire to injure is man's own, yet he cannot always deal out death just as he would.

7. Thus when our Lord Himself, Judge of the living and the dead, was brought before a human tribunal, He set us the pattern of humility and patience. Unconquered, He would teach His soldiers their plan of campaign. When the judge addressed to Him the high-sounding and arrogant threat: *Knowest thou not that I have power to release thee or to put thee to death?*, our Lord crushed the vainglorious pride with a reply which, so to speak, burst the bubble at a breath: *Thou shouldst not have any power against me*, He answered, *unless it were given thee from above.*[24] And Job also, what was his reaction? Bear in mind that the devil had just slain his children, the devil had taken away his substance. *The Lord gave, the Lord hath taken away*, he said. *As it hath pleased the Lord, so is it done. Blessed be the name of the Lord.*[25] The enemy need not congratulate himself upon his work, for I know, he said, who has granted him permission; to the devil belongs the malicious intent, but to my Lord the power to prove men. When his body is covered with sores, along comes his wife who has been left to him, like another Eve, to be the devil's colleague instead of being her husband's support. She continually upbraids him to shake his constancy: *Speak some word against God*, she tells him, *and die.* But the Adam on the dunghill was more prudent than the Adam in Paradise. Adam in Paradise gave ear to the woman, only to be thrust out of Paradise; Adam on the dunghill thrust aside the woman, only to enter into Paradise. And what had this Adam on the dunghill, inwardly begetting immortality, outwardly food for worms, what

had he to say to his wife? *Thou hast spoken like one of the foolish women. If we have received good things at the hand of God, why should we not receive evil?*[26] He repeated that it was the hand of God upon him when it was the devil who struck him, because he did not look at him who dealt the blow but at Him who gave the power. Even the devil himself in his turn called that power for which he begged, the hand of the Lord. Determined to impute sin to the man whose justice was attested by the Lord, Satan said to God: *Doth Job fear God in vain? Hast not thou made a fence for him, and his house, and all his substance round about, blessed the works of his hands, and his possession hath increased on the earth? Such wealth hast thou given him, therefore doth he worship thee. But stretch forth thy hand, and touch all that he hath, and see if he blesseth thee not to thy face.*[27] What did the devil mean by *stretch forth thy hand* when his own hand intended to strike? Yet because his own hand lacked the power to strike, he called the power to do so which he received from God, God's hand.

8. What are we to say, brethren, in the face of the sufferings our enemies have inflicted upon Christians, and of their delirious joy in their victory? And when will it be made obvious that their victory is illusory? When these are covered with confusion and the others with joy at the advent of the Lord our God, who will come bearing in His hand each one's recompense: to the reprobate, damnation; to the just, a kingdom; to evildoers, fellowship with the devil; to the faithful, fellowship with Christ. When therefore our Lord reveals all this, when the just stand forth in great boldness—I am going to quote the Scriptures, you will remember this lesson from the Book of Wisdom: *Then shall the just stand with great constancy*

*against those that have afflicted them; but they shall say
within themselves, repenting, and groaning for anguish of
spirit: What hath pride profited us, or what advantage hath
the boasting of riches brought us? For all those things are
passed away like a shadow.* And what will they say of the
just? *Behold how they are numbered among the children
of God, and their lot is among the saints.*[28] Then will be
celebrated the dedication of the house which we are building today amid tribulation; then will God's people sing
right heartily: *I will extol thee, O Lord, for thou hast
upheld me and hast not made my enemies to rejoice over
me.* These words therefore will be verified in the people
of God, that people at present beset with suffering, at
present borne down by the weight of so many trials, so
many scandals, so many persecutions, such deep distress.
The man who is making no headway in virtue feels none
of this mental anguish in the Church, and imagines that all
is at peace. But let him begin to advance and he will soon
find himself in difficulties, because when the blade sprang
up and brought forth fruit, it was then that there appeared
also the cockle;[29] and he that addeth knowledge addeth
also labor.[30] Let him make progress and he will see where
he stands: let there be fruit and the cockle will appear.
The Apostle has spoken the plain truth in words which
are true for all time: *Yet all that will live godly in Christ,*
he says, *suffer persecution. But evil men and seducers grow
worse and worse, themselves erring, and driving others
into error.*[31] Is not that the meaning of those words of the
Psalm: *Wait for the Lord, do manfully; and let thy heart
take courage, and wait thou for the Lord?*[32] Merely to say
once, *Wait for the Lord* would not be enough; the Psalmist
repeats it, for fear we should grow disheartened that two,
three or four days put no end to our trials and afflictions.

He then adds, *do manfully,* and later, *let thy heart take courage.* And as life must needs be thus from first to last, he ends as he began, *and wait thou for the Lord.* The evils that afflict you will pass, and He whom you patiently await will come; He will wipe away the sweat of toil, He will dry every tear, and weeping will be no more. Here below we must sigh amid tribulation: *What is man's life upon earth,* Job asks, *but a trial?*[33]

9. Nevertheless, brethren, whilst awaiting the day when the house is to be dedicated, we should consider that the dedication has already taken place in Him who is our Head: the house has already been dedicated in its Head as in the foundation stone. But a head crowns the summit, the foundation lies beneath: possibly I have been wrong in terming Christ the foundation; rather is He the topmost height, since He has ascended into heaven to sit at the right hand of the Father. No, I have not made any mistake, for the Apostle has told us: *For other foundation no man can lay, but that which is laid, which is Christ Jesus. Now if any man build upon this foundation, gold, silver, precious stones.*[34] Those who lead holy lives, who honor and praise God, who are patient under affliction, who long after their heavenly home, such as these build in gold, silver and precious stones; those who are still attached to the world, still entangled in secular affairs, enslaved by human loves of one kind and another, love of home, wife, possessions, yet who remain Christians in spite of all, so that their hearts are never separated from Christ and they prefer nothing whatever to Christ, just as in any building nothing is reckoned more important than the foundation— such as these really build, but they build in wood, in hay, in stubble. But what does the Apostle go on to say? *Fire shall try every man's work, of what sort it is:* the fire of

testing and affliction. Many martyrs have stood the test of this fire here below; the whole human race will face its ordeal at the last day. Martyrs are to be found who were bound by ties to the world. How many senators and men of wealth have undergone death! Some of them were building in wood, hay and stubble by reason of their pre-occupation with the world and human affections, and yet because Christ was the foundation stone upon which they built, the hay was burnt to ashes while they remained intact upon the foundation. Now the Apostle tells us: *If any man's work abide, he shall receive a reward,* and that without loss of any kind; he will find what he has loved. What then has the fire of tribulation done to them? It has tested them. *If any man's work abide, he shall receive a reward: if any man's work burn, he shall suffer loss; but he himself shall be saved, yet so as by fire.*[35] Now to pass unscathed through fire is very different from being saved by fire. Whence comes this salvation? From the foundation of the building. Therefore never allow this foundation to vanish from your heart. Do not make grass the ground-work of your building, that is to say, do not prefer grass to the foundation stone, so as to give the first place in your heart to grass, the second to Christ. But if grass you needs must have, at least let Christ hold the first place, and give grass the second.

10. Christ, then, is our foundation stone. As I have told you, the dedication of our Head has already taken place, and this summit of the building is also its foundation stone. Ordinarily, however, this stone is at the base of an edifice, whereas the summit is at its highest point. Listen carefully to my words, holy brethren; perhaps Christ will help me to explain clearly in His name. There are two kinds of weights. Weight is that force by which an object tends

to reach the place proper to its nature: that is its defini-
tion.[36] Hold a stone in your hand and you will feel the
weight; it presses against your hand because it is seeking
its center of gravity. Would you like to see what it seeks?
Withdraw your hand, it falls to the earth and lies on the
ground: it has reached its goal, it has found its proper
place. The weight was a kind of spontaneous movement,
without life or feeling. There are other objects which tend
to rise to their center. Pour water on top of oil, and its
weight will soon draw it to the bottom. It seeks its own
place, it wants its proper position, for it is contrary to the
nature of water to float on oil. Until it reaches its natural
place, therefore, until it occupies its true position, it sets
up a continual movement. By way of contrast, pour some
oil into water: supposing for instance a bottle of oil falls
into the water, into the sea or a rushing stream, and is
thereby broken, the oil cannot stay below the surface. Just
as water poured on oil tends to sink by its weight to its
proper level, so too oil poured out under water naturally
tends to rise by its weight to the surface. If this is so,
brethren, what is the tendency of fire and water? Fire
rises and seeks its natural place above; water likewise seeks
the place its weight assigns to it. Stone drops to the bottom,
so does wood, and so too the pillars and earth used to build
houses: they are to be classed among those objects which
are borne downwards by their own weight. It is obvious
therefore that at their base they have the foundation
which supports them, because they are drawn downwards
by their natural propensity; without this supporting
groundwork everything would fall to pieces, because
everything is attracted earthwards. Things that naturally
tend to drop to earth must have their foundations laid in
the earth. The Church of God, on the other hand, built

here on earth, tends heavenwards. It is there, you see, that its foundation stone has been laid, in other words, Jesus Christ our Lord seated at the right hand of the Father. If then, holy brethren, you have grasped that the dedication of the foundation stone has already been accomplished, let us listen and briefly run through the whole Psalm.

11. *I will extol thee, O Lord, for thou hast upheld me and hast not made my enemies to rejoice over me.* Which enemies? The Jews? In the dedication of the foundation stone, we must take into account the dedication of the house to come. What is said today of the foundation will be said tomorrow of the entire building. Who then are the enemies in question? Are they the Jews, or are they not rather the devil and his angels who were routed in confusion upon our Lord's resurrection? The prince of death had the mortification of seeing death conquered. *Thou hast not made my enemies to rejoice over me,* since hell is unable to hold me in bounds.

12. [V. 3] *O Lord my God, I have cried to thee, and thou hast healed me:* before His passion, our Lord pleaded on the mount with God, who healed Him. How could He heal one who had known no sickness? Was the Word who is God, the Word who is the Godhead, restored to health? No; remember He bore a mortal body, He bore your injury, for He was to heal you of your wound. So this human flesh of His was healed. When? When He rose from the dead. Listen to the Apostle and you will agree that the healing was perfect: *Death,* he says, *is swallowed up in victory. O death, where is thy sting? O death, where is thy claim?*[37] This song of victory, which Christ sings today, will be ours to sing hereafter.

13. [V. 4] *Thou hast brought back, O Lord, my soul from hell.* This passage requires no explanation. *Thou hast*

saved me from them that go down into the pit. Who go down into the pit? All the sinners who plunge headlong into the whirlpool, the pit symbolizing the whirlpool of the world. And what is meant by the whirlpool of the world? The ocean of self-indulgence and vice. They go down into the pit who wallow in their own impurity and gross desires. Such were Christ's persecutors. But what does He say here? *Thou hast saved me from them that go down into the pit.*

14. [V. 5] *Sing to the Lord, O ye His saints.* Since your Leader is risen, you His members left behind may hope to enjoy what you already see accomplished in your Head; hope for the members what you believe of the Head. The proverb which runs: "Where the head is, there also are the members," is both ancient and true. Christ has ascended into heaven; it is there we are to follow Him. He did not remain in hell, He has risen to die no more. When we too have risen again, we shall die no more. Therefore in the joy of these promises: *Sing to the Lord, O ye His saints, and give praise to the memory of His holiness.* What is the force of *give praise to the memory?* Why, you had forgotten Him, but He has never forgotten you.

15. [V. 6] *For wrath is in His indignation, and life in His good will.* In His anger, vengeance falls upon the sinner: *For on what day soever thou shalt eat of it, thou shalt die the death.*[38] They stretched out their hands, they tasted death, they were driven out of Paradise, *for wrath is in His indignation.* But their chastisement was not devoid of hope, because there is *life in His good will.* What is the meaning of *in His good will?* Not in our own strength any more than in our own merits; but He has saved us simply because He willed to do so, not because we deserved it. For what does a sinner deserve but punishment?

God has given life. And if He has bestowed life on the impious, what has He not in store for His faithful ones?

16. *In the evening weeping shall have place.* Do not be alarmed if after bidding us *Sing*, the Psalmist here speaks of lamentation. Song is the expression of joy, prayer of lamentation.

> Pray for today and its sorrow,
> Sing for the joy of tomorrow.[39]

In the evening weeping shall have place. What do we mean by *In the evening weeping shall have place?* Evening descends when the sun sets. Now the sun has set for man, that is to say, that light of justice which is the presence of God. Hence what does Genesis tell us of Adam's expulsion? When God walked in Paradise, God walked there at eventide. The sinner had already hidden himself among the trees, in order to avoid the face of God which formerly had been his delight.[40] His Sun of Justice had set, and he found no joy in God's presence. Thus began the course of this mortal life of ours. *In the evening weeping shall have place.* You will spend a long time in tears, O pitiable humanity; for you have Adam for father and there is no doubt about it; and we too are sons of Adam; and all those who have had children, and all who ever will have them, are sons of Adam as their fathers were. *In the evening weeping shall have place. And in the morning gladness,* when the faithful glimpse the dawning of that light which had departed from sinners. Thus, then, our Lord Jesus Christ rose from the tomb in the early morning,[41] so that the dedication of the foundation stone should be a pledge of the future for the whole building. With our Lord, evening was the time of His burial, and the morning of the third day saw His resurrection. You too were buried at eventide in Paradise, and on the third day you rose again. How on the third day? To sum up the course of time: there was one day before the Law, a second under the Law, a third under grace. What your Head Himself demonstrated during those three days is to be re-enacted also in yourselves during the three days of this life. When? Morning will be the time of hope and joy; at present it is the time of endurance and woe.

17. [V. 7] *And in my abundance I said: I shall never be moved.* What abundance prompted man to declare: *I shall never be moved?* But here we are listening, brethren, to man speaking from his abasement. Who enjoys abundance here below? No one. In what does mortal man's abundance consist? In care and calamity. But the rich, you retort, enjoy abundance? The more they possess, the poorer they are. They are consumed by envy, tossed by passion, racked by fear, wasted by melancholy: where, I ask, is their abundance? Man had real abundance when he dwelt in Paradise; he wanted for nothing when God was his joy. But said he: *I shall never be moved.* When did he say in so many words *I shall never be moved?* When he lent a willing ear to the invitation: *Taste, and you will be as gods;* when to God's warning, *In what day soever thou shalt eat of it, thou shalt die the death,* the devil opposed the assurance, *No, you shall not die the death.*[42] Whereupon the all too credulous man, yielding to the devil's persuasion, said: *I shall never be moved.*

18. But the Lord had spoken the truth when He threatened to deprive the proud man of what He had bestowed upon the humble at his creation; and so the Psalmist adds: [V. 8] *O Lord, in thy favor thou gavest strength to my beauty.* Of myself, that is to say, I had neither virtue nor strength; all my fair honor, all my power

came from thee. That loving favor which led thee to create me, made thee unite in me strength and beauty; and to teach me that I owed it solely to thy bounty, *Thou didst turn away thy face from me, and I became troubled.* God turned His face away from him whom He cast out of Paradise.[43] Now in his exile let him cry aloud in the words: [V. 9] *To thee, O Lord, will I cry, and I will make supplication to my God.* In Paradise you had not to cry aloud but to sing praise, in place of toil you enjoyed fruition. But now that you are driven forth, you must needs bemoan and plead aloud. He who left the proud to his own resources will come to the aid of the penitent, *for God resisteth the proud, but to the humble He giveth grace.*[44] *To thee, O Lord, will I cry, and I will make supplication to my God.*

19. What now follows applies to our Lord in person, who is our foundation stone: [V. 10] *What profit is there in my blood, whilst I go down to corruption?* What is the object of His prayer? His resurrection. If I go down into the grave, He argues, and if my flesh becomes the prey of corruption like other men's, to be restored to life only at the last day, why shed my blood? Unless my resurrection takes place at once, I can bring my message to no one, I can gain no disciple; but if I am to preach to others thy wondrous works, the praise that is thy due, and life everlasting, my body must rise from the dead, it must never taste corruption. If it must go the way of all men, what is there to gain by shedding my blood? *Shall dust confess to thee or declare thy truth?* Confession is twofold: that of sin and that of praise. In adversity, we should confess our sins with compunction; in prosperity, we should confess with joy the praise of God's justice. We must never be without one or other confession.

20. [V. 11] *The Lord hath heard and hath had mercy on me.* How? Remember the dedication of the house. God has answered the prayer, He has shown compassion. *The Lord became my helper.*

21. Now listen to His resurrection: [V. 12] *Thou hast turned for me my mourning into joy. Thou hast cut my sackcloth and hast girded me with gladness.* What sackcloth? His mortality. Sackcloth is woven from the hair of goats and kids, and both goats and kids are ranked among sinners.[45] The Lord as one of our race donned the sackcloth but not that for which it is the penalty. Sackcloth is the legacy of sin, while the sackcloth itself is mortality. He who did nothing to deserve death clothed Himself in a mortal body for your sake. One who sins deserves death, whereas He who was innocent of sin did not deserve the sackcloth. Our Lord's is the voice which cries out in another Psalm: *But as for me, when they were troublesome to me, I put on haircloth.*[46] What does *I put on haircloth* mean? I confronted my persecutors disguised in haircloth. In order that His persecutors should think Him a mere man, He hid Himself from their eyes, for they were unworthy of seeing Him who was clothed in haircloth. Therefore, *Thou hast cut my sackcloth and hast girded me with gladness.*

22. [V. 13] *To the end that my glory may sing to thee, and I may not be pierced.* As with the Head, so with the Body. What does *I may not be pierced* imply? I may no longer undergo death. For our Lord was pierced as He hung on the cross when He received the thrust of the spear,[47] and therefore He our Head cries out *I may not be pierced,* or, may I die no more.

But for our part, what are we to say concerning this dedication of the house? May our conscience no longer goad us with our sins. For all will be pardoned, and then we shall be free. *To the end that my glory*, not my humiliation, *may sing to thee*, says the Psalmist. If the glory is ours, it is also Christ's, because we are the Body of Christ. How is that? Because even though Christ is seated in heaven, He is to say to some: *I was hungry, and you gave me to eat.*[48] He is in heaven, and He is on earth: there in His own person, here in us. What then does He mean? *To the end that my glory may sing to thee, and I may not be pierced.* It is I who groan before thee in humility, as it is I who shall sing to thee in glory.

And finally: *O Lord my God, I will confess to thee forever.* What is the meaning of *I will confess to thee forever?* I shall sing thy praise for all eternity; as we have said, there is a confession of praise as well as of sins. Confess then today what you have done against God, and you will confess tomorrow what God has done in return for you. What have you done? Committed sins. And God? He forgives your sins as soon as you confess your guilt, to free you from the remorse of sin, that you may confess His praise hereafter forever and ever.

NOTES

NOTES

The set of discourses on Psalms 1–32 (or the first on each Psalm when there is more than one) are assumed to have been written down, *dictatae*, not actually preached. Some but not all are merely skeleton exegeses on the text. The rest may be examined as typical examples of treatises in sermon form.

[1] *Homo dominicus*, the Man of the Lord, in antithesis to *homo terrenus*, the man of earth. The phrase is incorrect usage when speaking of Christ, and for that reason is frequently discussed by theologians in treatises on the Incarnation. St. Thomas Aquinas devotes an article to this very title; see *Sum. theol.* 3, q. 16, a. 3. Although the phrase κυριακὸς ἄνθρωπος had been used by other Fathers, St. Augustine deliberately withdrew it in his *Retractationes* 1.19.8: "I do not see how He can rightly be called 'the Man of the Lord' who is the Mediator between God and man, considering that He is the very Lord Himself. Does not the title 'Man of the Lord' apply equally well to any amid the family of His elect? . . . Wherever I have used this phrase, I wish I had not done so."

[2] Cf. 1 Cor. 15.47.
[3] Cf. Gen. 3.6.
[4] 2 Tim. 2.17.
[5] 2 Tim. 1.9.
[6] John 8.56.
[7] Ps. 15.7.
[8] Ps. 64.10.
[9] Matt. 3.11.
[10] John 7.37.
[11] John 4.10,13,14.
[12] Apoc. 17.15.
[13] Isa. 40.6–8.
[14] Ps. 15.5,6.
[15] Ps. 36.34.
[16] Matt. 5.4.
[17] Ps. 35.9,12.

[18] Isa. 14.13,14.
[19] Gen. 3.6,8.
[20] Eccli. 10.9,10.
[21] 1 Cor. 3.13–15.
[22] Matt. 7.23.
[23] Exod. 3.14.

DISCOURSE ON PSALM 2

[1] Acts 4.26.
[2] Wisd. 12.18.
[3] Cf. Discourse on Ps. 47.5.
[4] 2 Cor. 3.18.
[5] Cf. Discourse on Ps. 60.8.
[6] Cf. Second Discourse on Ps. 21.30.
[7] Rom. 8.34.
[8] Cf. Discourse on Ps. 44.18.
[9] 1 Cor. 9.26,27.
[10] Cf. Discourse on Ps. 65.5.
[11] See above, § 4.

DISCOURSE ON PSALM 3

[1] 2 Kings 15.17.
[2] Ps. 3.6.
[3] Matt. 9.15.
[4] John 13.2.
[5] John 13.27.
[6] *Regnorum libri,* the Septuagint title of the Book of Kings.
[7] 2 Kings 18.33.
[8] Cf. Matt. 26.49.
[9] Matt. 27.42.
[10] 1 Cor. 4.7.
[11] St. Augustine here refers to the human mind of our Lord as distinct from the divine mind which as God He shares with the Father and Holy Ghost; cf. Luke 22.42.
[12] Dan. 13.44.
[13] Matt. 6.6.
[14] According to St. Thomas Aquinas, St. Augustine is here speaking of contemplative prayer in its strict sense; see *Sum. theol.* 2–2, q. 180, a. 8.2 and ad 2m.
[15] Cf. Discourses on Ps. 44.33 and Ps. 47.2.

[16] Dan. 2.35.
[17] Ps. 35.7.
[18] Cf. Discourses on Ps. 40.10, Ps. 56.11, Ps. 101.8, and Ps. 138.2.
[19] *Ego dormivi et somnum cepi.* Later on, St. Augustine states that some copies have *Ego dormivi et soporatus sum,* the Vulgate reading.
[20] John 10.18.
[21] 1 Thess. 4.12.
[22] Matt. 27.39.
[23] 2 Cor. 13.3.
[24] Gal. 5.15.
[25] Acts 10.13.
[26] Cant. 4.2; 6.5.
[27] Matt. 5.16.
[28] Matt. 22.40.
[29] Cf. Discourse on Ps. 145.9.
[30] Rom. 7.24,25.
[31] 1 Cor. 12.27.
[32] John 1.14.
[33] Eph. 2.6.
[34] Rom. 8.35.
[35] Col. 1.18.
[36] Eph. 5.14.
[37] 1 Thess. 5.7.
[38] Ps. 67.19.
[39] Cf. Matt. 9.37; John 4.36.
[40] Cf. Rom. 7.23.
[41] 1 Cor. 11.3.
[42] Rom. 7.25.
[43] *Pacata.* Some MSS read *peccata,* an obvious error.
[44] 1 Cor. 15.54.
[45] Ps. 62.9.

DISCOURSE ON PSALM 4

[1] Rom. 10.4. *Unto the end* is considered by most modern exegetists to mean "For the choirmaster," the title implying that the Psalm to which it is prefixed belongs to the official songs in charge of the chief singer. St. Augustine constantly acknowledges that he finds great difficulty in elucidating these introductory titles. In *Conf.* 9.4 he describes the powerful effect his study of

Psalm 4 while he was still a catechumen in the country house at Cassiciacum had upon his soul.

2 1 Par. 13.8; 16.5.

3 See Note 1 to Ps. 1.

4 Rom. 2.9.

5 Rom. 5.3,5.

6 Matt. 25.35.

7 Rom. 5.3,5.

8 Rom. 8.25.

9 *Vanitas est vanitantium:* see *Retract.* 1.7.3, in which St. Augustine declares his preference for the generally accepted reading *vanitas vanitatum,* a truer rendering of the Greek. It was only towards the close of his life that he perceived his error. See Dom de Bruyne, in *Rev. biblique,* 1932, p. 554; and J. Colleran, *St. Augustine, The Greatness of the Soul, The Teacher* (ACW 9, Westminster, Md., 1950) 215, note 104.

10 Cf. Eccle. 1.2,3.

11 See Second Discourse on Ps. 25.3.

12 Rom. 7.25.

13 Isa. 29.13.

14 Matt. 6.6.

15 Dom de Bruyne points out (*Miscell. Agost.* 2.556) that St. Augustine's manuscript was defective. The obvious reading is κατανοίγητε.

16 Ps. 50.19.

17 Gen. 1.26.

18 Matt. 22.21.

19 Eph. 3.17.

20 John 14.6.

21 2 Cor. 13.3.

22 Matt. 6.6.

23 John 6.51.

24 Ps. 35.9.

25 Ps. 22.5.

26 Luke 17.21.

27 Wisd. 9.15.

28 Wisd. 1.1.

29 1 Cor. 15.54.

30 Rom. 8.25.

31 Acts 4.32.

32 To translate *Dominus* as "our good" or "our blessed" Lord

is to follow in the Biblical tradition of St. John Fisher and St. Thomas More.

DISCOURSE ON PSALM 5

[1] Matt. 5.4.
[2] Ps. 141.6.
[3] Ps. 15.5.
[4] Ps. 2.8.
[5] John 14.6.
[6] Sabellius, leader in Rome of the Monarchians, was excommunicated by Pope Callistus, *ca.* 220. These heretics held that in the Godhead the only differentiation was a succession of modes or operations, not Persons. In the West they were usually called Patripassians, as it was a corollary of their doctrine that God the Father appeared on earth and suffered as the Son; in the East they were commonly known as Sabellians.
[7] Rom. 11.36.
[8] Rom. 8.24.
[9] Ps. 3.7.
[10] Deut. 13.3.
[11] Cf. Second Discourse on Ps. 26.8.
[12] Cf. Exod. 1.19. See also *Liber de mendacio* 5 and 17.
[13] Matt. 5.37.
[14] Wisd. 1.11.
[15] John 16.12.
[16] 1 Cor. 3.1.
[17] Ps. 8.5.
[18] 1 Cor. 3.17.
[19] Cf. Eph. 2.20.
[20] 1 John 4.18.
[21] John 15.15.
[22] Matt. 5.45.
[23] Ps. 7.15–17.
[24] Ps. 4.3.
[25] Matt. 12.34.
[26] Ps. 79.3.
[27] Rom. 2.15.
[28] Cf. Ps. 5.5.
[29] Ps. 72.28.
[30] Matt. 25.21,30.

[31] *Quoniam inamaricaverunt te;* Vulgate reads *irritaverunt,* "they have provoked."
[32] John 6.51.
[33] John 6.27.
[34] Ps. 33.9.
[35] Rom. 3.23.
[36] Rom. 8.30.
[37] Rom. 8.33.
[38] Rom. 8.31,33.
[39] Rom. 5.8–10.

DISCOURSE ON PSALM 6

[1] Acts 1.7.
[2] Matt. 24.36; Mark 13.32.
[3] 1 Thess. 5.2.
[4] Deut. 13.3.
[5] Ps. 3.7.
[6] Cf. Eph. 4.22.
[7] Cf. Rom. 5.14.
[8] Col. 3.10.
[9] Cf. Deut. 6.5; Matt. 22.37.
[10] Rom. 2.5.
[11] Wisd. 12.18.
[12] Cf. 1 Cor. 3.11.
[13] Isa. 65.24.
[14] 1 Peter 4.18.
[15] Zach. 1.3.
[16] Osee 6.3, according to the Septuagint.
[17] John 1.10.
[18] Luke 16.23–31.
[19] Cf. 1 Cor. 15.56.
[20] Rom. 1.28.
[21] Rom. 7.25.
[22] Ps. 5.5.
[23] See First Discourse on Ps. 36.9.
[24] Rom. 1.28.
[25] Cf. Matt. 25.30.
[26] 1 Tim. 6.16.
[27] Matt. 25.21,23.
[28] Eph. 4.26.
[29] See Discourse on Ps. 102.9.

[30] Cf. Col. 3.9,10.
[31] Ps. 33.19.
[32] Cf. Ps. 125.5.
[33] Cf. Matt. 5.5.
[34] Matt. 10.32; Luke 9.26.
[35] Cf. Ps. 111.9.
[36] 1 Tim. 6.7,8.
[37] Wisd. 5.3–9.
[38] Cf. 1 Thess. 5.3.
[39] Almost all manuscripts read *sine confusione;* Louvain reads *confessione,* "without confession."
[40] Rom. 6.21.

DISCOURSE ON PSALM 7

[1] Cf. 2 Kings 16.
[2] Cf. 2 Cor. 3.16.
[3] Cf. Discourse on Ps. 3.1.
[4] Cf. Matt. 9.15.
[5] John 20.17.
[6] Cf. Rom. 8.29.
[7] Rom. 11.33,34.
[8] John 15.15.
[9] Matt. 6.3.
[10] 1 Peter 5.8.
[11] Matt. 5.48,45.
[12] Cf. Matt. 6.6.
[13] Prov. 16.32, according to the Septuagint.
[14] Gen. 3.14,19.
[15] Cf. Ps. 1.4.
[16] 1 Cor. 1.31.
[17] Ps. 52.6.
[18] Eccli. 10.15,14.
[19] Acts 7.59.
[20] Cf. Rom. 4.5.
[21] Gen. 3.5.
[22] Ps. 2.1.
[23] Rom. 11.25.
[24] Ps. 2.8.
[25] John 7.39.
[26] Ps. 17.11,12.
[27] Luke 18.8.

[28] Matt. 24.8.
[29] Cf. Amos 8.11.
[30] Matt. 10.22.
[31] Luke 18.8.
[32] John 5.22.
[33] Matt. 6.10.
[34] Cf. Luke 5.32.
[35] Ps. 6.5.
[36] Ps. 17.29.
[37] John 1.8.
[38] John 5.35.
[39] Apoc. 22.11.
[40] Cf. Matt. 6.21.
[41] Cf. Gal. 1.16.
[42] Cf. 1 John 2.16,17.
[43] Ps. 6.3.
[44] Ps. 6.5.
[45] Cf. Rom. 4.5.
[46] Rom. 5.8,9.
[47] Ps. 4.7.
[48] Ps. 15.7,8.
[49] Ps. 15.9.
[50] Cf. Matt. 16.27.
[51] *Non iram adducens:* an early example of St. Augustine's independent treatment of the text of the Psalms.
[52] Cf. Rom. 2.5.
[53] *Homo dominicus:* see Ps. 1, note 1. The phrase recurs at the end of this discourse, § 20.
[54] Ps. 16.13.
[55] Cant. 2.4, following the Septuagint.
[56] Ps. 119.3,4.
[57] Rom. 8.35,38,39.
[58] 1 Cor. 11.19.
[59] 2 Cor. 2.16.
[60] Gen. 3.17.
[61] Matt. 11.28,30.
[62] Cf. Eccli. 10.14.
[63] Ps. 9.17.
[64] John 8.34.
[65] Ps. 3.4.
[66] Matt. 11.25.
[67] Eccli. 39.19–21.

[68] Gen. 1.3.
[69] Gen. 1.4,5.
[70] Isa. 58.10.
[71] 1 John 2.11.
[72] Rom. 13.12.

DISCOURSE ON PSALM 8

[1] Cf. Discourse on Ps. 83.1.
[2] Luke 3.17.
[3] Num. 13.24.
[4] John 19.29.
[5] Cf. Luke 22.18.
[6] 1 Cor. 3.1,2.
[7] Matt. 21.16.
[8] 1 Cor. 2.6.
[9] Cf. Eph. 3.18,19.
[10] Isa. 7.9, following the Septuagint.
[11] John 20.29.
[12] Matt. 11.25.
[13] *Defensorem*, "defender." When discussing this text again in his Discourse on Ps. 102 (composed in 412), St. Augustine replaces this word by *vindicatorem*, "avenger," adding: *Nonnulli codices defensorem habent, sed verius vindicatorem:* "Some manuscripts have 'defender,' but 'avenger' is more accurate."
[14] Cf. Exod. 31.18; Deut. 9.10.
[15] Exod. 8.19.
[16] Isa. 34.4.
[17] Ps. 17.10.
[18] Ps. 10.3.
[19] Cf. 1 Cor. 15.49.
[20] Cf. Eph. 4.22–24.
[21] Ps. 118.155.
[22] Ps. 4.7.
[23] Ps. 35.7–11.
[24] 1 Cor. 3.1–3.
[25] See Ps. 1, note 1. The phrase recurs in § 13.
[26] 1 Cor. 15.27.
[27] Cf. Heb. 2.8.
[28] Cf. Matt. 18.12.
[29] Cf. Gen. 2.22.
[30] Deut. 25.4. Cf. 1 Cor. 9.9 and 1 Tim. 5.18.

[31] Cf. Matt. 3.12; 13.24.
[32] Cf. Matt. 13.47.
[33] Cf. Gen. 7.8.
[34] Cf. Matt. 7.13.
[35] Cf. Gen. 4.8.
[36] Ps. 35.7.
[37] Ps. 72.9.
[38] Ps. 11.5.
[39] 1 John 2.15,16.
[40] Matt. 4.3.

DISCOURSE ON PSALM 9

[1] Ps. 3.1.
[2] John 8.36.
[3] Cf. Rom. 11.25.
[4] 1 Peter 4.7.
[5] John 5.24, slightly adapted.
[6] John 3.18.
[7] Wisd. 12.25,26.
[8] Rom. 5.3.
[9] Cf. Ps. 4.7.
[10] Ps. 30.21.
[11] Cf. John 6.38.
[12] Matt. 4.10.
[13] Cf. 1 Cor. 15.47.
[14] John 1.15.
[15] Cf. Phil. 3.13.
[16] Cf. 1 Cor. 15.49.
[17] Matt. 19.21.
[18] Cf. Ps. 89.1.
[19] Gal. 2.20.
[20] John 19.11.
[21] Isa. 66.1.
[22] 2 Cor. 5.19.
[23] Cf. Eph. 5.27.
[24] Cf. Cant. 1.3.
[25] Ps. 7.13.
[26] John 12.31.
[27] Rom. 6.12.
[28] Cf. Ps. 2.1.
[29] Cf. Matt. 25.33.

[30] Cf. Rom. 2.15.
[31] Cf. Heb. 12.6.
[32] Jer. 33.2.
[33] Exod. 3.14.
[34] Cf. Matt. 6.24.
[35] 1 Cor. 3.17.
[36] Eph. 3.16,17, slightly modified.
[37] Isa. 53.1.
[38] Ps. 43.22.
[39] Cf. 2 Cor. 8.9.
[40] Cf. 1 Tim. 6.10.
[41] Cf. 1 Tim. 5.6.
[42] Cf. Matt. 7.6.
[43] Cf. Gen. 3.7.
[44] Cf. 2 Cor. 4.18.
[45] Cf. 1 Cor. 2.9.
[46] Cf. 1 Cor. 1.24.
[47] *Muscipula,* "mousetrap."
[48] Cf. 1 Tim. 6.10.
[49] Cf. Matt. 13.5.
[50] Eph. 3.17.
[51] Cf. Rom. 1.24.
[52] Inserted from the Septuagint.
[53] Cf. Rom. 1.28.
[54] 2 Thess. 2.3.
[55] Cf. Gen. 1.34.
[56] 2 Thess. 2.4.
[57] Cf. Acts 8.9–23.
[58] Matt. 5.3.
[59] Cf. Matt. 8.26; Mark 4.39; Luke 8.24.
[60] Gal. 6.14.
[61] Matt. 23.9.
[62] Matt. 12.48.
[63] That is, the Manicheans.
[64] Ps. 56.8.
[65] Rom. 8.25.
[66] *Extulit patrem.* This looks like a flagrant example of St. Augustine's wordplay, and as such defies translation. *Effero* does in fact mean "proclaim"; but it is also the regular term for carrying out to burial.
[67] Cf. Matt. 24.36.
[68] Matt. 20.30.

⁶⁹ Luke 1.32.
⁷⁰ Matt. 22.44.
⁷¹ Cf. John 1.1.
⁷² Cf. Rom. 1.3.

DISCOURSE ON PSALM 10

¹ That is, the Donatists.
² Ps. 83.4.
³ Ps. 9.10.
⁴ *In obscura luna*, the Septuagint version. Vulgate reads *in obscuro*, "in the dark."
⁵ Cf. 1 Cor. 15.33.
⁶ See Discourse on Ps. 8.9.
⁷ An allusion to the introductory dialogue *Sursum corda* with its response *Habemus ad Dominum* of the Preface of the Mass, and a witness to its antiquity. See also Discourse on Ps. 90.13.
⁸ Namely, the Manichees. See *De Genesi contra Manich.* 1.3,6 and 2.25,38; *De moribus Manich.* 8.13; and *De haeresibus*.
⁹ The Donatists accused the Catholics of having treacherously surrendered the Holy Scriptures and Church documents to her persecutors, whereas many African municipal records proved that the Donatists were in fact the culprits. See St. Augustine's *Letters* 76.2 and 105.2.
¹⁰ The Donatists swore by the grey hairs of Donatus.
¹¹ Jer. 17.5.
¹² Matt. 7.16.
¹³ The Circumcellions were thus named by their Catholic opponents from their encircling attacks on their dwellings; cf. Discourse on Ps. 132.3: *quia circum cellas vagantur*. The fanatics themselves preferred to be known as *Agonistici*, "soldiers of Christ."
¹⁴ The Donatists complained of the bitter persecution they had endured at the hands of Macarius and Paul, whom the Emperor Constantius had sent to Africa to relieve the poor and convert the schismatics about A.D. 348, six years before Augustine's birth. Cf. Optatus, *Contra Parmen.* 3.4; and *Letter* 44.4.
¹⁵ Matt. 13.47.
¹⁶ A reference to the Constitutions promulgated in the year 405.
¹⁷ Cf. Ps. 8.3.
¹⁸ John 14.27.

[19] Cf. Luke 22.19,21.

[20] John 6.71.

[21] John 12.6.

[22] Matt. 10.5.

[23] In his struggle against the Donatists, St. Augustine constantly emphasized the teaching of the Church that the validity of the sacraments in no way depends upon the worthiness of the minister, since the true minister is Christ. Cf. *In Joann. tract.* 6, read at Matins on January 13, the Commemoration of Our Lord's Baptism: "Should Peter baptize, it is Christ who baptizes; should Paul baptize, it is Christ who baptizes; should Judas baptize, it is Christ who baptizes."

[24] 1 Cor. 3.17.

[25] Cf. Col. 2.19.

[26] Cf. Eph. 4.16.

[27] Cf. *Serm.* 336.1: "When we are instructed, baptized and guided, we are, so to speak, cut into shape, put into line and laid side by side; yet we do not form the Lord's dwelling unless we be cemented by charity."

[28] *Principatus sui:* the Donatists largely drew upon African national feeling against Rome.

[29] Gen. 3.19.

[30] Cf. Ps. 9.10.

[31] See Discourse on Ps. 8.10.

[32] Cf. Discourses on Ps. 93.1 and Ps. 100.4.

[33] 2 Cor. 2.16.

[34] Gen. 2.24.

[35] Eph. 5.32.

[36] Matt. 15.11.

[37] Cf. Ps. 22.5.

[38] Cf. Ps. 35.9.

[39] This way of referring to our Lord seems strange to modern minds, yet it is not without scriptural support. Cf. Acts 2.22: *Jesus of Nazareth, a man approved of God among you.* See also Mark 15.39; Acts 4.27.

DISCOURSE ON PSALM 11

[1] See Discourse on Ps. 6.2.

[2] Rom. 13.10.

[3] Rom. 2.9.

[4] See Discourse on Ps. 93.7.

[5] Matt. 9.37.
[6] Matt. 5.3.
[7] Luke 2.30.
[8] Matt. 7.29.
[9] Cf. Phil. 1.17.
[10] Isa. 11.2.
[11] Matt. 5.3–9.
[12] Matt. 7.29.
[13] See Discourse on Ps. 139.13.
[14] Prov. 20.26, according to the Septuagint.
[15] Wisd. 9.15. See Discourse on Ps. 4.9,10.
[16] Cf. Ps. 83.8.

DISCOURSE ON PSALM 12

[1] Rom. 10.4. See also Discourse on Ps. 4.1.
[2] Both St. Augustine's text and the Vulgate read *Respice.* Douai translates *consider,* but the context here demands *look.*
[3] Cf. Job 1.22.

DISCOURSE ON PSALM 13

[1] Rom. 10.4. See Discourse on Ps. 4.1.
[2] Rom. 1.28.
[3] Cf. Discourse on Ps. 10.7.
[4] Acts 10.13.
[5] Cf. Ps. 57.5,6.
[6] Matt. 11.28–30.
[7] John 11.48.
[8] Rom. 1.25.
[9] Rom. 11.25.
[10] Rom. 11.26; Isa. 59.20.

DISCOURSE ON PSALM 14

[1] *Peregrinabitur,* "shall sojourn," an accurate rendering of the Hebrew. Douai, following the Vulgate, translates "shall dwell," *habitabit.*
[2] Cf. 2 Cor. 5.1,2.
[3] *Animus:* St. Augustine uses *animus* rather than the more

usual *anima* in this context to denote the soul's specifically rational functions. See J. Colleran, ACW 9.200, note 24.

[4] Cf. Ps. 110.10; Eccli. 1.16.

[5] See Third Discourse on Ps. 36.6.

[6] Matt. 5.37.

Discourse on Psalm 15

[1] P. Boylan translates this title: "A monumental poem of David." He remarks that the title denotes the abiding worth of the Psalm which, containing as it does prophecy and deep theology, deserves to be carved like a royal inscription on a pillar (*The Psalms:* Ps. 15.1 and note 1).

[2] See Discourse on Ps. 69.7.

[3] See Discourse on Ps. 58.8.

[4] See First Discourse on Ps. 34.12.

[5] Cf. John 17.5.

[6] Cf. Num. 18.20.

[7] *Emendaverunt,* where Vulgate reads *increpuerunt,* "corrected." Cf. Ps. 1.2.

[8] St. Thomas teaches that our Lord's human intellect or understanding, from the first moment of His Incarnation, possessed the fulness of human intellectual knowledge; the only knowledge by which Christ could be said to learn was "experimental knowledge," here referred to by St. Augustine. See *Sum. theol.* 3, qq. 9–12.

[9] See Discourse on Ps. 7.11.

Discourse on Psalm 16

[1] Matt. 27.29.

[2] Cf. 1 Peter 5.8.

[3] John 8.44.

[4] See First Discourse on Ps. 34.4.

[5] Cf. Matt. 7.6.

[6] Matt. 27.25.

[7] The Septuagint may read either υἱῶν, "sons," or ὑειῶν, "swine." St. Augustine discusses this verse in *Letter* 149.5 to Paulinus, in which he tells his correspondent: "I have been revising a very short commentary on this same Psalm which I committed to paper some time ago."

DISCOURSE ON PSALM 17

[1] Cf. 2 Kings 22.
[2] Cf. 2 Kings 8.5–9.
[3] Cf. Rom. 13.10.
[4] Cf. Isa. 11.2. St. Augustine is possibly referring here to contemplative prayer, which is a fruit of the gifts of the Holy Ghost enumerated in Isa. 11.2,3.
[5] Cf. 2 Cor. 5.7.
[6] Cf. Rom. 8.25.
[7] The Latin *prae fulgore* of the Latin text may mean "compared with" or "at the brightness." St. Augustine adopts the first reading and couples it with the preceding verse; Douai reads "at."
[8] Cf. 2 Cor. 2.16.
[9] Cf. John 4.14.
[10] Luke 10.9.
[11] Luke 13.5.
[12] Eph. 5.27.
[13] Cf. Gal. 5.6.
[14] Cf. 2 Cor. 4.18.
[15] Cf. Prov. 5.22.
[16] See Discourses on Ps. 44.17 and on Ps. 72.7.
[17] Ezech. 18.25.
[18] Cf. Rom. 10.3.
[19] Cf. Eph. 3.19.
[20] *Salutis meae*, a translation from the Septuagint. The Vulgate *salutis tuae*, "thy salvation," corresponds with the Hebrew. See St. Jerome's *Epist. 353, ad Suniam.*
[21] The two feet of the soul are love of God and love of one's neighbor. See Discourse on Ps. 9.15.
[22] Cf. Matt. 7.13.
[23] Cf. John 11.48.
[24] John 8.44.
[25] Cf. Matt. 15.2.
[26] Rom. 8.6.
[27] John 19.6.

FIRST DISCOURSE ON PSALM 18

[1] The ancients thought of the firmament as an immense canopy of solid material resting on supports. St. Augustine here sees

in the story of Gen. 1.6–8 a symbol of the apostles who before Pentecost were timid and earth-bound, but by the power of the Holy Ghost rose above earthly things to become as it were the heavens.

[2] Cf. John 1.1.
[3] See Discourse on Ps. 44.3.
[4] Cf. Matt. 10.34.
[5] Cf. Ps. 1.1.
[6] See First Discourse on Ps. 58.10.
[7] Cf. John 1.14.
[8] Cf. Matt. 5.17.
[9] Cf. 1 Peter 2.22.
[10] Cf. Matt. 11.27.
[11] Cf. Matt. 11.25.
[12] Cf. James 4.6.
[13] Cf. 1 John 4.18.
[14] Cf. John 5.22.
[15] See Discourse on Ps. 39.20.
[16] Cf. Eccli. 10.14.
[17] Cf. James 4.6.

SECOND DISCOURSE ON PSALM 18

[1] Preached at Hippo, at the end of 411 or the beginning of 412. Note reference to the singing of the Psalm by the assembly.
[2] Ps. 88.16.
[3] Cf. 2 Cor. 11.3.
[4] John 1.14.
[5] Cf. Rom. 3.22–25.
[6] Cf. Titus 3.5.
[7] Ps. 58.11.
[8] Ps. 113.9.
[9] Cf. Ps. 102.10.
[10] Cf. Gen. 1.
[11] Cf. John 1.3.
[12] Ps. 101.26.
[13] Ps. 101.27.
[14] Ps. 94.5.
[15] Cf. 1 Cor. 1.24.
[16] Luke 15.21.
[17] Cf. Eph. 2.10.
[18] Cf. Ps. 99.3.

[19] Matt. 5.14.
[20] Cf. Acts 2.4.
[21] 2 Kings 12.12.
[22] Luke 15.32.
[23] Luke 12.13.
[24] Cf. Acts 2.3.
[25] Cf. 1 John 4.18.
[26] Gen. 2.24.
[27] Cf. Luke 23.34.
[28] Ps. 35.12.
[29] Ps. 118.133.
[30] Eccli. 10.15,14.
[31] Luke 15.13.
[32] Cf. James 4.6; 1 Peter 5.5.
[33] 2 Cor. 1.12.

DISCOURSE ON PSALM 19

[1] John 17.1.
[2] Cf. Gen. 25.23.
[3] See Discourse on Ps. 2.5.
[4] Luke 12.36.
[5] For *diapsalma*, see Discourse on Ps. 4.4.
[6] Cf. John 15.13.
[7] Cf. John 12.25.
[8] Cf. Rom. 11.25,26.
[9] Cf. John 17.1.
[10] Cf. Rom. 8.34.
[11] Cf. Acts 2.
[12] Cf. 2 Cor. 12.10.
[13] Cf. Ps. 59.13.
[14] See Discourse on Ps. 146.19.
[15] Cf. John 11.48.
[16] Cf. Rom. 9.32.
[17] Cf. Rom. 11.25.
[18] Cf. Rom. 10.3.
[19] Cf. Matt. 3.9.
[20] Cf. Rom. 9.30.
[21] "Our sacrifices": a possible reference to the Mass. The use of the plural, as seen for instance in the phrase *haec sancta sacrificia* of the Canon, is not unusual in the early Church.

DISCOURSE ON PSALM 20

[1] Cf. Luke 22.15.
[2] Cf. John 10.18.
[3] John 14.27.
[4] See Discourse on Ps. 4.4.
[5] John 17.1.
[6] Our Lord's human nature attained its full prerogatives only when He entered into heaven on Ascension Day.
[7] John 11.50.

FIRST DISCOURSE ON PSALM 21

[1] Cf. Matt. 28.1; John 20.1–17.
[2] Cf. Rom. 6.9.
[3] Cf. Rom. 6.6.
[4] See Discourses on Ps. 37.6; Ps. 43.2; and Ps. 87.14.
[5] Cf. Ps. 118.155.
[6] St. Augustine here stresses the solidarity existing between Christ our Head and us His ignorant and sinful members. For a complete exposition of this Psalm and a fuller explanation of the punctuation of the verse adopted by St. Augustine, see his *Letter* 140 to Honoratus.
[7] See Discourse on Ps. 53.5.
[8] Not that Adam was blind before but because his gaze now stirred up unholy desires; cf. Gen. 3.
[9] *Sine semine.* Owing perhaps to the apparent absence of coition in propagation, the ancients considered worms to be asexual. See St. Augustine's *Letter* 140.21.
[10] John 9.28.
[11] John 19.6.
[12] Matt. 26.56.
[13] Cf. Ps. 1.4.
[14] On this and the two following verses see Discourse on Ps. 84.3: "Reading these words is like reading the Gospel."
[15] Cf. John 17.6,21.
[16] Cf. Ps. 21.3.
[17] See First Discourse on Ps. 48.3.
[18] The Vulgate adds the word *coeli:* the "heavens" shall show forth His justice. St. Augustine here follows the Septuagint reading.

SECOND DISCOURSE ON PSALM 21

[1] Preached to the people at Hippo, March 23, 395.
[2] Cf. 1 Peter 3.18.
[3] Rom. 6.9.
[4] Jer. 9.1.
[5] This is directed against the Donatists.
[6] Cf. Matt. 26.7.
[7] 2 Cor. 2.14,15.
[8] Matt. 26.8-10,13.
[9] Matt. 27.46.
[10] Cf. John 13.23.
[11] John 1.1,14.
[12] Cf. Eph. 1.23.
[13] 1 Peter 2.22.
[14] Matt. 26.39.
[15] Cf. Matt. 10.25.
[16] Phil. 1.23.
[17] 2 Cor. 12.9.
[18] Cf. Job 1.11.
[19] Cf. Matt. 8.31.
[20] *Deo gratias.* The Donatists said *Deo laudes,* "Praise be to God."
[21] Cf. Exod. 12.51.
[22] Cf. Dan. 3.
[23] Cf. Dan. 14 and 13.
[24] John 1.1.
[25] Cf. Job 42.10.
[26] Matt. 27.
[27] *Deus meus ab uberibus* etc. In the previous discourse on this Psalm, St. Augustine read this text as *Spes mea* etc.
[28] John 19.6.
[29] Matt. 10.16; Luke 10.3.
[30] Cf. Matt. 27.15.
[31] John 20.25,27,28.
[32] John 19.23.
[33] Cf. Gen. 8.11.
[34] Cf. 1 Peter 5.8.
[35] Cf. Ps. 18.7.
[36] Two of the principal towns of the Donatists.
[37] The Donatists declared that they had preserved the books

of Holy Scripture whereas the Catholics had handed them over to the persecutors.

[38] Ps. 2.8.
[39] Ps. 7.
[40] Cf. 1 Cor. 3.7.
[41] Cf. Matt. 24.23.
[42] Cf. Ps. 112.1.
[43] Matt. 12.30.
[44] Council held at Bagai, A.D. 394.

DISCOURSE ON PSALM 22

[1] Cf. Matt. 7.14.
[2] Cf. 1 Cor. 3.2.
[3] See Discourse on Ps. 35.14.

DISCOURSE ON PSALM 23

[1] See Discourse on Ps. 4.4.
[2] Cf. Gen. 25.23.
[3] John 16.33.
[4] Cf. 4 Kings 17.16. The exaggerated cult paid to the angels by certain heretical sects in the early days of Christianity is reflected in St. Paul's Epistle to the Colossians 2.18, and possibly also in Hebrews, where the Apostle lays special emphasis on Christ's superiority to the angels. It was one of the tenets of the Manicheans that angels and souls were emanations of the Godhead.
[5] Cf. Rom. 8.34.
[6] Cf. Eph. 2.2.
[7] Cf. Rom. 8.38,39.
[8] Cf. Ps. 117.9.
[9] Cf. 1 Cor. 1.31.

DISCOURSE ON PSALM 24

[1] Cf. *Conf.* 2.6: "Thus even those who go from You and stand up against You are still perversely imitating You" (tr. by F. J. Sheed, *The Confessions of St. Augustine* (New York 1943) 35.
[2] Cf. Matt. 7.13.
[3] Cf. Gen. 3.23.
[4] Cf. Luke 15.13.

⁵ Cf. Rom. 8.20.
⁶ Cf. Matt. 11.30.
⁷ See Discourse on Ps. 60.9 and Twenty-Ninth Discourse on Ps. 118.8.
⁸ Cf. Ps. 50.19.
⁹ Cf. Matt. 10.22.
¹⁰ Cf. Matt. 24.12.
¹¹ Cf. Matt. 10.22.

FIRST DISCOURSE ON PSALM 25

¹ A possible reference to the Holy Eucharist, which each communicant received into cupped hands, *conjunctis manibus*, after which he replied "Amen."
² Cf. 1 Tim. 6.5.
³ The foot is the symbol of love. See Discourse on Ps. 9.15.

SECOND DISCOURSE ON PSALM 25

¹ This sermon was preached at Hippo, after the year 410.
² Eph. 4.21-24. In his "Saint Augustin reviseur de la Bible," Dom de Bruyne has set forth compelling arguments for attributing to St. Augustine a minute revision of St. Paul's Epistles based on the Greek text. In this passage, St. Augustine's *concupiscentias deceptionis*, "deceitful lusts," is replaced in the Vulgate by *desideria erroris*, "the desire of error."
³ The Priscillianists, an heretical sect of the 4th-5th centuries, taught that in order to conceal their doctrines it was lawful to deceive pagans. See Augustine, *Contra mendacium* 2.2.
⁴ Eph. 4.25,26.
⁵ Eph. 4.26.
⁶ 1 John 3.15.
⁷ 1 John 2.9.
⁸ Luke 8.23.
⁹ Luke 8.24.
¹⁰ Cf. Isa. 40.6,8.
¹¹ Eph. 4.26-28.
¹² Cf. 3 Kings 19.10; Rom. 11.3.
¹³ Ps. 25.9.
¹⁴ Ps. 42.1.
¹⁵ An allusion to the Donatists; see Discourse on Ps. 10.5.
¹⁶ Ps. 18.7.

[17] Luke 12.49.

[18] Gal. 6.4.

[19] This passage reads like a prophecy of what was to befall in the following year. At the Conference of Carthage, A.D. 411, held after the Donatists had for years obstructed all St. Augustine's efforts to meet in friendly discussion, the Donatists refused the courteous invitation of Marcellinus the tribune to be seated. Quoting Ps. 25.5, they were forbidden, they said, to sit with the wicked. Their Catholic opponents retorted that if the words of Psalm 25 were to be taken literally, the Donatists had already committed sin by entering in at all. The heretics refused to yield the point, with the result that about eight hundred persons had to stand from early morning till late at night for two out of the three days. See *Serm.* 99.8; *Collatio* 1.44; *Lib. ad Donatistas post collationem* 5.

[20] Matt. 13.9.

[21] Eph. 5.8.

[22] In the early Church those catechumens whose petition for admission to baptism had been approved were termed *illuminandi.* The sacrament itself was often referred to as "illumination."

[23] John 1.9.

[24] 1 Cor. 4.7.

[25] Cf. 1 Cor. 1.31.

[26] Cf. Rom. 3.23.

[27] Cf. John 12.6.

[28] Cf. *Code of Theodosius* 16: *De episcopali iudicio.*

FIRST DISCOURSE ON PSALM 26

[1] Cf. 1 Cor. 15.54.
[2] Cf. Rom. 10.10.
[3] Cf. Rom. 8.10.
[4] Cf. Rom. 7.22.
[5] Cf. Wisd. 1.11.

SECOND DISCOURSE ON PSALM 26

[1] Preached at Hippo, at the end of 411 or the beginning of 412.
[2] Cf. Gen. 3.19.
[3] Cf. 1 Kings 16.13,
[4] Cf. Rom. 8.34.

[5] Cf. 1 Cor. 15.53.
[6] 1 Cor. 15.44.
[7] Cf. Job 1.
[8] Luke 22.31.
[9] Even a slight acquaintance with Hebrew would have spared St. Augustine a good many misinterpretations. Here, however, he correctly surmises that the feminine form, *unam*, has the force of the neuter, *one thing*.
[10] Ps. 83.5.
[11] Ps. 101.28.
[12] Rom. 1.24.
[13] 2 Cor. 12.8,9.
[14] Ps. 5.5.
[15] Cf. John 3.13.
[16] 2 Cor. 5.6.
[17] Matt. 6.13.
[18] Cf. Rom. 5.6.
[19] Cf. Heb. 9.3.
[20] Col. 3.3.
[21] Cf. 1 Cor. 10.4.
[22] Acts 9.4.
[23] Cf. Matt. 28.20.
[24] Cf. 1 Cor. 15.54.
[25] 1 John 1.5.
[26] Matt. 5.8.
[27] Ps. 50.11.
[28] Cf. Ps. 33.15.
[29] Cf. Matt. 10.22 and 24.13.
[30] Possibly a reference to the Pelagians.
[31] John 8.44.
[32] Cf. Eph. 2.2.
[33] A reference to the Roman Empire, already growing old and weakening beneath enemy attacks.
[34] Eph. 5.8.
[35] John 14.6.
[36] Prov. 31.26.
[37] Ps. 83.8.
[38] Job 9.24.
[39] Eccli. 2.16.
[40] Cf. Gal. 3.28.

Discourse on Psalm 27

[1] See Discourse on Ps. 17.1.
[2] Cf. Matt. 11.20.
[3] John 3.2.
[4] Cf. Rom. 10.3.
[5] Ps. 2.8.
[6] John 17.10.

Discourse on Psalm 28

[1] See Discourse on Ps. 17.1.
[2] Cf. 1 Cor. 4.15.
[3] Cf. Luke 13.1–5.
[4] Cf. 1 Cor. 1.28.
[5] Cf. Isa. 53.7.
[6] Ps. 2.2.
[7] Cf. Phil. 2.7.
[8] Cf. Rom. 10.3.
[9] Cf. John 7.41; 7.12.
[10] Cf. Eph. 2.12.
[11] A reference to the ancient belief that stags by their breath drew serpents from their holes and afterwards killed and devoured them. Cf. Pliny, *Hist. nat.* 8.32.
[12] Cf. Gen. 7.
[13] John 14.27.

First Discourse on Psalm 29

[1] See Discourse on Ps. 28.1.
[2] See Discourse on Ps. 17.51.
[3] For this blindness signified by "hell," see Discourse on *Ps.* 6.6.
[4] See Second Discourse on Ps. 58.10.
[5] Cf. Ps. 15.10.
[6] Cf. Luke 15.22.
[7] Cf. 1 Cor. 15.28.

Second Discourse on Psalm 29

[1] This sermon was preached at Hippo, between the years 414–415.

[2] Eph. 6.12.

[3] Mark 1.35–38.

[4] John 1.1–5.

[5] John 1.14.

[6] Rom. 8.34.

[7] Luke 3.6.

[8] Eph. 6.12.

[9] Apollinaris (*ca.* 310–*ca.* 390), the originator of the first great Christological heresy, taught the coexistence in man of body, soul and spirit, but asserted that while Christ had a human body and soul, He had no human spirit, the spirit being replaced by the divine Logos. Christ consequently possessed perfect Godhead but lacked complete manhood.

[10] Ps. 44.8.

[11] Cf. Matt. 11.11.

[12] Cf. Mark 1.7.

[13] See Discourse on Ps. 10, note 39.

[14] Cf. Gen. 1.26.

[15] Ps. 31.9.

[16] Apollinaris held to the Platonic division of human nature into body, soul and spirit. The soul, *anima* or *anima humana*, was the principle of sense or animal life; the spirit, *mens, mens humana*, or *rationale*, was the principle of intellectual life. See Discourse on Ps. 3.3.

[17] John 1.14.

[18] It is probable that the presence of Apollinarians at his sermon gave rise to this long digression with its direct questions obviously aimed at the audience. St. Augustine frequently framed his exposition for the sake of some among his listeners. See Discourses on Ps. 21.5 and Ps. 61.22,23.

[19] Luke 24.39.

[20] Matt. 26.68.

[21] Matt. 27.42.

[22] Cf. Judges 10.7; 13.1. The foreigners, as the Septuagint calls them, were the Philistines. The Vulgate, which ordinarily terms them Philistines, gives them this title *alienigenae*, "foreigners," in Ps. 59.10.

[23] Cf. Job 1.12.

[24] John 19.10,11.

[25] Job 1.21.

[26] Job 2.9,10.

[27] Job 1.9–11.

[28] Wisd. 5.1,8,9.
[29] Cf. Matt. 13.26.
[30] Cf. Eccle. 1.18.
[31] 2 Tim. 3.12,13.
[32] Ps. 26.14.
[33] Job 7.1.
[34] 1 Cor. 3.11,12.
[35] 1 Cor. 3.11–15.
[36] Cf. *Conf.* 13.9. Augustine follows the theory disproved by Galileo, that the fall of a solid body is proportionate to its weight. See Augustine, *De quantitate animae* 22 (ACW 9.57–58; also note 51, *ibid.* 204).
[37] 1 Cor. 15.54.
[38] Gen. 2.17.
[39] *Geme de praesentibus, psalle de futuris; ora de re, psalle de spe.*
[40] Gen. 3.8.
[41] Matt. 28.1.
[42] Gen. 3.4,5.
[43] Gen. 3.23.
[44] James 4.6.
[45] Matt. 25.32.
[46] Ps. 34.13.
[47] Cf. John 19.34.
[48] Matt. 25.35.

INDEXES

INDEXES

1. OLD AND NEW TESTAMENT

2. GENERAL INDEX